During the twentieth century the number of people who

speak English as a first or second language has increased dramatically. The covers of

the Voyages series reflect the fact that English is the most widely read language in the world.

This year our Voyages in English book takes us to the Middle East.

VOYAGES in English

Revised Edition

Carolyn Marie Dimick

General Editor

Marie T. McVey

Revision Editor

Jeanne M. Baker

Maria Byers

Carolyn Marie Dimick

Marian E. Metz

Susan Mary Platt

Joan I. Rychalsky

Authors

Loyola University Press · Chicago

Contributors	Jane Mary Carr
	Martina Anne Erdlen
	Marie T. McVey
Managing Editor	Juanita Raman (revision)
Project Editor	Kathleen Schultz
Production/Design Manager	Carol Tornatore
	Frederick Falkenberg (revision)
Designer	William A. Seabright

ISBN 0-8294-0756-1

In every grade, language development challenges teachers and students to explore their world through the spoken and written word. Language in all its aspects is essential to the development of the individual on both personal and social levels. We use language as a vehicle for expressing wonder and delight, a tool for exchanging ideas, a medium for transmitting information, and a resource for bridging the differences among peoples. These are the ultimate goals of language and the underlying philosophy of *Voyages in English*.

Integration of the language arts

The revised *Voyages in English* series is designed to include the major areas of the language arts curriculum: writing, grammar, correct usage, mechanics, dictionary and library skills, speaking and listening skills, and literature. These areas should not be considered separate and distinct from one another even though, for purposes of instruction, the skills may be taught in isolation.

The challenge of the teacher is to present the areas as integrated so that the students can perceive the seemingly discrete parts of the curriculum as an interrelated whole. Ultimately, students should view the entire program as essential to building competency and success in other curricular areas.

Parts I and II. Before teaching the material in *Voyages in English*, the teacher should become acquainted with the format of the textbook. There are two distinct sections: writing and grammar. (Literary selections are incorporated into each chapter of the grammar section.) Neither section is meant to be taught in continuity without reference to the other. Familiarity with the chapters in both sections will enable the teacher to move with ease between the two sections.

For example, when working with the students in the proofreading stage of the writing process, the teacher will discover areas of weakness in correct usage and mechanics. At this point it is recommended that the teacher turn to the lesson in the grammar section that corresponds to the particular problem area and teach the concept in the context of the writing activity.

While teaching an area of grammar such as adjectives, teachers may refer to the lessons on word substitution, sentence expansion, or descriptive writing so as to integrate grammar and writing. At all times the instructional goal should be integration, not isolation.

Illustrations. The full-page illustration that opens each chapter relates directly or indirectly to the chapter that follows, but it may often be as appropriately used with other subject matter.

In the writing section of the book, the captions are "lead" questions designed to serve as a springboard for class discussion. The ideas explored through the illustrations can often inspire a composition. Teachers having an overview of the illustrations in the book can refer to a specific one to prompt a writing activity.

In the grammar section a credit line identifies photographs and fine art. Illustrations may inspire a poem, a theme, or different kinds of sentences (declarative, interrogative, exclamatory, imperative). A simple sentence about the picture might be expanded with words, phrases, or clauses—all of which might include various types of figurative language. The inclusion of much regionalist (especially American) and other art from different periods provides opportunities for cross-curricular links.

Practice Power. This feature provides a skill-extension or a writing activity following each grammar lesson. Sometimes it is simply writing sentences or completing a review exercise; at other times it is writing a brief paragraph or poem. With teacher assistance, the students should be led to realize the importance of integrating correct grammar, usage, and mechanics with writing skills.

You Are the Author. This feature extends the integration of the language arts, replacing the final Practice Power activity in each chapter with an assignment related in some way to the literary opener. The students learn to apply the grammatical concept taught in the chapter to writing that draws on the genre, subject, or content of the literature. In addition, students engage in cooperative learning, which teaches them to take pride in sharing both their individual skills and the rewards of group achievement.

The writing process

Exploring and discovering meaning through written language should be part of every child's educational experience. Schools that make the development of writing skills a high priority foster the writing process within the curriculum.

Developing good writing skills is essential at every grade level. The teacher should become familiar with the elements of the writing process. The goal is for writing to be a natural, enjoyable means of expression in which the students engage frequently.

When the writing process is begun in the early school years, children have no fear or anxiety about writing. Instead, building on their ability to communicate through speech, they find writing an exhilarating and happy experience. There is a sense of satisfaction in knowing a piece is well written and has expressed exactly what the writer intended to say. Although research on the composing, or writing, process is ongoing, most authorities agree that the process has four stages: prewriting, writing or drafting, revision, and editing. These are not mutually exclusive, however, so should not be taught in isolation. Writing is a cyclic process; thus its components overlap, allowing the writer to wander in and out of all stages at will.

Prewriting. Observing, discussing, reading, journal writing, note-taking, interviewing, brainstorming, imagining, and remembering are some activities that take place before the writer begins an actual draft. In this stage the writer hones in on a subject, narrows it, and makes decisions about the purpose and audience of the piece. Why is it being written? For whom? (The teacher, parents, principals, other students, and the community are all appropriate audiences.) What form should the writing take? In this stage enthusiasm is generated. Interaction between student and teacher helps attest to the value of the project. Teachers should encourage students to share their ideas so as to "hear" their own ideas and others', ultimately helping them to evaluate their material, to be selective about it, and to make associations.

Writing. During the creation of the first draft, the student puts the information on paper. At this stage the writer should be encouraged to keep the ideas flowing without worrying about sentence structure or correct usage. Maintaining momentum is important, so completing this process at one sitting is the ideal. The first draft is the visible form of what took place in the prewriting stage. It allows the student to see a dim shape of what the material is to become. Teachers should encourage students to write without making corrections—on alternate lines so as to provide room for revision.

Revision. This can be the most difficult stage of writing yet the most vital to its success. Here students look over the work again and again. First drafts are rarely well organized or cohesive. Ideas need clarification, sentences need variety, and vocabulary needs development. Such refining takes more than one revision. Teachers should encourage students to write as many drafts as seem necessary.

Editing and proofreading. In the final stage before "publication," the students must look to the correctness of the piece. Correct punctuation, spelling, capitalization, and usage are important if the work is to be taken seriously. The students should be taught the importance of reviewing their own work for accuracy. Frequently at this stage, however, they can get caught up in refining content, which is not the domain of proofreading, instead of being attentive to mechanical details. The teacher can help control the proofreading process by suggesting four or five areas to check so that all the students proofread for at least those specific prime areas of concern.

Having another student proofread the work is another way to help avoid major revisions at the proofreading stage. To increase objectivity and foster cooperative learning, students should be encouraged to do what real publishers do: select "a second pair of eyes." Teachers may wish to assign a team of students who are good in proofreading to serve as a class resource in this area.

It is important to note again that writers wander in and out of the various writing stages. Many times one begins to revise while writing a first draft. Frequently it may be necessary to return to prewriting in order to gather more information or think about an idea. Bits of proofreading are done while revising. No student should be locked into writing stage by stage, although it is often productive to restrict the critical faculty during a creative time.

Finally, students are ready to publish their work—as close to perfection as possible. The audience has the right to require that finished writing be comprehensible and stylistically consistent. The students can learn a great deal from total involvement in the process of writing. If the audience receives the work well, the students learn to take pride in achievement.

Write Away! This extension of the activities in each writing lesson may or may not be completed by students, depending on their ability to manage the assignment. Some will respond to the challenge. Others may perform better on a version modified to address individual interests, learning styles, or needs.

Grammar, usage, and mechanics

Part II of the *Voyages in English* program offers the students a traditional approach to grammar in a handbook-reference format. Lessons include definitions, explanations, and then exercises that allow for abundant practice in each concept. The activities and recurring features build on learning by providing opportunities for practical application and language-arts integration.

Recalling What You Know. A few review questions in the first lesson of each grammar chapter set the stage for learning and relate loosely to a literary selection in the chapter. The questions are intended not to test students' previous learning but to remind them of what they already know, to show them that they can do the exercises that follow, and so to instill self-confidence.

Chapter Challenge. At the end of each grammar chapter is a paragraph that incorporates all the grammar skills the students have learned in the chapter. Identifying various grammatical structures is more difficult in paragraphs than in isolated sentences. In most cases, therefore, this feature should be teacher directed rather than used as a testing tool.

Literature

New to the *Voyages in English* program is literature-based traditional grammar. The series' ample poetry component has now been expanded to include other literary genres drawn from a broad range of ethnic backgrounds, social contexts, and historical periods. Not only is the literature integrated into the other language arts; it suggests many cross-curricular applications as well.

Literary opener. The literature that opens each chapter in the grammar section of the book includes fiction, drama, history, fables, folktales, fantasy, and biography. Topics often relate to other academic subjects. Exciting, thought-provoking subject matter stimulates discussion of current issues, introduces students to new cultural perspectives, and has personal relevance.

The Writer's Craft. This feature relates the literary selection the students have just read to their experience. Open-ended questions stimulate discussion and encourage interpretation, teaching students to think and developing an appreciation for writing style. By eliciting the students' feelings, opinions, and judgments, the reader-response questions create interest and reinforce the literary intent. Subsequent questions highlight the author's application of the grammatical concept being taught in the chapter.

Creative Space. The poetic selections that close each grammar chapter should be enjoyed first and then analyzed. They open up new writing possibilities for students, including using the literature as a model for students' original work.

The Teacher's Edition

The teacher's text sets the objectives and presents directives for the lessons. Some lessons may require two or three days of instruction. The pacing depends on class as well as individual needs.

It is hoped that *Voyages in English* will provide students with a thorough knowledge of the English language and will lead them to a greater appreciation for the gift that language is. A good textbook, when combined with a teacher's own love of language and attentiveness to its many subtle nuances, can be a vehicle for growth and development in all areas of the curriculum.

Teacher-student interaction is of paramount importance in implementing the writing process. When trust is built up, students readily share their work. The teacher can act as a guide by asking essential questions: What are you writing about? Should you say more about your subject? Have you expressed what you have written in the best way you can? What part do you like best? least? Deleting, adding, and rearranging ideas are essential to the revision process.

Students should be taught to look for specific things as they examine their own work: Is the opening sentence effective? Is there one topic sentence? enough sentence variety? strong action verbs? Does the ending sentence draw the whole to a close?

Peer response is important, so students should ask these questions when critiquing one another's work too. The more response from others, the better the revision will be. Language at this point is exciting and challenging. Trying to select just the right word in the right place is the challenge of revision.

Likewise, teachers creating original pieces of writing *along with* the students reinforce the feeling that the challenge and effort involved in the writing process are worthwhile.

The satisfaction that comes from creating a good piece of writing is immeasurable. The hard work is well worth the effort.

Contents

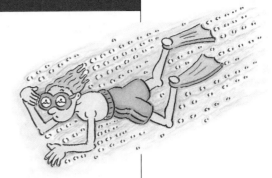

Part I   Written and Oral Communication

Part II   Grammar, Correct Usage, Mechanics

Exploring Our Language

Part I

Written and Oral Communication

Chapter 1

Learning to Write a Paragraph

Lesson 1 Understanding the Paragraph

A paragraph is a group of sentences that talks about one specific idea.

A paragraph tells about one idea. Each sentence in the paragraph is about this same idea. The first sentence of a paragraph is *indented*. This means that the sentence begins a few spaces to the right of the margin. Read this paragraph. What is the specific idea?

Seeds don't have legs to help them get around, but they have many clever ways to travel. Some seeds are "hitchhikers." They have tiny hooks that catch onto animals. They are carried around, then fall off, and grow in a new location. Some seeds, like dandelions, are "parachuters." They are so light that they can float on the wind from one place to another. "Winged" seeds, like those from a maple tree, let the breeze fly them to new places. "Shooting" seeds grow in pods that burst open and send them firing out. Nature provides seeds with many ways to journey out and take root in new places.

Would you like to go exploring in this meadow? What do you think you would find? Colorful flowers, green grass, bumblebees...

There are three parts to a paragraph:
The *beginning sentence*, which gives the specific idea.
The *middle sentences*, which give information about the specific idea.
The *ending sentence*, which gives the last fact or detail, or tells how the writer feels.

In this paragraph, the specific idea of the beginning sentence is that seeds have many ways to travel. Each middle sentence tells about a way in which they travel. The ending sentence closes the paragraph.

Activity A

Read this paragraph and point out the beginning sentence, the middle sentences, and the ending sentence.

The Fourth of July explodes like a firecracker in our town. Bold brass bands march to a cheerful beat up the crowded streets. Drums bang, whistles blow, and children shout in celebration. In the evening, fireworks whistle through the dark sky. Then with each new bold explosion and bright flare of light, people applaud and cheer. It may be noisy, but our Fourth of July is always a day to remember!

Activity B

The sentences in this paragraph are mixed up. Find the beginning, middle, and ending sentences.

—I'll never know if it was, though, because I had to take my little brother.

—His last trick was a trampoline bounce onto the lap of a rather grouchy man.

—First, he spilled popcorn all over a lady's hat.

—The movie I went to see was supposed to be a comedy.

—Next, he got his leg stuck between two of the seats.

—This was one comedy act I hope I *never* see again!

Write Away!

Write the sentences in activity B in correct order to form a paragraph. Underline the beginning and ending sentences.

Lesson 2 Writing Beginning and Ending Sentences

The beginning sentence introduces the specific idea of a paragraph and catches the interest of the reader. The ending sentence gives the last fact or detail or tells how the writer feels.

The beginning sentence has two jobs—it should tell the specific idea of the paragraph and should capture the reader's attention. The ending sentence may give the last fact or detail or it may tell how the writer feels. The ending sentence should leave the reader with something to think about.

A writer can use different kinds of sentences to begin and end a paragraph. A beginning or ending sentence might make a statement (declarative sentence), it might ask a question (interrogative sentence), or it might be an exclamation (exclamatory sentence).

The snake slithered under the bed. (*declarative*)
Whose softball broke the window? (*interrogative*)
What a day that was! (*exclamatory*)

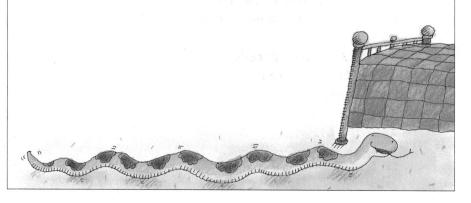

Read this paragraph. Then look at the beginning and ending sentences. What kinds of sentences are they? Why do you think the writer used these kinds of sentences?

Do you have a pair of shoes that uses restickable tape instead of shoelaces? This tape is called Velcro. A Swiss man named George de Mestral got the idea for Velcro as he was hiking in the mountains. Some stubborn burrs caught on his clothes. When he looked closely, he noticed that the burrs had tiny hooks that hooked onto the loops in the material of his clothes. George's careful examination of these burrs gave him the idea that led to his inventing Velcro. *Today Velcro is even used on space suits!*

Activity A

Remember that a beginning sentence should tell the specific idea of a paragraph. It should also capture the reader's attention. Read the paragraph below and choose the sentence (1, 2, 3, or 4) that makes the best beginning sentence.

He wrote a piece of music he called the *Surprise Symphony,* which started out quietly and sweetly. The gentle melody went on and on. After the audience was relaxed and drowsy, a sudden, unexpected blast came from the orchestra. The audience woke up with a start!

1. Joseph Haydn was an Austrian composer.
2. Joseph Haydn, an Austrian composer, loved to play practical jokes.
3. Loud music wakes people up.
4. Joseph Haydn wrote beautiful music.

Activity B

Remember that an ending sentence gives the last fact or detail or tells how the writer feels. Read the paragraph below and choose the sentence (1, 2, or 3) that makes the best ending sentence.

Not every bird can fly. Some birds are much better divers and swimmers. The auk is a tiny bird that lives in cold climates and exists mainly on fish. Diving into frigid waters, an auk uses its wings to paddle and its feet to steer.

1. The auk is a different kind of bird.
2. The auk is like a penguin.
3. Maybe the auk is really a fish with feathers!

Activity C

Read the following group of sentences. Then write a beginning and an ending sentence to complete the paragraph. When you finish, answer the questions below the paragraph.

Bob cranked and cranked until it seemed as if the sharpener had swallowed his pencil. The teacher waited for him to sit down. He quickly slid back to his seat. Then Bob realized he had used his last piece of paper to write a note to Phil. Everyone watched as Sarah passed him a piece of paper across three rows.

—Will your beginning sentence capture your reader's interest?
—What kind of sentence did you use for your ending sentence?
—Do your beginning and ending sentences fit with the other sentences in the paragraph?

Write Away!

Read the following group of sentences. Then use the directions below to write a beginning and an ending sentence to complete the paragraph.

Snow drifted higher and higher against the house until we could hardly see the trees. As the wind whistled around the corners, we could imagine how the houses in our neighborhood were being covered with a white blanket. Early morning weather reports stated that roads were being closed. We scrunched further and further under our quilts, hoping to hear good news.

—Write an exclamatory sentence for the beginning and an interrogative sentence for the ending.

Lesson 3 Writing Middle Sentences

The middle sentences of a paragraph develop the specific idea. They give details.

The beginning sentence introduces the specific idea of the paragraph. Each middle sentence should tell something about this idea. In the paragraph below, the beginning sentence tells you that the paragraph is about different ways animals sleep in the water. Notice how each of the middle sentences tells about one of these ways.

> Different animals have different ways to sleep in the deep blue sea. When the sea otter sleeps, it uses seaweed as a blanket. The parrot fish makes a sleeping bag by blowing a big bubble around itself. Many fish lie down on the floor of the sea to take their naps. Sea mammals need to stick their noses out of the water for oxygen, so they float near the surface while they slumber. None of these animals has to worry about falling out of bed!

—How many middle sentences are there in this paragraph?
—What are some of the different ways animals sleep in the sea?

Activity A

Here is a beginning and an ending sentence. Use the questions to help you write three middle sentences to complete the paragraph.

Beginning: My birthday celebration last year would have made anyone dizzy.

Ending: Next time I go to the amusement park, I'll ride the Triple Loop only once!

—Where did you go?
—What was the ride like?
—How did you feel after three turns?

Activity B

Below are three sets of beginning and ending sentences. Choose one set and write three middle sentences that add details.

<u>Set 1</u>

Beginning: One night I woke up and saw a shadow dancing on my bedroom wall.

Ending: I laughed when I realized how a lost balloon had fooled me.

<u>Set 2</u>

Beginning: Dad always warned us to close the door of the hamster cage.

Ending: I rushed to the kitchen and saw the hamster climbing on Dad's shoe.

<u>Set 3</u>

Beginning: At the last moment our band leader decided to have us play a new piece for our part in the recital.

Ending: Nobody had told the announcer about our change of plans!

Write Away!

Here is a beginning and an ending sentence. Write some middle sentences to complete the paragraph. Think about the questions below before you begin to write.

Beginning: I like to experiment with new activities on rainy afternoons.

Ending: Sometimes I just sit and watch the rain pour down.

—Are there any unusual games you know?
—Do you have any hobbies or work on any projects?
—What do you think is the best way to spend a rainy day?

Lesson 4 Organizing Your Ideas

Before you begin a paragraph, you must have a specific idea about which you can write.

When you are choosing a topic, think about things that you like to do. Think about these questions:

What kind of games do you like?

Do you take part in any sports?

Have you done an experiment or an art project?

Have you visited a museum, an amusement park, or another city?

Has anything funny or interesting happened at school or at home?

Think of topics that interest you. Think of topics you know something about.

A paragraph is like a sandwich. If your topic is too large, it's like a sandwich that is too clumsy to eat. For example, if your topic was "Philadelphia," there would be too many things that you could write. You should narrow your topic down to a specific idea—"My First Trip to Philadelphia."

The beginning and ending sentences introduce and sum up the topic. They are like the pieces of bread. The middle sentences develop the topic and provide the interesting details. They are the "ham, cheese, and tomato" of the paragraph.

Look at the paragraph sandwich below. How is it organized? What are its contents?

I took a trip to Philadelphia. (*beginning sentence*)
I saw traffic, buildings, and trolleys. (*middle sentence*)
I met shoppers and salespeople. (*middle sentence*)
I bought gifts and a pretzel. (*middle sentence*)
I was happy that I went. (*ending sentence*)

Now read this paragraph. Notice how the writer used the paragraph sandwich to construct a well-organized, interesting story.

Hustle and Bustle

Yesterday, my older sister and I *toured Philadelphia* in style. We circled the city on the Mid-City Loop bus, a fast and easy way to see the heart of the city. *Traffic* poured from side streets that seemed wedged between *towers of glass and steel buildings*. Rumbling *trolley cars* screeched, and *cars and taxis* rushed to be first to the light. We met *shoppers and salespeople* as we purchased clothes and books as *gifts* for our family. We had been told that no trip to Philadelphia is complete without having a giant *hot pretzel*. So, we each had one spread with mustard. Then, tired but *happy*, we headed for the station. We finally fell into our train seats and on the trip home, we relived our first trip to the city.

Activity A

Choose *three* of these topics and narrow each of them down to one specific idea. The first one is done for you.

Topic	Specific Idea
1. boats	a ride in a canoe
2. games	
3. outer space	
4. vacation	
5. states	
6. clothing	
7. television shows	
8. famous people	

Activity B

Choose one of your specific ideas from activity A and make your own paragraph sandwich. Decide how you will begin and end the paragraph. Then choose the ideas that will go in the middle.

Write Away!

Look at your paragraph sandwich. Do you have a beginning that will introduce your specific idea? Do the middle ideas go together? Do you have an ending idea that will sum up your paragraph? Now is the time to write your paragraph. Get ready! Get set! Write!

Lesson 5 Giving the Paragraph a Title

A title is the name of a piece of writing.

Has a title ever caught your attention? Often, people will decide to read a story because they like the title. Read the titles below. Would you want to read these books?

How to Eat Fried Worms
Chocolate Touch
Help, I'm a Prisoner in the Library
Treasure Island

A good title has sparkle. It should be short and should give a clue about your paragraph.

Good titles are made up of colorful words that attract the reader's attention. Choose the titles from the ones listed below that sound interesting. Tell why.

Help!   My Vacation
My Nose Knows   Midnight Caper
Skateboard 500   Mario's Magic Touch
My Pet   The Boa in the Basement
Asleep on Nails   Just in Time
Too Many Tubas   My Cat's Career

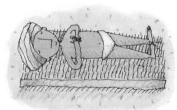

Activity A

Titles give a hint about the topic of your paragraph. Below are two paragraphs. Choose the title that you think best fits the paragraph.

The first man to die for the freedom of our country was Crispus Attucks. Attucks was a runaway slave and ex-sailor. When British soldiers attacked some Boston colonists in 1770, Attucks told the colonists not to be afraid. He showed them how to defend themselves. Attucks lost his life in the fight for freedom. Crispus Attucks's name can be seen on a statue in Boston Commons.

1. Colonial Days
2. The First American Hero
3. The British in Boston
4. A Famous Statue

Full moons have helped farmers since ancient times. The first full moon after the first day of autumn is called the Harvest Moon. During this time, the moon rises just after the sunset for several days. The extra light helps farmers work longer hours so that they can harvest their crops. The Hunter's Moon is the next full moon after the Harvest Moon, but its light is not so bright.

1. The Farmer's Ancient Helper
2. Two Moons of Autumn
3. Harvesting the Crops
4. Autumn Days

Activity B

Read each of these paragraphs. Create an interesting title. Remember, your title should be short and should attract your reader's attention.

The chameleon, a member of the lizard family, has many disguises. It can change its body color under certain situations. Sometimes it is bright green and blends with its surroundings. When it is basking in the sunshine, it becomes the color of black coffee. During sleeping time, it turns to a pale green. If the chameleon is frightened, it may change to any color from yellow to gray to white. Do you know any other animal that owns such a wardrobe?

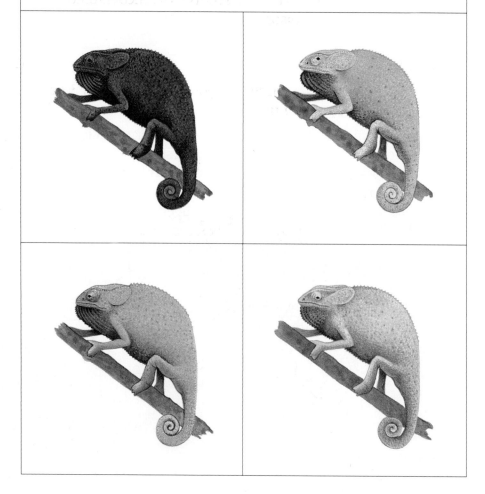

Do you know that a hamster has its own built-in pantry? Its two large cheek pouches make excellent baskets. Into these, the hamster packs seeds and grains. Then the hamster can easily carry food supplies to its underground home. This thrifty habit gives it something to eat in the winter when food is in short supply.

I had an unhappy experience at camp last summer. One day I joined a group of friends and took a long hike through the woods. Soon after I had gone to bed that night my legs began to itch all over. I turned on my flashlight to look at them, and saw they were all covered with little bumps. It seems I had encountered my first case of poison ivy.

Write Away!

Go back and read any paragraph you wrote in lesson 3 or 4. Give it an interesting title.

Word Study 1

Synonyms

Synonyms are words that have the same or almost the same meaning.

When you write, you might notice that you use the same word over and over again. Look in the dictionary to find synonyms that you can use instead. *Synonyms* are words with similar meanings. Using synonyms will help make your writing more interesting.

Can you give a synonym for each of these words? The first one is done for you.

save *rescue*	cool	empty
kind	thin	fast
big	reply	strange
sport	quiet	old
smart	almost	car

Although many synonyms have the exact same meanings, some synonyms have slightly different meanings. Notice how the synonyms *kind* and *gentle* are used in these sentences. How does each fit the meaning of the sentence?

A. It was *kind* of Anna to lend me her umbrella.
B. Anna is *gentle* when she pets the kittens.

Use the dictionary to help you choose the best synonyms for your sentences.

Activity A

Match each word in column A with its synonym in column
B. Use a dictionary to find the meaning of any word you
do not know. The first one is done for you.

Column A		Column B
still	f	a. wish
tardy	___	b. tale
afraid	___	c. street
story	___	d. scared
fix	___	e. bundle
loud	___	f. quiet
hope	___	g. place
put	___	h. noisy
package	___	i. late
road	___	j. mend

Activity B

Choose the synonym that best fits each sentence.
1. That robot (starts, begins) when you push the button.
2. That seven-foot man is very (high, tall).
3. The printing on the pirate's map is (faint, weak).
4. The Amish people live (still, quiet) lives.
5. The flash from the camera (hurts, harms) my eyes.
6. I'm going swimming with my best (companion, friend).
7. City buses don't always (race, run) on time.
8. A trained dog (guides, leads) George's blind brother.
9. Checkers is a fun (sport, game).
10. The grapes (ripen, develop) very quickly in the sun.

Chapter 2

Improving the Paragraph

Lesson 1 Writing Sentences in Order

Sentences in a paragraph should follow in correct order.

Imagine that you want to learn to play the harmonica. It is important to learn the steps in correct order. For example, you will need to know how to hold the harmonica before you learn the notes. Look at the following paragraph that explains how to play a harmonica. Are the sentences in correct order?

Did you know Abraham Lincoln played the harmonica? You can, too. First, rest the harmonica on the thumb of your left hand with one or two fingers on top. Next, bring the harmonica up to your mouth. Then, pucker your lips and blow gently into one of the holes. Now, make a note by drawing your breath in instead of pushing it out. Finally, try a simple tune.

Words such as *first*, *next*, *then*, and *finally* help you write your sentences in correct order. They connect one sentence to the other. These words are called *order words*. What order words are used in the paragraph you just read?

Did you know Abraham Lincoln played the harmonica? What facts do you know about his life?

Activity A

Put each set of sentences in the correct order to make a paragraph.

A

1. First, I slice a banana in half.
2. After that, I sprinkle some brown sugar on top of the sour cream.
3. It's always perfect—not too sour, not too sweet!
4. Then, I spread a big spoonful of sour cream on top of the banana.
5. I never liked sour cream until I discovered the following recipe.
6. Finally, I take a sample bite out of my creation.

B

1. If they need air, I borrow Dad's air pump to fill them.
2. Finally, I am ready to enjoy bike riding.
3. First, I dust it off.
4. As soon as the weather is warm enough, I get my bike out.
5. Then, I check the tires.
6. If anything is wrong, I take it to my uncle's bike shop.
7. After that, I go for a short ride to test the bike.

Activity B

Put the following sentences in the correct order to make a paragraph. Add order words to help connect the sentences.

1. Carry a flashlight and search the water's edge for a frog.
2. Feed your frog earthworms, flies, and small fish.
3. Put your frog in a large box with a tray of water on the bottom.
4. When you see one, point the light at the frog's eyes.
5. Find a pond, small stream, or even a big puddle in your neighborhood.
6. Slowly walk over to the frog and grab it gently from behind.

Write Away!

The sentences in the following paragraph are not written in the correct order. Rewrite the paragraph with the sentences in the correct order. Add order words to help connect the sentences.

Nancy found a recipe for a chocolate cake with fudge filling and chocolate frosting. There was only one thing wrong. Nancy and I wanted to bake a cake for our brother on his birthday. The top layer kept sliding down the crooked bottom layer. We baked the cake. We made the batter and we poured it into two cake pans. When it cooled, we put lots of fudge filling between the layers. My sister's solution was to stick chopsticks through the layers. That did the trick!

Lesson 2 Finding the Exact Word

Use exact words to add color, feeling, interest, or excitement to your paragraph.

A writer paints pictures with words. When you write, use vivid adjectives and strong verbs to create a clear picture. When you use words that help to create pictures, readers will enjoy your writing. Look at the following sets of sentences.

> An army of ants *walked* up the hill.
> An army of ants *marched* up the hill.

Notice how a strong verb like *marched* makes the second sentence more interesting.

> The *mean* dragon roamed the forest.
> The *snorting* dragon roamed the forest.

Notice how a vivid adjective like *snorting* makes the second sentence more interesting.

Replace the italicized words with colorful words to make these sentences come alive.

> The helicopter *flew* overhead.
> Did you see that *nice* dolphin?
> What a *big* wave that was!

Activity A

Find the picture words in these sentences. Some will be verbs; some will be adjectives.

1. We dashed to the corner to see the gigantic steamroller.
2. Horace's paper airplane fluttered over our desks and then plunged to the ground.
3. The gooey bubble gum stretched from the sidewalk to my shoe.
4. The elephant waved his trunk and let out a thunderous roar.
5. A fuzzy green caterpillar inched through the grass.

Activity B

Replace the italicized word in each sentence with a word from the Word Bank.

1. The train *moved* along the tracks.
2. The sea otters *went* down the muddy riverbank.
3. Sean *said*, "I can't move this box."
4. The campers listened to the *good* story.
5. Suddenly, the call of a crow echoed through the *quiet* forest.
6. "I got a hit!" *said* Nancy.

WORD BANK

peaceful	grumbled
slid	screamed
exciting	silent
raced	scary
rattled	bragged

Activity C

Add a picture word to complete each sentence.

1. The sailboat _____ on the calm blue water.
2. "Hurry!" _____ Marco. "We will miss the bus."
3. The _____ alien _____ behind a tree.
4. Tiny fish _____ among the plants in the aquarium.
5. Charlie's _____ pet scared his neighbors.
6. We _____ as we _____ the steep hill.

Write Away!

Complete each sentence in the following paragraph with a picture word. The word in parentheses will tell you what kind of word to use in each sentence.

The air grew thinner as we ___(verb)___ up the mountain. ___(adj.)___ trees gave way to smaller plants. The wind was cold, and we ___(verb)___ in our cotton jackets. ___(adj.)___ clouds threatened overhead. In the distance, we could hear an eagle ___(verb)___. Suddenly, there was a clap of thunder, and lightning ___(verb)___ the sky. Because of the ___(adj.)___ storm, we ___(verb)___ for shelter.

Lesson 3 Using Similes in Writing

A simile compares two seemingly unlike things that actually have something in common. The words *like* and *as* are used in similes.

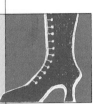

Try these riddles. Each riddle compares two things that are very different, but that are alike in some way.

What do an old shoe and a skunk's den have in common?
Both are smelly.

What do peanut butter and wet cement have in common?
Both are thick and sticky.

What do a ship's horn and a bullfrog have in common?
Both sound loud and deep.

You can change these riddles into similes by using *like* or *as*. For example:

The old shoe was *as* smelly *as* a skunk's den.
The peanut butter stuck in my mouth *like* wet cement.
The ship's horn bellowed *like* a bullfrog across the water.

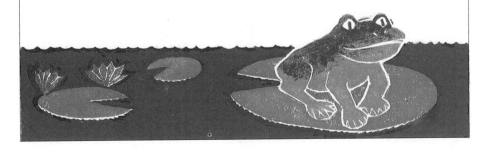

Activity A

Think of an answer to each of these riddles. Then complete the simile following each riddle.

1. What do a bouquet of flowers and a rainbow have in common?

   A bouquet of flowers is as _____ as a rainbow.

2. What do a kite and a comet have in common?

   A comet has a _____ like a kite.

3. What do snowflakes and diamonds have in common?

   Snowflakes _____ like diamonds.

Activity B

Find the simile in each of these sentences.

1. The runner sprinted like a jackrabbit across the finish line.
2. Kevin slithered like a snake under the fence.
3. The snow lay as heavy as a blanket over the city.
4. The kites soared like birds in the brisk wind.
5. Joan giggled as mischievously as a chimpanzee.

Activity C

Complete each of these similes.

1. The cat's eyes glowed like...
2. The giraffe's neck was as long as...
3. The deer stood as still as...
4. The steak was as tough as...
5. He walks like...

Write Away!

Write two different similes to describe each topic below. Try to paint a vivid word picture with your similes.

joggers   elephant   balloon

Lesson 4 Expanding Sentences

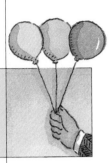

Some sentences give only a simple fact. Other sentences include details that help give the reader a clear picture.

Picture words and similes can help you add interesting details to your sentences. To help expand your sentences, ask yourself these questions: *what, what kind, how, when, where, why.* Look at the following sentence.

> The gorilla swung across his cage.

This sentence gives basic information, but it does not give interesting details.

> What is the gorilla's name?
> What does he look like?
> How did he swing?
> What kind of a cage is he in?

With the answers to these questions, you can expand your sentence with interesting details.

> Samson, a three-hundred-pound gorilla, swung across his giant cage with a mighty screech.

Activity A

Use the following chart to help you expand each sentence. The first one is done for you.

	What Kind?	When?	Where?	How?
1. Snow fell.	soft	today	from the sky	gently
2. The penguins strolled.	stout	in the morning	across the ice	calmly
3. The cook complained.	cranky	at noon	in the kitchen	loudly
4. The pitcher threw the ball.	nervous	last evening	from the mound	wildly

1. Soft snow fell gently from the sky today.

Activity B

Make a chart to help you gather ideas about each of these pictures. Then expand the sentence.

1. The helicopter landed.
2. The porpoise jumped.
3. The trumpet sounded.
4. The dancers danced.

Write Away!

Imagine that you and a friend are the first people to have traveled outside our galaxy. Write five sentences in which you describe some of the sights you have seen. Use the questions from the chart of activity A to help expand your sentences.

Lesson 5 Trimming Long Sentences

Sentences that contain too many words or ideas should be trimmed to make shorter sentences.

Long, confusing sentences are called rambling sentences. Sentences ramble when you use too many ideas connected by words such as *and, and so,* or *and then.* Look at the following sentence.

> Elephant-foot plants can grow to be thirty feet high and they have leaves that may be four feet long and they have bark that is grayish-brown and wrinkled.

In this sentence, *and* is used too many times. Do not use *and* to connect more than two ideas in a sentence, or you will confuse your reader. This sentence can be broken into three clear sentences.

> Elephant-foot plants can grow to be thirty feet high. Their leaves can be four feet long. Their bark is grayish-brown and wrinkled.

Read the following rambling sentence. Can you rewrite it to form three clear sentences?

> Red Riding Hood was on her way to Grandmother's house and when she arrived she noticed that Grandmother looked different and then she saw the big ears and big eyes and big teeth and she was scared.

Activity A

Trim each of these sentences to make shorter, clearer sentences.

1. One day I went roller-skating in my cousin's neighborhood and I forgot to look where I was going and some sticks were in my way and over I went.

2. Our class learned how to use a computer the first month of school and then we enjoyed learning how to write a computer program and one group even created a math game.

3. George picked blueberries on the farm and he was in a hurry and he didn't pick them carefully and then he got stains on his new shirt.

4. The artist unwrapped the wet ball of clay and she molded it in her hands and then she used the potter's wheel to fashion a vase.

5. Jeremy built a model of the space shuttle for the science fair and he was excited when he won first prize and he received a trophy.

Activity B

Rewrite each paragraph. Trim each rambling sentence to make shorter, clearer sentences.

A

Yesterday, Pierre and his friends decided to go tubing on the Delaware River and they bicycled to East Grove to rent their tubes. It was a warm, sunny day and they floated lazily down the river and they watched the wild geese make perfect landings on the water and farther down they saw people waving to them from other floating tubes and they waved back. The boys finally came ashore and as soon as they landed they saw Pierre's father in his van and while they rode back to their starting point they described their wonderful river experience to him.

B

Quilts are beautiful bedspreads and they are made by sewing together many types of cloth patches. Old shirts and dresses and other scraps of colorful clothing are very good material for patches and some people even go to used clothing stores to buy the fabric for these patches. In the past, neighbors, friends, and relatives gave each other scraps of clothing to make the quilts and so for each scrap there was an interesting story to tell about its owner.

Schoolhouse quilt from 1900

Quilt from the 1840s

Write Away!

Use your imagination to create a story for this cartoon. Be careful not to use *and* too often.

Lesson 6 Practicing Revision

**When you revise, you take a careful look at your
sentences and paragraphs and try to improve them.**

Each lesson in this chapter has shown you a way to
improve your sentences. You were taught to write
sentences in order, to use colorful words, to write similes,
and to expand and trim sentences. The subject of this
lesson is *revision*.

Think of the following questions when you revise your
sentences.
   a. Have I made sure my sentences are in logical order
      and make sense?
   b. Have I used interesting, colorful words to paint a clear
      picture?
   c. Have I used similes where possible to add exciting
      comparisons?
   d. Have I used *and, and so,* and *and then* too often?
   e. Have I tried to expand my sentences by adding
      important details?

Activity A

In each set, sentence A has been revised. Sentence B is the
revised sentence. Tell how sentence A was revised by
choosing the correct letter from the questions above.
   A. Tears ran down the child's face.
   B. Tears trickled down the child's freckled face.

   A. Leon made a pizza with pickles and grape jelly and he
      put it into the oven and then he forgot to take it out.
   B. Leon made a pizza with pickles and grape jelly. He put
      it into the oven. He forgot to take it out.

A. He fed his fish each day. Peter bought a guppy at the store. Peter enjoyed his new pet.

B. Peter bought a guppy at the store. He fed his fish every day. Peter enjoyed his new pet.

A. The campers huddled.

B. Around the campfire, the young campers huddled together to sing songs and tell stories.

A. The leopard streaked through the forest.

B. The leopard streaked through the forest like a bolt of lightning.

Activity B

Follow the directions given below to revise the paragraph.

Going Under the Water

1. I went into the submarine excitedly. 2. It took me below the surface of the water and I could see oyster beds and then I could see sea urchins and I could even see starfish. 3. Some of the starfish had bright colors. 4. The sea is interesting.

1. In sentence 1, write a more exact word for *went*.
2. Trim sentence 2 to make shorter, clearer sentences. Also, use more exact words for *see*. Add picture words where needed.
3. Help brighten the paragraph by using a simile in sentence 3.
4. Expand sentence 4.
5. Select a better title for the paragraph.

Lesson 7 Learning to Proofread

Learning to proofread will help make your final copy perfect.

Proofreading is the last thing you do before you write your final copy. Proofreading symbols mark the places where you should make corrections. You should use a colored pencil so that you can spot the symbols easily.

Carefully study this list of proofreading symbols.

≡	Make a capital letter	Alice in wonderland
∧	Add a word or phrase	Alice Wonderland
⑤℗	Correct spelling	Alise in Wonderland
○	Change end punctuation	Alice in Wonderland!
ℯ	Omit a word or letter	Alice in in Wonderland
¶	Begin a new paragraph	¶ Alice in Wonderland

Activity A

Discuss the meaning of each symbol in this paragraph.

A dinosaur could never be a house pet. They are to^(sp) big and they eat too much?⊙What would your mother say if you brought a dinosaur home?¶Today dinosaurs can be found only in museums. ṣcientists have studied ancient bones so they can tell us how dinosaurs once lived.

Activity B

Use proofreading symbols to mark the places where corrections should be made in this paragraph.

saddle up your ponies, we're off to a rodeo! You mite want to enter the bronco-riding contest. Could you stay on a twisting, plunging horse for ten seconds. Remember to use only one hand on the reins! Rodeos began as contests among cowboys. Modern day cowhands practice many hours roping steers and riding bareback soo they can win prizes at the rodo. Maybe you would rather sit safely the grandstand and watch the pros wrestle the wild ones.

Word Study 2

Antonyms

Antonyms are words that have opposite meanings.

When you play games, you try to win. But only one team wins. The other team loses. The words *win* and *lose* have opposite meanings. They are called *antonyms*.

Can you give an antonym for each of these words? The first one is done for you.

wide *narrow*	warm	young
poor	common	dry
polite	thick	shout
sharp	over	true
strong	win	better

Activity A

Match each word in column A with its antonym in column B. Use a dictionary to find the meaning of any word you do not know. The first one is done for you.

Column A		Column B
large	i	a. common
fast	___	b. asleep
right	___	c. young
old	___	d. easy
awake	___	e. dim
strange	___	f. long
difficult	___	g. slow
bright	___	h. idle
busy	___	i. small
short	___	j. left

Activity B

Choose an antonym for the word in italics from the words in parentheses.

1. The old king was *poor*. (wise, rich, honest)
2. Slowly the puppy crept up the *narrow* stairs. (steep, wooden, wide)
3. In winter, the nights are *short*. (long, cold, dark)
4. The zookeeper showed us the *tiny* cage. (messy, huge, tall)
5. We found an *old* chart in the bottle. (green, ancient, new)
6. Hail can *help* crops. (harm, feed, water)
7. When lava cools, it *softens* into rock. (grows, breaks, hardens)
8. The ogre *shut* his fierce eyes. (rolled, opened, winked)

Activity C

Use an antonym in place of the word in italics in each sentence.

1. Anna is always *early* for her saxophone lesson.
2. Wolves are very *careless* with their young.
3. Who was the *last* person to swim the English Channel?
4. A porcupine's quills are *dull*.
5. Sandy *whispered* to James over the cheers of the fans.
6. Suzie was the *worst* gymnast in the Olympics.
7. The lights in the theater became very *bright*.
8. The *polite* princess poured tea on the butler's sleeve.

Chapter 3
Exploring Writing

Lesson 1 Writing Instructions

Instructions explain how to do or make something.

Imagine that you are the chairperson of your club's Valentine project—making bookmarks for children in a hospital. You need to write instructions so that the other club members will understand how to make bookmarks. When you write instructions, you must give all the information needed in the correct order.

In your instructions, first state the *specific idea*. The specific idea tells what you will explain how to do or make. Then tell the *materials* that are needed. Next list the *steps* that should be followed to complete the project. Lastly you might like to say why the project is helpful.

Have you ever made a special card? How did you make it?

Read these instructions carefully. Then answer the questions that follow.

The All-around Bookmark

A bookmark is a useful and colorful gift. To make one, you need a 2″ by 5″ piece of plain fabric, a 6″ piece of elastic, some felt scraps, glue, a needle and thread, and scissors. First, cut out small designs, such as stars or hearts, from the felt. Then, glue them onto the piece of fabric. You can also use markers to write a message around the design. Finally, use the needle and thread to sew one end of the elastic to the top and the other end to the bottom of the bookmark. The back of the decorated fabric goes against the book's spine. The elastic goes between the pages to mark your place. This bookmark is a bright and neat way to keep the correct page for you.

A. What is the specific idea?
B. What materials are needed?
C. What order words are used in the steps to follow?
D. Are the steps given in the proper order?
E. Why is this project helpful?

Activity A

Below are instructions for applying an iron-on patch to your T-shirt. The first and last steps are in the correct order. Can you put the middle steps in the correct order?

__1__ Here is your iron-on patch.

_____ Last, iron over the patch for 20 seconds. Now you can peel off the paper on the back of the patch.

_____ Next, place the piece of plain paper on the ironing board.

_____ First, use scissors to trim the edges of the patch.

_____ You will need scissors, a cotton T-shirt, a piece of plain paper, and an iron.

_____ Slide the T-shirt over the ironing board. The place on the shirt where the patch will go should be on top of the paper.

_____ Then put the iron-on patch face down on the shirt.

__8__ Your T-shirt is ready to wear!

Activity B

Write instructions for one of these ideas. Be sure to list all the materials needed. Give your instructions a colorful title.

  a. How to make your favorite sandwich
  b. How to find the school lunchroom
  c. How to make a social studies diorama
  d. How to use common objects to show a five-year-old that $2 + 3 = 5$

Write Away!

Be an artist! First, draw a simple picture and color it. Next, write instructions that tell how you did it. Give your instructions a title. Then give these instructions to a classmate to follow. After your classmate completes your instructions, compare the two pictures. Do they look alike? How clear were your instructions?

Checkpoint: Revising and Proofreading Instructions

Revision: Time to Take Another Look

Reread your instructions carefully and then ask yourself these questions:

—Did I clearly state the main idea?
—Did I include all the necessary information?
—Did I put the steps in the correct order?
—Did I use specific verbs and adjectives?
—Does the ending sentence tell why you would want to do this project or make this object?

Now is the time to make any changes. Discuss your changes with another student or with your teacher. Rewrite your paragraph and then go on to proofreading.

Proofreading: Time to Look at Capitalization, Punctuation, and Spelling

≡	make a capital letter
/	do not capitalize a letter
ʌ	add a word
ℰ	omit a word
(SP)	incorrect spelling
O	new mark of punctuation
¶	begin a paragraph

—Did I begin each sentence and proper noun with a capital letter?
—Did I indent the first word of my paragraph?
—Did I use the correct mark of punctuation at the end of each sentence?

Start at the last word of the paragraph and work backward to check for correct spelling. If necessary, rewrite the paragraph in your best handwriting.

Lesson 2 Writing a Feature Story

A feature story gives interesting information about a particular person or event.

A feature story spotlights people or happenings that would be interesting to others. It focuses attention on what makes a person or event special. A feature story usually includes a *direct quote*. A direct quote is the exact words of the person being featured, or of a person involved in the featured event.

Here is a feature story about a fourth-grade boy. Read it carefully. Then answer the questions that follow.

> What makes a champion? Sometimes it means not just being the best but becoming the best in spite of great odds. Harrison Roberts, a fourth-grade boy, is a champion gymnast. Harrison is also blind. He learned gymnastics by listening to his instructor's commands and by touching every piece of equipment until he knew it by heart.
> This year, Harrison won a gold medal in his division finals. "Nothing ever felt as great as that heavy gold medal around my neck," he exclaimed. That day a small nine-year-old boy showed everyone how to be a winner.

A. Who is the important person in the story?
B. What is his special talent?
C. What challenge did he have to face?
D. What did he win?
E. What did he say?
F. What did he show other people?

Activity A

Choose *one* of these five people to spotlight in a feature story. Think of five questions that you could ask him or her to gather information for a story.

1. Lionhearted Larry, lion tamer
2. Andrea Kim, deep-sea explorer
3. Joe Perez, 10-year-old magician
4. Wendy Walker, adventure story author
5. Daniel Newthing, inventor

Activity B

Think of a person you know who has an interesting hobby or talent. Interview that special person. Then write a feature story. In the first paragraph, tell why the person is special. In the second paragraph, give more information and include a direct quote.

Write Away!

Clip and bring to class a feature story from a newspaper or magazine. Use a marker to highlight the important person in the story and what he or she did. Highlight any direct quotes.

Checkpoint: Revising and Proofreading a Feature Story

Revision: Time to Take Another Look

Reread your feature story and then ask yourself these questions:

—Did I use colorful adjectives to describe people or events?

—Did I use a direct quote in my feature story?

—Did I trim any rambling sentences and expand others?

—Is my story interesting?

Now is the time to make any changes. Discuss your changes with another student or with your teacher. Rewrite your feature story and then go on to proofreading.

Proofreading: Time to Look at Capitalization, Punctuation, and Spelling

	make a capital letter
/	do not capitalize a letter
	add a word
	omit a word
(SP)	incorrect spelling
O	new mark of punctuation
	begin a paragraph

—Did I begin each sentence and each proper noun with a capital letter?

—Did I indent each paragraph?

—Did I use the correct mark of punctuation at the end of each sentence?

—Did I use correct punctuation for the direct quote?

Start at the last word of the story and work backward to check for correct spelling. If necessary, rewrite the feature story in your best handwriting.

Lesson 3 Writing a Story: Characters

Characters are the actors in a story. A story is about characters and events in their lives.

Think of some of the stories you have enjoyed reading. Characters make a story come alive through what they say and do. Characters can be people or animals. What are the names of characters you remember from stories you have enjoyed?

When you write a story, you must give your characters *personalities*. Your personality is a total of the qualities that make you act differently from other people. You can give your characters personalities by using

> clear descriptions
> interesting dialogue
> colorful words

Read this excerpt from the story *Chan's Philly Summer*. Then answer the questions that follow.

> "I can hear some guys playing," Chandler said with a question in his voice. "Do any live near you, Uncle Ray?"
>
> "Sure do. There's Leroy Conn and Sid Berman right on the block. I told them you were coming for the summer, and they said they'd be glad to show you the ropes. In fact, I see them over by the garage now. Are you up to some introductions?"
>
> Chandler felt a tiny sliver of fear begin to slide around his insides and to poke holes in his confidence.
>
> "Don't get upset," he said to himself.

Sneakers came thump-thumping up the driveway and two voices shouted a hello. Leroy, a powerhouse of energy, had a Phillies cap smashed on his afro, giving it the appearance of a curly black halo. Sid jogged behind him, tall and lanky, a cool, distant look hiding a brain like a steel trap. They carefully eyed Chandler.

A. What advice does Chandler give himself? Does this tell you something about his personality?
B. What does Leroy Conn look like?
C. What does Sid Berman look like?
D. What colorful words does the author use?

Activity A

Choose one sentence from each set that would make the character of Big Al come alive. Then write the descriptive sentences in order. They will form a paragraph.

Big Al works on Pier 52 along the river.

A. Big Al is tall and strong.
B. Big Al is a giant of a man and as strong as an ox.

A. His muscles are rock hard from tossing heavy boxes on board the ships.
B. He has very big muscles from throwing boxes on board the ships.

A. Big Al's curly blond hair brushes over smiling brown eyes that sparkle when he talks.
B. Big Al has blond hair, brown eyes, and a nice smile.

A. Everyone likes to work with Big Al because he is fun.
B. Everyone likes to work with Big Al because he makes hard work seem like fun.

A. "My job working along the river is nice," says Big Al.
B. "I like using my muscles, I like being outside on the docks, and I love this mighty river," says Big Al.

Activity B

Choose *one* of these five characters. Write a description of the character in four or five sentences.

1. Sir Richard Schaeffer, worldwide explorer
2. Margaret Wong, U.S. astronaut
3. Amazing Amelia, 80-year-old marathon runner
4. Murderous Marty, mystery book author
5. Short-circuit Sam, talking, walking robot

Write Away!

Now decide on a character you would like to use in a story. Give your character a name and then describe him or her. Save your description for the next lesson.

Lesson 4 Writing a Story: Plot and Setting

Every story has a plot and a setting. The events in a story make up the plot. The place where the events happen is the setting.

Stories introduce *characters* and describe a *setting*. The action that happens is the *plot*. In the plot, characters face problems or *conflicts*. Throughout the story, the characters try to solve the conflict.

Here are the first two paragraphs of a story. Read them carefully. Then answer the questions that follow.

> Thirty-two tons of steel sped with a clickety-clack across the Nebraska plains. Captain Raimos sat in an empty dining car. His hair fell down on his forehead as he bent over a piece of scrap paper on the table. Beads of perspiration trickled down his cheeks. Feverishly, he worked to put together the pieces of a crazy puzzle. The jewels were somewhere on board, in someone's suitcase. The wail of the engine's whistle reminded him that his time was short. He had to begin his search now.
>
> Quickly, he moved from one compartment to the next. From under the closed door of the last room, he saw something sparkle. Cautiously, he entered the room. Without warning, the door slammed behind him and he heard the jiggle of a key in the lock.

A. Who is the first character you are introduced to in the story?

B. What is the setting of the story? How do you know?

C. What is the problem or conflict?

D. What do you think will happen?

Activity A

Choose one character and one setting from the lists below. Then write the introduction to a story. Tell what conflict your character will face. Use the story in the introduction as a model.

Characters	Settings
Crafty Christopher	on a surf-splashed beach
Handsome Harry	in a giant circus tent
Incredible Ingrid	in an abandoned gold mine
Practical Pat	in a detective's office
Fearless Freda	out in space

Activity B

A story should have a strong ending. It might be a surprise ending or a solution to a problem. Here are the last two paragraphs of the detective story.

    With a lurch and a hiss of steam, the train ground to a stop. Quickly Captain Raimos lowered the window and swung himself onto the steps of the car's entrance. The jewel thief had locked him in the compartment, and he knew who it was!

    In the small room, along with the jewels, the captain had seen a familiar hat, a hat that belonged to someone who had many keys. "No one will believe it," he thought as he watched the jolly conductor walking down the platform. Captain Raimos grabbed him from behind and cuffed him. "You are the one," he said, "the one who has the keys to all the compartments—and the only conductor without a hat!"

Write Away!

Now plan your own story.
1. Use the character you wrote about in lesson 3.
2. Choose the setting—where your story will take place.
3. Jot down ideas for your plot—what will happen, what the conflict will be.
4. Think of a surprise ending or a solution to the problem.

When you are finished planning, write your story.

Checkpoint: Revising and Proofreading a Story

Revision: Time to Take Another Look

Reread your story carefully and then ask yourself these questions:

—Did I use colorful words to describe my character?

—Is the setting of the story clear?

—Does my character have a problem to solve?

—Is the plot in correct order?

—Did I trim long sentences and expand very short sentences?

—What kind of ending did I write?

Now is the time to make any changes. Discuss your changes with another student or with your teacher. Rewrite your story and then go on to proofreading.

Proofreading: Time to Look at Capitalization, Punctuation, and Spelling

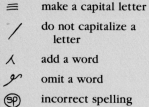

≡	make a capital letter
/	do not capitalize a letter
⋏	add a word
℘	omit a word
ⓢⓟ	incorrect spelling
◯	new mark of punctuation
¶	begin a paragraph

—Did I begin each sentence and proper noun with a capital letter?

—Did I indent each paragraph?

—Did I use the correct mark of punctuation at the end of each sentence?

—Did I use correct punctuation for any direct quote?

Start at the last word of the story and work backward to check for correct spelling. If necessary, rewrite the paragraph in your best handwriting.

Lesson 5 Writing a Book Report

A book report is a way to share information about a book you have read.

When you read a book, you meet new characters and learn about new places. A book report gives you a chance to share interesting and exciting experiences with other students. In a book report, you should give just enough information to make someone else want to read the book.

In your book report, you should tell the *title* and the *author* of the book and just a hint about *what happens*. Don't tell too much! The reader shouldn't know how the story ends. The last part of the report should tell your *personal opinion*. Here you can tell why you enjoyed the story, or why you didn't enjoy it.

Read these model book reports. Then answer the questions that follow.

Title: Shoeshine Girl
Author: Clyde Bulla

    In the book Shoeshine Girl by Clyde Bulla, Sarah's best friend gets into trouble for shoplifting. Sarah's parents want to keep their ten-year-old daughter out of trouble. They send her to live for a while with her Aunt Claudia. Sarah treats everybody in her new neighborhood in a mean way, including her aunt. Sarah is angry. She feels that no one trusts her. Then she gets a good job as a shoeshine girl and her adventures begin.

    I enjoyed reading how Sarah solved the problem of how to get her own spending money. She got a job. Many things happened to her when she was a shoeshine girl. These things showed me that ten-year-old people can make a big difference.

Title: <u>Man from the Sky</u>
Author: Avi

In the book <u>Man from the Sky</u> by Avi, Jamie is not imagining things. There really is a man dropping from the sky! He is a dangerous criminal using a parachute to escape with a million dollars. From a distance, Jamie can see the man using a gun to take Jamie's neighbor, Guilliam, hostage.

I really admired the way Jamie acted. It was very hard for him to figure out the important evidence, but he did it. He took the chance that people would make fun of him so that he could get help for Guilliam. I liked sharing Jamie and Guilliam's adventure.

A. What is the title of each book?
B. Who is the author of each book?
C. What is the plot of *The Shoeshine Girl*? What is the plot of *Man from the Sky*?
D. What reasons are given for liking *Man from the Sky*?
E. Do you think you would enjoy reading these books?

Activity A

Write a book report. In the first paragraph, include the name of the book, the author, and just enough about the plot to interest your reader. In the second paragraph, give your personal opinion about the story. Tell why you feel the way you do.

Writing about Book Characters

The characters in your stories are often very interesting people. They may have exciting adventures or do great and important things for others. You might like to introduce a book character to your classmates. When you write about a book character, it is called a *character sketch*.

Read the *character sketch* below to find out about a special person—Annie Sullivan.

> *Title:* Annie Sullivan
> *Author:* Mary Malone

Helen Keller and Annie Sullivan

> Annie Sullivan was a winner. But to be a winner she had to come from last place and jump over a lot of hurdles. When she was ten, she became almost blind. Her parents had died. She had to take care of her little brother Jimmy. They lived in a place called a poor house.
>
> Annie soon learned Braille, a way that blind people read by touching raised dots on a page. When Annie was about twenty-one years old, she was asked to teach Helen Keller. Helen was six years old, blind, and could not hear or speak. She was wild and stubborn. How could anyone teach her? Annie could.
>
> To find out how she helped Helen become one of the most educated and respected women in the world, read <u>Annie Sullivan</u> by Mary Malone.

Activity B

Think of a few special book characters you have read about. They may be people who actually lived or imaginary characters. Introduce a character to other students. Write a character sketch.

Write Away!

Write a riddle about a character or the plot of a story. You can try to rhyme the riddle if you wish. First see if you can guess something about the books Jennifer and Stan read. Begin your guess by writing, "I think Jennifer (or Stan) read a book about...."

Here is Jennifer's riddle:

I read a book that got me all wet.
A hand-shaking octopus is someone I met.

Here is Stan's riddle:

Before these folks landed, they traveled awhile.
Strange-looking guests, but they made readers smile.

Word Study 3

Homophones

Homophones are words that sound alike but are spelled differently and have different meanings.

Sometimes you hear words that sound the same but have different meanings. These words can be very confusing when you write. You need to know the *meaning* of each word and how to *spell* it. Read this sentence.

> I heard a herd of elephants run past my bedroom window.

Can you find the homophones in it? Why are they called homophones?

A dictionary will give you the meaning of a homophone. Here are some homophones with their meanings. Study them carefully.

hair—threadlike growth from
    the skin
hare—animal like a rabbit

right—correct, opposite of left
write—to make letters or words

sail—to travel on water
sale—act of selling

so—in that way
sew—work with needle and thread

scene—view, picture
seen—past participle of *see*

plain—clear, not fancy
plane—flat surface, short form of airplane

peace—freedom from war, quiet
piece—one of the parts of something

way—means, method
weigh—find out how heavy

Activity A

Choose the correct homophone to complete each sentence.
1. We saw some donkeys for (sale, sail).
2. My mom wanted some (piece, peace) and quiet.
3. How much does this little calf (way, weigh)?
4. My little sister didn't want her (hair, hare) cut.
5. I haven't (seen, scene) the magic show yet.
6. Skippy likes a (plane, plain) peanut butter sandwich.
7. Paul can (sew, so) the patch on his sweatshirt.
8. (Write! Right!) A dolphin is not a fish.
9. The (hair, hare) beat the tortoise in the race.
10. Trish is painting a jungle (scene, seen).
11. Toy boats (sale, sail) in the pond.
12. "Wrong (weigh, way)" was printed on the sign.
13. (So, Sew), you would like to be an acrobat?
14. Use that (piece, peace) of string to tie the package.
15. Did you ever (right, write) a letter on a puzzle?

Activity B

Use your dictionary to find the meaning of each
homophone. Then use each word in a sentence.

sense	tale	wear	pale
cents	tail	where	pail

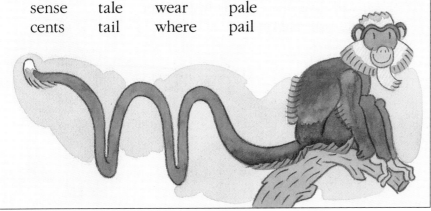

To, Too, and Two

> *To, too,* and *two* are easy to confuse because they sound alike. These words are *homophones*.

To means *in the direction of a person, place, or thing*.
Tomorrow, I will go *to* the zoo.
I gave my glue *to* Dave.

Too means *also, more than enough*.
Marty will go with me, *too*.
Don't use *too* much glue on the paper!

Two means the *number 2*.
There will be *two* of us going to the zoo.
Two globs of glue will be enough.

Activity C

Complete each sentence with the correct homophone.
1. Amy and her friends ran ___ the corner.
2. She, ___, wanted a good view of the parade.
3. Now, she could see ___ floats coming down the street.
4. This morning, I received ___ letters.
5. I was writing one, ___.
6. I took it ___ the mailbox.
7. That Mexican sombrero was ___ big.
8. Pedro wanted ___ small ones.
9. He will give one ___ his little sister.
10. Would you like one, ___?

Their, *There,* and *They're*

Their, *there,* and *they're* are easy to confuse because they sound alike. These words are *homophones.*

Their is an adjective. It shows *ownership* or *possession.*
　Don't take *their* peanuts.
　Their feet made footprints in the wet sand.

There is an adverb. It shows *place.*
　Our peanuts are *there.*
　Look over *there* at all the birds!

They're is a contraction. It means *they are.*
　They're my peanuts on the bench.
　I think *they're* sandpipers.

Activity D

Complete each sentence with the correct homophone.
　1. _____ slippers are too big.
　2. Mine are _____, under the table.
　3. _____ the biggest slippers I've ever seen.
　4. _____ catching butterflies.
　5. I love to look at _____ colorful wings.
　6. I see some over _____ in the bushes.
　7. _____ are the hens in the chicken coop.
　8. They laid _____ eggs this morning.
　9. _____ going to lay some more.
　10. _____ for breakfast tomorrow morning.

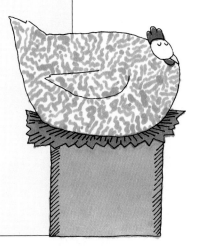

Chapter 4

More to Explore about Writing

Lesson 1 Using Your Senses

Use your senses to gather important information about a topic.

Once you choose a topic, think about what senses you could use to gather important information about the topic. Your senses of sight, sound, smell, taste, and touch can be used to help you describe your topic clearly.

When you describe a topic, you are giving the reader a "picture" of a person, place, or thing. In descriptive writing, you use words that help your reader see, hear, smell, taste, and touch what is in the "picture" you are describing.

Here are some examples of words that describe the senses.

Sight	Sound	Smell	Taste	Touch
silvery	shrill	flowery	juicy	silky
spotted	hissing	moldy	sour	sharp

Some of these words give a pleasant feeling. Which words are they? Some of these words give an unpleasant feeling. Which words are they? Can you add other words to these lists?

What day of the year do you think it is? What do you like to do on this special day?

Look at these ideas about a vegetable garden. The writer used his or her senses to create a "picture" of this garden. What "picture" do you have in your mind?

Sight

green leaves
red radishes

Taste

tart tomatoes
sweet corn

Sound

buzzing bees
chirping birds

Touch

smooth leaves
thorny stems

Smell

strong onions
spicy peppers

Activity A

Here are some topics:

snowstorm   camp fire   party   supermarket   zoo

Complete this chart. First, think of things you would see, hear, smell, taste, or touch for each topic. Then think of a descriptive word to help paint a clear picture of each thing. The first one is done for you.

	Sight	Sound	Smell	Taste	Touch
snowstorm	*sparkling* *flakes*				
camp fire					
party					
supermarket					
zoo					

Activity B

Not every topic uses all the senses. For some topics, it is more logical to use only one or two senses. Select one of the topics below and decide upon one sense. Write three groups of words using that particular sense. Then write one or two sentences about your topic. First, look at this example topic.

TOPIC: clown's costume

SENSE: sight

GROUPS
OF WORDS: orange curly hair
            bright red nose
            colorful patches on clothes

SENTENCES: Hector, the circus clown, has a bright red
            nose and orange curly hair that sticks out
            from his head. His colorful patches give his
            clothes a funny appearance.

A. radio
B. sand castle
C. library
D. pizza

Write Away!

Choose two topics from activity A. Look at the sense words next to these topics in your chart. Now write two descriptive sentences for each topic, using the words in your chart.

Lesson 2 Writing a Descriptive Paragraph

A descriptive paragraph paints a picture with words.

An artist uses colors to make a painting come alive. A writer is like an artist. A writer paints a picture with words. In a descriptive paragraph, the words you use are important. Your reader should be able to see, hear, smell, touch, or taste what you are describing.

Greg wants to write a descriptive paragraph about a roller coaster ride. He knows he won't use all his senses to help write his paragraph. He decides he will use *sight, sound,* and *touch.* To help picture his ideas, Greg makes a chart like this:

Roller Coaster Ride

What did I see?	*tiny cars, blurred ground, colorful booths*
What did I hear?	*rumbles, screeches, clanks, shouts, chugs*
What did I touch (feel)?	*cold metal bar, wind*

Here is what Greg wrote. What ideas from the chart are in his paragraph?

Roller Coaster Thrills

When I reached the front of the line, I knew there was no turning back. I squeezed my legs into the tiny car and clanked the cold safety bar in place. With a rumble and a snap, the car chugged up the first hill. It reached the top and then dove into space. I grabbed the bar and felt the wind whip against my face and through my hair. The ground below was a blur of tiny people and cars and colorful booths. My stomach dropped and my head spun. Soon the cars screeched to a stop. On shaky legs, I headed for the line again. I couldn't wait to try it again!

Activity A

Choose three of these topics. Decide which senses will help you gather the most information. Make a chart like Greg's that asks questions about each topic.

A. Being lost in a jungle
B. Landing on the moon
C. Sitting on a mountaintop
D. Sliding into a swimming pool
E. Eating in a fancy restaurant

Activity B

Ask these questions about the picture below.

What do I see?	What do I taste?
What do I hear?	What do I touch?
What do I smell?	

Now write a short paragraph using as many senses as you can.

Write Away!

Write a short paragraph like Greg's. Choose one topic from activity A. Try to include most of the ideas from your chart. You can also add new ideas. Remember, your descriptive paragraph should paint a picture with words.

Macaws

Checkpoint: Revising and Proofreading a Descriptive Paragraph

Revision: Time to Take Another Look

As you look over your descriptive paragraph, ask yourself these questions:

—Have I used as many senses as possible? (sight, sound, smell, touch, taste)

—Could I use more exact verbs and adjectives?

—Could I trim any rambling sentences?

—Could I expand any sentences by asking *what kind*, *when*, and *where*?

—Could I use a simile in any of my sentences?

—Does the paragraph make sense?

Now is the time to make any changes. Discuss your changes with another student or with your teacher. Rewrite your paragraph and then go on to proofreading.

Proofreading: Time to Look at Capitalization, Punctuation, and Spelling

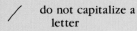 ≡	make a capital letter
/	do not capitalize a letter
⅄	add a word
℘	omit a word
⑤Ⓟ	incorrect spelling
○	new mark of punctuation
¶	begin a paragraph

—Did I begin each sentence and proper noun with a capital letter?

—Did I indent the first word of my paragraph?

—Did I use the correct mark of punctuation at the end of each sentence?

Start with the last word of your paragraph and work backward to check for correct spelling. If necessary, rewrite the paragraph in your best handwriting.

Lesson 3 Making a Word Map

A word map is a fun way of organizing your ideas. It will help you write an outline.

When you write a report, you will need to write more than one paragraph. Each paragraph should contain a separate specific idea.

This train is overloaded. Paragraphs can also become overloaded when they have more than one specific idea.

On this train, each car holds only one item. If each car were a paragraph, it would contain only one specific idea.

In order to write more than one paragraph, you must learn to organize your information. Making a *word map* can help you do this. Word maps are fun and easy to do. In the next lesson, they will help you learn to write an outline. Here is a word map about trains. Study it carefully.

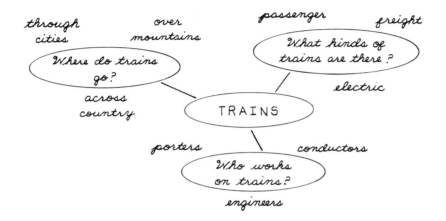

Activity A

The circle in the middle of the word map contains the *topic*.
—What is the topic of this report?

Three "arms" extend from the circle in the middle. The three circles at the end of each arm are the *questions* to be answered in your report. Each question will be answered in a separate paragraph.
—What are the questions to be answered in this report?

The answers to each question are written around the circles.
—What are the answers to the question *What kinds of trains are there?*
—What are the answers to the question *Who works on trains?*
—What are the answers to the question *Where do trains go?*

Activity B

This word map contains the topic of the report. Write three questions that you would like answered in a report about *elephants*.

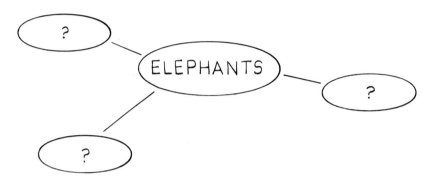

? ELEPHANTS ?

?

Activity C

This word map contains the title of the report and three questions. Below are nine answers. Put three correct answers around each question.

Answers:
1. Each frog gets a number.
2. June
3. Find a grassy area in your yard.
4. Each frog has three turns to jump.
5. Put a string around the area.
6. Hartford, Connecticut
7. The frog with the longest jump is the winner.
8. Mark Twain Memorial
9. Make up your own contest rules.

Write Away!

Choose one of these topics. Make a word map that includes the topic and three questions to be answered. Exchange your paper with a partner and have your partner give two or three answers to each question.
   A. A special school event
   B. An interesting animal
   C. A vacation
   D. A famous person

Lesson 4 Writing an Outline

An outline helps to put your ideas in order when you are writing more than one paragraph.

You have learned how to make a word map. Now, you will learn to turn the map into an *outline*. Outlines are very useful because they keep your thoughts in order as you write. Look below at how a word map becomes an outline.

Trains

I. What kinds of trains are there?
   A. There are electric trains.
   B. There are passenger trains.
   C. There are freight trains.

II. Where do trains go?
   A. Trains go across the country.
   B. Trains go through cities.
   C. Trains go over mountains.

III. Who works on trains?
   A. Engineers run them.
   B. Conductors collect tickets.
   C. Porters help with baggage.

Can you see how each part of the map becomes a part of the outline? The writer uses the word in the center as the *topic*. Then the *question* for each paragraph follows a roman numeral. The question gives the specific idea for the paragraph. The *answers* to the questions are indented and follow a capital letter. A period comes after each roman numeral and capital letter.

—What is the topic of this outline?

—How many questions are there? What comes before each question?

—How many answers to each question are there? What comes before each answer?

—Why do you think the questions are in this order?

Activity A

Add roman numerals and capital letters to this outline. Indent wherever necessary.

Spices

In what parts of plants are spices found?
Spices are found in bark.
Spices are found in stems.
Spices are found in seeds.
Spices are found in leaves.
What are their uses?
Spices are used in medicine.
Spices are used in food.
Spices are used in soap.
Spices are used in perfumes.

Activity B

Look at the word map on famous cures. Decide which question would be answered first, which would be second, and which would be third. Then make an outline from the word map.

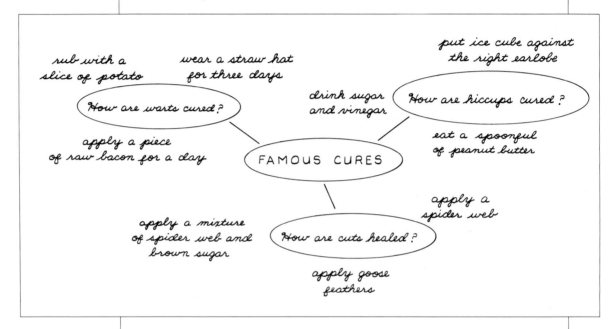

rub with a slice of potato

wear a straw hat for three days

put ice cube against the right earlobe

How are warts cured?

drink sugar and vinegar

How are hiccups cured?

apply a piece of raw bacon for a day

FAMOUS CURES

eat a spoonful of peanut butter

apply a mixture of spider web and brown sugar

How are cuts healed?

apply a spider web

apply goose feathers

Write Away!

Choose one of the topics below. Ask two or three questions about the topic. Go to the library to discover the answers. Make a word map and then write an outline.

    An invention
    Ice cream
    My hobby
    Volcanoes
    A sport

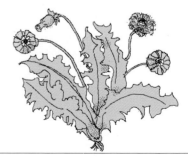

Lesson 5 Writing a Short Report

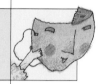

A report is a piece of writing that gives facts about a certain topic.

Pam chose the topic "Dinosaurs." First, she began to make a word map. Pam asked questions about dinosaurs and then found her answers in an encyclopedia and other books. After she gathered the facts, Pam made an outline. Then it was easy for her to write a report.

Tyrannosaurus rex

Pam's report has three paragraphs because there are three roman numerals in her outline. In column A is the outline. In column B are the paragraphs that contain the information under each roman numeral. Carefully study Pam's outline and report.

Dinosaurs

I. When and where did dinosaurs live?
   A. Most lived between 225 million and 65 million years ago.
   B. Some areas had small dinosaurs and some had giant ones.
   C. Most lived in warm, swampy areas because of food and water.

II. What kinds of dinosaurs were there?
   A. Plant eaters were very large.
   B. Meat eaters were fast and fierce.
   C. Meat eaters preyed on plant eaters.

III. Why did dinosaurs disappear?
   A. Mountains dried up swamps.
   B. Climate became cooler.
   C. Diseases killed many.

Dinosaurs

Between 225 and 65 million years ago, dinosaurs ruled the earth. Some regions of the earth had small dinosaurs, and some had giant ones. These animals lived in warm, swampy places where there was plenty of food and water.

There were two types of dinosaurs. Plant eaters were huge animals who ate many pounds of food each day. Meat eaters were fierce and fast. Tyrannosaurus, the largest meat eater, would prey on plant eaters that were larger than he was.

As the earth changed, dinosaurs began to disappear. Mountains formed and caused the swamps to dry up and the climate to become colder. Plant eaters died, and without them, the meat eaters had no food. Disease also helped to destroy the dinosaur. The once proud rulers of the earth now live only in museums.

At the end of her report, Pam wrote down the names of the encyclopedia and the other books from which she gathered her information.

"Dinosaurs," *World Book Encyclopedia*, Vol. 4.

Jones, Peter. *The World of the Dinosaur.*

Scott chose the topic "Masks." Here is the first part of his outline and the first paragraph of his report.

Masks

I. From where did masks come?
  A. Prehistoric people used them in ceremonies.
  B. Actors in Greece used them in plays.
  C. Clowns in Italy entertained audiences.
  D. Today, masks are worn at Halloween.

Masks

    Masks have been used by many people. Prehistoric people probably used masks for their ceremonies. In ancient Greece, actors wore masks to tell who they were. Masks were made to look happy or sad. In Italy, around 1500, clowns wore masks to entertain their audiences. Today, Halloween is the most popular time to wear a mask.

Activity A

Scott wasn't able to finish the second paragraph of his report. Use his outline to write the second paragraph. The beginning sentence is done for you.

II. How are masks made?
    A. Indians carved them out of wood.
    B. Some are molded out of metal and leather.
    C. Children make them from construction paper.

Beginning sentence:

Many materials can be used to make masks.

Native American mask

Early 20th century African mask

Activity B

Here is the third part of Scott's outline on masks. The report needs one more paragraph to be complete. Use his outline to write the third paragraph. The beginning sentence is done for you.

III. *How are masks used today?*
    A. *Surgeons protect themselves and patients from germs.*
    B. *Steelworkers protect themselves from blasts of heat and light.*
    C. *Skiers protect themselves from cold wind.*

Beginning sentence:

    There are many different uses for masks today.

Egyptian mask from 1700 B.C.

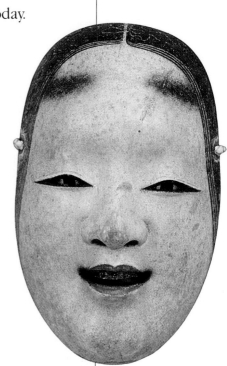

15th century Japanese mask

Write Away!

Choose one of the topics below. Complete the outline by writing two or three answers under each question. If necessary, use an encyclopedia or other books to find your answers. Then use your outline to write a report.

My Favorite Sport

    I. Who invented it?
   II. How is it played?
  III. Why do I like it?

You are the "Tasty Treat Eater" on television. Write a report on your favorite restaurant.

My Favorite Restaurant

    I. Where is it and what kind of restaurant is it?
   II. What kind of food does it serve?
  III. Why do I like it?

Checkpoint: Revising and Proofreading a Report

Revision: Time to Take Another Look

As you look over your report, ask yourself these questions:

—Do I have a separate paragraph for each question?
—Are the answers to each question in one paragraph?
—Could I substitute more exact verbs and adjectives?
—Have I used *and*, *and so*, or *and then* too often?
—Does the report make sense? Is it easy to read?

Now is the time to make any changes. Discuss your changes with another student or with your teacher. Rewrite your report and then go on to proofreading.

Proofreading: Time to Look at Capitalization, Punctuation, and Spelling

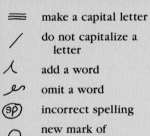

≡	make a capital letter
/	do not capitalize a letter
⅄	add a word
℮	omit a word
⑤℗	incorrect spelling
○	new mark of punctuation
¶	begin a paragraph

—Did I begin each sentence and each proper noun with a capital letter?
—Did I indent each paragraph?
—Did I use the correct mark of punctuation at the end of each sentence?

Start with the last word of your report and work backward to check for correct spelling. If necessary, rewrite the report in your best handwriting.

Word Study 4

Contractions Using Pronouns

A contraction is formed by joining some words together. An apostrophe takes the place of the missing letter or letters.

A contraction is a short way to write some words. In a contraction, there is always a missing letter or letters. Use an apostrophe to take the place of the missing letter or letters.

In this lesson, you will form contractions by joining a *pronoun* and a *verb*. Study this list of contractions.

I am—I'm	we have—we've
I will—I'll	he is—he's
I would—I'd	she is—she's
I have—I've	it is—it's
we will—we'll	they will—they'll
we are—we're	they have—they've

Can you name the missing letters in each of these contractions?

Activity A

Match each group of words in column A with its contraction in column B. The first one is done for you.

<u>Column A</u>   <u>Column B</u>

they have   __d__   a. I'll
I would   ____   b. we'll
we will   ____   c. I'm
she is   ____   d. they've
I have   ____   e. it's
they will   ____   f. I've
we are   ____   g. she's
I am   ____   h. I'd
it is   ____   i. they'll
I will   ____   j. we're

Activity B

Use a contraction in place of the words in italics in each sentence.

1. *I have* never seen a pink flamingo.
2. *He is* going to try wonton soup.
3. In the play, *I am* a talking dragon.
4. *We are* playing on the trampolines.
5. *I would* rather meet a cat than a tiger.
6. If you start to walk, *they will* follow you.
7. I think *it is* the same color as mine.
8. If we can, *we will* do it.
9. *They have* walked from the Pacific to the Atlantic Ocean.
10. *I will* take a pound of jelly beans, please.

Activity C

Use each of these contractions in a sentence.

we'll   I'd   they're   I'm   we've   it's

Chapter 5
Writing Letters

Lesson 1 The Parts of a Social Letter

A social letter has five parts.

It is fun to write letters and to receive letters. A *friendly letter* is a special type of social letter. Writing a friendly letter is a good way to "visit" with a person who lives far away, your favorite relative or a pen pal. Letters are even fun to write to someone who lives nearby. In a letter, you can share ideas or news of different events. You can keep your letters and reread them whenever you wish.

Think of all the ways people can travel. When you write and send a letter, your words can travel too!

Look at this letter. Can you name the five parts of a social letter?

Model: A Friendly Letter

624 Maple Leaf Drive
Milwaukee, Wisconsin 53207
January 15, 19—

Dear Mary Lou,

It was fun having you home for Christmas. I wish the holidays had been just a little longer. I miss having you around.

Last weekend, dad took Jay and me ice-skating. We went to the new rink in the center of the city. You'll never guess! I can skate backwards. It has taken a lot of practice, but I'm finally getting it. When you come home again, maybe we can go there.

I am mailing you a present. I found something special in the gift shop at the rink. Hope you like it! Let me know what is happening at college.

Your sister,
Jane

The Heading

The heading of a letter has three lines.

Write your street address on the first line.
Write your city, state, and zip code on the second line.
Write the month, day, and year on the third line.

Write the heading about an inch from the top of the paper and a little to the right of the center. You may use the two-letter postal abbreviations for the states. These can be found on page 362. Notice where the commas are placed.

123 Addison Avenue
Toledo, OH 43607
*March 1, 19_*

The Salutation (Greeting)

The salutation begins at the left-hand margin. The first word of the salutation and the person's name begin with a capital letter. A comma always follows the salutation of a friendly letter.

Dear Aunt Mary,   *Dear Grandpa,*

Dear Mike,   *My dear cousin,*

The Body (Message)

The body is the most important part of a letter. This is where you write your message. Each paragraph is indented. The first word of each paragraph begins with a capital letter.

The Complimentary Close

The complimentary close comes at the end of the letter. It begins one line below the last sentence. It starts a little to the right of the center of the paper and is in line with the heading. Only the first word of the complimentary close begins with a capital letter. A comma always follows the last word of the complimentary close.

Your loving son,   *Your pal,*

Your grandson,   *Your friend,*

                              Love,

The Signature

The signature is written under the first word of the complimentary close. Do not forget to use a capital letter when you write your name.

Jill   *Henry*

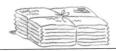

Activity A

Can you solve these riddles about friendly letters?
1. I include the street address, city, state, and date.
   What am I?
2. I help the writer say good-bye.
   What am I?
3. I am the written name of the writer.
   What am I?
4. I am how the writer says hello.
   What am I?
5. I am the message the writer wants to share.
   What am I?

Activity B

Proofread the following parts of a friendly letter by adding punctuation and capital letters where needed.
1. 653 mitchell street
   ridley park pa 19067
   october 3, 19_____
2. your best friend
   mary sue
3. dear gus
4. my dear aunt jean
5. 6490 south lane
   raleigh nc 27603
   february 10, 19_____
6. your niece
   jennifer

Activity C

Below are all the parts of a friendly letter. Put them together in the proper form to create a friendly letter. Remember to use the correct punctuation.

1. 234 holland road montrose pa 19087 october 24 19____
2. dear danny
3. Bermuda is a great place for a vacation!
4. I wish you could have been there with me.
5. I spent most of the time wearing my mask, snorkel, and flippers.
6. My dad and I found time though, to ride around the island.
7. Did you know they drive on the left side of the road there?
8. I have two albums of pictures for you to see.
9. I hope you can come for a visit soon.
10. your friend gerry

Write Away!

Follow these directions to write your own friendly letter.

1. Decide to whom you will write.
2. Think of a message you want to share.
3. Begin your letter with your own address in the heading.
4. Write your letter using correct form and punctuation.
5. Proofread your letter carefully.

Lesson 2 Kinds of Social Letters

Besides the friendly letter, three other types of social letters are letters of invitation, letters of acceptance, and thank-you letters.

I would like to invite you to a party. I will write a letter of *invitation*.

I am happy to come to your party. I will write a letter of *acceptance*.

I was thrilled with the present you sent. I will write a *thank-you* letter.

A Letter of Invitation

When you invite your friends to a party, you should send a *letter of invitation*. You should tell your friends *what kind* of a party you are giving, the *day*, the *date*, the *time*, and the *place*. Here is a letter of invitation.

2703 Hill Road
Boise, Idaho 83702
April 1, 19_

Dear Laura,

Please come to my birthday party. It will be at my house on Saturday, April 10, at 3:00 P.M. There will be lots of games and good things to eat. Please let me know if you can make it.

Your friend,
Gloria

Activity A

Important information has been left out of the invitation below. Rewrite the invitation and fill in the missing information.

521 Mystery Lane
Lincoln, Nebraska 68506
February 2, 19___

Dear Keith,

    I am having a Presidents' Day Party. Everyone must dress up as one of the U.S. Presidents. It will be held at my house. I hope you will be able to come.

Your friend,
Pete

Activity B

Choose *one* of these beginning sentences. Write a letter of invitation.

A. On Saturday, October 31, I am having a Halloween party.

B. Would you like to see a hockey game next Sunday afternoon?

C. Something special is happening at my house.

D. Next Thursday, December 15, our class is having a Christmas play.

A Letter of Acceptance

When you are invited to a party, the person who invites you would like to know if you can come. Answer an invitation with a *letter of acceptance* as soon as possible. Here is a letter of acceptance.

2157 Warm Springs Avenue
Boise, Idaho 83701
April 4, 19__

Dear Gloria,

Thank you for inviting me to your birthday party. I can't wait until the big day. Your parties are always so much fun. I will see you on Saturday!

Your friend,
Laura

Activity C

Write a letter of acceptance in response to the invitation you wrote in activity B.

A Thank-You Letter

When someone does something nice for you or gives you a
gift, you should write the person a *thank-you letter*. If you
have received a present, you should mention it in your
letter and tell why you like it. Here is a thank-you letter.

1855 River Drive
Grand Falls, Montana 59405
November 17, 19__

Dear Aunt Terri,
What a lovely surprise the
beautiful sweater was! I received the
package in the mail on Tuesday, just in
time for my birthday. My new blue
skirt matches the sweater perfectly.
Thank you for the thoughtful gift.

Love,
Pam

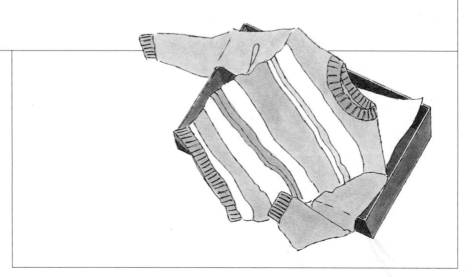

Activity D

Choose one of these situations. Write a thank-you letter.
A. You spent the weekend visiting a friend or relative.
B. A friend gave you a birthday gift you always wanted.

Write Away!

Write a letter for *one* of these situations.
A. Your aunt sent you a tape for your birthday.
B. Your favorite cousins invite you to visit them in Florida.
C. You are having a surprise birthday party for your best friend.

Checkpoint: Revising and Proofreading a Social Letter

The Heading

—Does the heading include a separate line for the street address, city, state, zip code, and date?
—Did I use a comma between the city and the state? Is there a comma between the date and the year?
—Did I use the correct two-letter state abbreviation?

The Salutation

—Does the salutation begin at the left-hand margin?
—Did I use a comma after the salutation?
—Did I begin the first word and the person's name with a capital letter?

The Body

—Does every sentence and every proper noun begin with a capital letter?
—Does every sentence end with the proper mark of punctuation?
—Did I indent the first word of every paragraph?

The Complimentary Close and the Signature

—Did I write the complimentary close and signature in line with the heading?
—Did I begin the complimentary close with a capital letter?
—Did I use a comma after the last word of the complimentary close?
—Did I write my name neatly and carefully?

Start with the last word of the letter and work backward to check for correct spelling. If necessary, rewrite the letter.

Lesson 3 Addressing the Envelope

An envelope should have a mailing address and a return address.

Mr. O'Brien works at the post office. It is easy for him to put the letters in the right pile when they are addressed correctly. He likes an envelope to look like this:

Jack March
231 Barber Street
West Chester, PQ 19380

RETURN ADDRESS

Mr. Ray Thomas
213 West Avenue
Willow Grove, PQ 19090

MAILING ADDRESS

An envelope should always be addressed carefully. In the top left corner put *your* name, street name and number, city, state, and zip code. This is the *return address*. In the middle of the envelope put the name of the person to whom you are writing, his or her street name and number, city, state, and zip code. This is the *mailing address*.

Activity A

These addresses are not in the correct order. Draw three envelopes on a piece of paper. Then write the addresses in the correct order and in the proper place on the envelopes.

Return Address

1. 501 Adams Avenue
   Kelly Schmidt
   New Orleans, LA 70101

2. Bethlehem, PA 18096
   450 Sinnet Road
   Jeb Parker

3. Augusta, MA 04330
   Susan B. Anthony
   5 North Lyn Road

Mailing Address

Arlington, VA 22213
Mrs. Ann Saldo
672 South High Street

Santa Fe, NM 87022
10 Parks Avenue
Sarah Tobin

211 Beach Run Drive
Col. Robert Stayer
Tampa, FL 33605

Activity B

Draw an envelope on a piece of paper. Write your own address as the mailing address. Write the school address as the return address. Do you have all the information you need? Are the addresses in the correct order? Are they in the proper place on the envelope?

Write Away!

Bring the following items to school: a sheet of writing paper, an envelope, and a stamp. Write a letter to a member of your family. When you finish your letter, address the envelope. Write the school address as the return address. Write your home address as the mailing address. Don't forget to stamp and mail your letter.

Lesson 4 Filling Out Forms

A form is an easy way to give information.

A form is also an easy way for people to collect information. Sometimes it is necessary that you give information by filling out a form. There are many different kinds of forms: bicycle registrations, library cards, pet licenses, contest applications. Can you think of some others?

When you fill out a form, you should remember three things:
1. Read the entire form first.
2. Answer all the questions.
3. Check over your answers.

Activity A

Copy these forms onto a sheet of paper. Fill in the correct information.

Win Free Tickets to the Zoo!!!

NAME _____ AGE _____

HOME ADDRESS _____

CITY _____ STATE _____ ZIP _____

(_____) _____ _____
PHONE NUMBER   TODAY'S DATE

NUMBER OF PEOPLE IN YOUR FAMILY _____

PET LICENSE FORM

YOUR NAME _____

HOME ADDRESS _____

CITY _____ STATE _____ ZIP _____

(_____) _____ _____
PHONE NUMBER   KIND OF PET

PET'S AGE _____ PET'S NAME _____

Activity B

Enter this contest. Copy the entry form onto a separate piece of paper. Fill in the correct information. Then tell why you would like to win this trip.

WIN A TRIP TO THE LAND OF OZ
(June 10–12)

Win a trip for you and your family to The Land of Oz. Meet your favorite characters. You'll get to shake hands with the Scarecrow, the Lion, and the Tin Man. Of course, you'll talk with Dorothy, and even to the Wizard himself.

It's easy to enter.

1. You must be between the ages of 8 and 12.
2. Fill in the entry form below.
3. Tell why you would like to win this trip to The Land of Oz.
4. Entry form must be mailed by March 15.
5. Winners will be notified by mail no later than April 20.

ENTRY FORM

Name _____

Address _____

City _____ State _____ Zip Code _____

Name of Parent or Guardian _____

Phone Number (_____) _____ Birth Date _____ / _____ / _____

Why I would like to win a trip to The Land of Oz.

_____

_____

_____

_____

Write Away!

Create your own contest. Write an advertisement that tells about the contest. Then make up a form to fill out. Give it to a classmate to complete.

Contractions Using *Not*

A contraction is formed by joining some words together. An apostrophe takes the place of the missing letter or letters.

In this lesson, you will form contractions by joining a *verb* with the word *not*. The apostrophe will take the place of the letter *o* in the word *not*. Study this list of contractions.

do not—don't	are not—aren't
does not—doesn't	were not—weren't
did not—didn't	was not—wasn't
cannot—can't	has not—hasn't
could not—couldn't	have not—haven't
is not—isn't	will not—won't

Activity A

Use a contraction in place of the words in italics in each sentence.
1. Scuba diving *is not* an unusual sport.
2. My cat *does not* like garlic.
3. Jellyfish *do not* really have jelly in them.
4. The mule *will not* move for anyone but Jessie.
5. *Were* you *not* the first in line?
6. *Cannot* the Christmas lights go on now?
7. The scientist *did not* have a cure for hiccups.
8. Sally *has not* learned to tie her shoes.
9. George *could not* find the mustard.
10. *Is not* there such a thing as a paper house?

Activity B

Find the contraction in each sentence. Name the two words that are joined to make the contraction.

1. Isn't the Sears Tower the tallest skyscraper?
2. I won't rake the leaves until tomorrow.
3. Shirley and Jeff don't believe in flying saucers.
4. Wasn't that a purple cow?
5. She can't rub her head and pat her stomach at the same time.
6. Ricardo couldn't see the lighthouse through the fog.
7. There aren't any mushrooms in the store.
8. Hasn't the movie begun yet?
9. The turtle won't come out of its shell.
10. They weren't as heavy as I thought.

Activity C

Use each of these contractions in a sentence.

don't	isn't
won't	weren't
couldn't	haven't

Adam Win
Aº 1730.

Chapter 6

Speaking and Listening Skills

Lesson 1 Oral Presentations

You can share information about things you have learned, things you like, and opinions you have through oral presentations.

An oral presentation is similar to what you do each day when you speak with others and share your ideas. When you have a conversation with your friends, answer in class, or talk with your family at dinner, you share your ideas. Speaking is part of your everyday experience.

An oral presentation is given to a group of people, for example, your class. To give a good oral presentation, it is important to *plan* and *practice* it before you give it to your class. Improving your speaking skills will help you present your ideas more effectively.

Follow these steps as you plan an oral presentation.
—Think about a topic that would interest you and your audience.
—Go to the library and read about your topic.
—Look for pictures or charts that explain your topic.
—Write the specific ideas of your talk on note cards.
—Study your notes carefully.

When and where do you think this boy lived? What ideas about your life would you like to share with him?

115

Lori decided to write a report about deep-sea divers. First, she thought of questions she would like answered. Then she went to the library and read about her topic. Here are the notes Lori wrote.

I. What do divers wear under the sea?
  A. Divers wear breathing equipment called aqualungs.
  B. Divers wear rubber suits that keep their bodies warm. These are called wet suits.

II. What do divers do under the sea?
  A. Divers check oil wells, build bridges, and study sea life.
  B. Divers search for sunken treasures.
  C. Divers hunt for lost ships.

III. How can divers stay under the sea for a long time?
  A. They can live in an underwater sea house that is equipped with electricity and fresh water.
  B. They can stay for a few days in a submersible. These are like submarines with very large windows. They can hold three people.

Follow these guidelines as you prepare and as you give an oral presentation.

Before you give a presentation
—study the information on your note cards
—organize your pictures or charts
—practice your speech before you give it

When you give a presentation
—be enthusiastic
—stand up straight
—speak in a clear, distinct voice
—look at your audience when you speak
—use pictures or charts to explain your ideas

Activity A

Think of a topic that would be of interest to you and your audience. Then go to the library to gather information. Write down the important ideas on note cards. Look for pictures or charts to help explain your presentation.

Activity B

Give an oral presentation of the report you planned in activity A. Review the guidelines for preparing and giving a presentation.

Activity C

After you listen to other students' presentations, it is valuable to tell them *how they did* and *what you learned*. Make a chart like the one below to evaluate a presentation.

Speaker's name _____

	Yes	No
Was the speaker well prepared?		
Was the speaker's voice clear and distinct?		
Did the speaker stand up straight?		
Did the speaker look at the audience?		
Did the speaker use pictures or charts?		

From listening to the presentation, I learned _____

_____

_____

Lesson 2 Choral Speaking

It is fun to read poems aloud as a group. This is called choral speaking.

Poems are filled with descriptive words. Poems contain sense words to help paint pictures. In choral speaking, these words come to life when they are read by voices that are expressive and interesting. Sometimes the meaning of a poem is best expressed by a *group of voices*. Sometimes it is best expressed through *one voice*, or a *solo* reading. Voices can make the sound of a roaring lion or a whispering breeze. They can make you feel happy, excited, sad, or lonely.

Tuning-up Exercises

Just as you warm up in gym class, you can warm up or tune your voice with a few simple exercises. Some exercises help you breathe slowly and evenly. Other exercises help you pronounce words clearly. Try these exercises.

Breathing

Take a deep breath. Do not move your shoulders. Hold your breath while your teacher counts "one, two, three." When your teacher says "exhale," let out your breath slowly and silently through your mouth. Repeat this breathing exercise several times and gradually increase the number of counts.

Enunciation

Practice the long sound of *o* (ō) and the short sound of *o* (ŏ) by repeating ō—ŏ several times. Pronounce these words clearly and distinctly:

go	hot	row	pond
so	top	cold	rock
rope	not	comb	knock
hope	odd	home	bottle

The sound of the consonant *b* is made with the lips. Practice a clear *b* sound by repeating these sentences:

Buzz goes the big black bumblebee.
Baby Bess broke the big brown box.
Barbara bikes near Barber's barn.

Activity A

This poem explains why lions cannot be petted at the zoo even though they might like to be. Do you agree with the speaker's explanation? As you read this poem, notice that the words at the end of each set of lines rhyme.

Why Nobody Pets the Lion at the Zoo

LIGHTER VOICES:
The morning that the world began
The Lion growled a growl at Man.

DEEPER VOICES:
And I suspect the Lion might
"If he'd been closer" have tried a bite.

LIGHTER VOICES:
I think that's as it ought to be
And not as it was taught to me.

DEEPER VOICES:
I think the Lion has a right
To growl a growl and bite a bite.

LIGHTER VOICES:
And if the Lion bothered Adam,
He should have growled right back at 'im.

DEEPER VOICES:
The way to treat a Lion right
Is growl for growl and bite for bite.

LIGHTER VOICES:
True, the Lion is better fit
For biting than for being bit.

DEEPER VOICES:
But if you look him in the eye
You'll find the Lion's rather shy.

ALL:
He really wants someone to pet him.
The trouble is: his teeth won't let him.

He has a heart of gold beneath
But the Lion just can't trust his teeth.

John Ciardi

This poem is divided into solo and unison. *Solo* means one voice, and *unison* means all voices together. In the second stanza, which task would you like to have?

Oh, Who Will Wash the Tiger's Ears?

SOLO 1:   Oh, who will wash the tiger's ears?
SOLO 2:   And who will comb his tail?
SOLO 3:   And who will brush his sharp white teeth?
SOLO 4:   And who will file his nails?

UNISON: Oh, Bobby may wash the tiger's ears
          And Susy may file his nails
          And Lucy may brush his long white teeth
SOLO 5:   And I'll go down for the mail.

Shel Silverstein

Tuning-up Exercises

Breathing

Inhale slowly. Hold your breath for six counts. Then exhale in short puffs, as if you were blowing out a candle.

Enunciation

Practice the long sound of *u* (ū) and the short sound of *u* (ŭ) by repeating ū—ŭ several times. Pronounce these words clearly and distinctly:

tune	cup	due	duck
dune	tub	cube	rung
fruit	rub	duke	under
duty	nut	fume	study

The sound of the consonant *p* is made with the lips. Practice a clear *p* sound by repeating these sentences:

Paul purchased pickles, peppers, peas, and peaches.
Patsy and Polly pressed pretty pink petals.
Peter pedaled proudly down the path in the park.
Patricia promptly pruned the potted palm.

Activity B

In your dictionary, find the meaning of the word *brigade*. Have you ever seen an umbrella brigade near your school or in your neighborhood?

The Umbrella Brigade

SOLO 1:
"Pitter patter!" falls the rain
On the school-room window-pane.

SOLO 2:
Such a plashing! such a dashing!
Will it e'er be dry again?

SOLO 3:
Down the gutter rolls a flood,
And the crossing's deep in mud;

SOLO 4:
And the puddles! oh, the puddles
Are a sight to stir one's blood!

UNISON:
But let it rain
Tree-toads and frogs,
Muskets and pitchforks,
Kittens and dogs!
Dash away! plash away!
Who is afraid?
Here we go,
The Umbrella Brigade!

SOLO 1:
Pull the boots up to the knee!
Tie the hoods on merrily!

SOLO 2:
Such a hustling! such a jostling!
Out of breath with fun are we.

SOLO 3:
Clatter, clatter, down the street,
Greeting everyone we meet,

SOLO 4:
With our laughing and our chaffing,
Which the laughing drops repeat.

UNISON:
So let it rain
Tree-toads and frogs,
Muskets and pitchforks,
Kittens and dogs!
Dash away! plash away!
Who is afraid?
Here we go,
The Umbrella Brigade!

Laura E. Richards

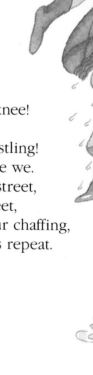

This poem tells what one grandmother was told her grandchild saw on Halloween. Does the child really see the things he or she tells Granny? What do the two lines at the end tell Granny? Do you think this is a clever way to end the poem?

Halloween

DEEPER VOICES: "Granny, I saw a witch go by,
I saw two, I saw three!
I heard their skirts go swish, swish, swish"

LIGHTER VOICES: "Child, 'twas leaves against the sky,
And the autumn wind in the tree."

DEEPER VOICES: "Granny, broomsticks they bestrode,
Their hats were black as tar,
And buckles twinkled on their shoes—"

LIGHTER VOICES: "You saw but shadows on the road,
The sparkle of a star."

DEEPER VOICES: "Granny, all their heels were red,
Their cats were big as sheep.
I heard a bat say to an owl—"

LIGHTER VOICES: "Child, you must go straight to bed,
'Tis time you were asleep."

DEEPER VOICES: "Granny, I saw men in green,
Their eyes shone fiery red,
Their heads were yellow pumpkins—"

LIGHTER VOICES: "Now you've told me what you've seen,
WILL you go to bed?"

UNISON: "Granny?"
SOLO: "Well?"
UNISON: "Don't you believe—?"
SOLO: "What?"
UNISON: "What I've seen?
Don't you know it's Halloween?"

Marie Lawson

Tuning-Up Exercises

Breathing

Inhale slowly. Hold your breath for four counts and then exhale in short puffs.

Enunciation

Practice the long sounds of vowels by pronouncing these words clearly and distinctly:

say	me	find	go	tune
day	she	kind	old	duke
play	be	grind	know	June

The consonant *t*, made by the tongue almost touching the back of the teeth, should be a sharp, light sound. Practice a distinct *t* sound by repeating these sentences:

Tommy, teach Toby to touch his toes.
The teacher told Teddy to trim the tree.
Take these, Terry, to Tom, Tim, and Tad.

Activity C

Have you ever had a wozzit in your closet? Can you draw a picture of what it looks like?

The Wozzit

UNISON: There's a wozzit in the closet
        And it's making quite a mess.

SOLO 1: It has eaten father's trousers,

SOLO 2: It has eaten mother's dress,

SOLO 3: And it's making so much noise
        As it gobbles down my toys,

UNISON: There's a wozzit in the closet—
        Oh I'm certain…yes, oh yes!

UNISON: There's a wozzit in the closet
        And I don't know what to do.

SOLO 1: It has swallowed sister's slippers,

SOLO 2: It has chewed upon my shoe,

SOLO 3: Now it's having its dessert
        For it's stuffing down my shirt,

UNISON: There's a wozzit in the closet—
        Yes, oh yes, I know it's true!

UNISON: And I also know I'll never never
        Open up that closet,
        For I never never never
        Ever
        Want to meet that wozzit.

Jack Prelutsky

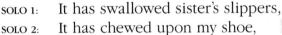

Lesson 3 Listening to Directions

When you listen to directions, pay close attention to details.

When directions are being given, listen very closely. Not only are the *details* very important, but so is the *order of the details.*

Directions help us understand how to get from one place to another place. Directions must be clear and exact, especially if they are not written.

Look at this map carefully.

Imagine that you want to go from Kathy's house to Alvin's house. If these directions were given to you, would you arrive at Alvin's house?

> Go down the street.
> Go around the circle.
> Go up the street.

You would probably not reach Alvin's house.

If you received clear and exact directions, it would be much easier to find the house.

> From Kathy's house turn right and go south on First Avenue. Turn left and go east on Oak Street.
> Go around the circle halfway and continue east on Oak Street.
> At the fork in the road, turn left.
> Follow Second Avenue for a short distance.
> Alvin's house is on the right.

Study these guidelines to follow and give directions.
1. Know which way is north, south, east, and west.
2. Think about landmarks—buildings or signs that are easily noticed.
3. Concentrate on the logical order of the directions.
4. Try to picture the directions in your mind.

Activity A

Your teacher will read a set of directions. Listen carefully, and then answer these questions.
1. What were some of the landmarks mentioned?
2. Where did you start and where did you end?
3. Can you follow these directions on the map?

Activity B

Choose two points on the map. *Write* directions from one point to the other. Then *read* them to another student. Have him or her answer the questions in activity A.

Activity C

You have a robot in your house. "Feed" into the robot a set of directions showing him or her how to bring food from the kitchen to your bedroom. Make sure your directions are clear and in logical order.

Lesson 4 Supporting Your Opinion

An opinion is the way a person thinks or feels about something.

Everybody sees things in a different way. You may want to go to camp for a week, but your mom has a different opinion. You and your friend both read the same book. Your friend liked it very much. You didn't like it at all. You each had a different opinion. Listening to a person's opinion helps you see things in a way different from your own.

Whenever you give an opinion, you should have specific reasons for the way you feel.

> Why do you want to go to camp?
> > It's a good experience to be away from home.
> > To learn different sports, games, and crafts.
> > To make new friends.

> Why didn't you like the book?
> > It was supposed to be funny and it really wasn't.
> > It was too easy to figure out what was going to happen.
> > There wasn't enough action in the story.

Activity A

Your teacher will read two paragraphs. They express two different opinions on the same topic. Answer these questions after your teacher reads the first paragraph.

What is the specific idea of the paragraph?
What is Tod's opinion about his experience?
Give reasons that support his opinion.
Why might Tod feel the way he does?

Listen carefully to the second paragraph. Answer these questions.

What is Marcia's opinion about her experience?
Give reasons that support her opinion.
Why might Marcia feel the way she does?

Activity B

Select one of these situations. With another class member, role-play the situation. Make sure you give reasons for the way you feel.

1. Two students took the same test. One thought it was easy; the other thought it was difficult.
2. Two friends went to a dance. One liked the music; the other did not.
3. Twins went to a fancy restaurant with their uncle. One enjoyed the meal; the other did not.

Lesson 5 Listening to Poetry

The language of poetry is often different from the language you use every day.

A poet uses words in such a way that you can *see* people and places and *hear* sounds. Poets do not always use many words. Sometimes in five or six lines you can see and hear many things.

Close your eyes and listen to the sounds around you. How many can you name? To hear and see things in poetry, you must listen closely to the words the poet uses. The words will create a feeling or a picture. Sometimes the feeling is happy or sad. Sometimes the picture is funny or scary.

Listen carefully to the poem your teacher will read to you. Can you discover the answers to these questions?

    What kinds of shoes can you *see*?
    What kinds of shoes can you *hear*?
    What feelings do the words of the poem create?

Activity A

Listen to these poems as they are read by your teacher. Write on a piece of paper all the things you *hear*, *taste*, *smell*, and *feel*. Think about the feelings and picures these poems express.

A Matter of Taste

What does your tongue like the most?
Chewy meat or crunchy toast?

A lumpy bumpy pickle or tickly pop?
A soft marshmallow or a hard lime drop?

Hot pancakes or a sherbet freeze?
Celery noise or quiet cheese?

Or do you like pizza
More than any of these?

Eve Merriam

Galoshes

Susie's galoshes
Make splishes and sploshes
And slooshes and sloshes,
As Susie steps slowly
Along in the slush.

They stamp and they tramp
On the ice and concrete,
They get stuck in the muck and the mud;
But Susie likes much better to hear

The slippery slush
As it slooshes and sloshes,
And splishes and sploshes,
All around her galoshes!

Rhoda W. Bacmeister

Now listen to two other poems. What do you *hear*, *taste*, *smell*, and *feel* in these poems?

Activity B

Poems let us picture objects and people in our imagination. Listen to these two poems and tell what things you *see*. Can you *hear*, *smell*, and *feel* things, too?

The Kite

How bright on the blue
Is a kite when it's new!

With a dive and a dip
It snaps its tail

Then soars like a ship
With only a sail

As over tides
Of wind it rides,

Climbs to the crest
Of a gust and pulls,

Then seems to rest
As wind falls.

When string goes slack
You wind it back

And run until
A new breeze blows

And its wings fill
And up it goes!

How bright on the blue
Is a kite when it's new!

But a raggeder thing
You never will see

When it flaps on a string
In the top of a tree.

Harry Behn

Homework

Homework sits on top of Sunday, squashing Sunday flat.
Homework has the smell of Monday, homework's very fat.
Heavy books and piles of paper, answers I don't know.
Sunday evening's almost finished, now I'm going to go
Do my homework in the kitchen. Maybe just a snack,
Then I'll sit right down and start as soon as I run back
For some chocolate sandwich cookies. Then I'll really do
All that homework in a minute. First I'll see what new
Show they've got on television in the living room.
Everybody's laughing there, but misery and gloom
And a full refrigerator are where I am at.
I'll just have another sandwich. Homework's very fat.

Russell Hoban

Now listen to two other poems. What pictures do you see
in your imagination?

Compound Words

Compound words are two or more words joined together to make one word.

These compound words begin with the same word. Can you think of other compound words beginning with the word *book*?

   *book*shelf   *book*mark   *book*store   *book*seller

What two words make up each of these compound words? Can you use each word in a sentence?

   handshake   something   fireplace
   toenail   ladybug   toothpaste

Activity A

Match each word in column A with a word in column B to make a compound word. The first one is done for you.

Column A		Column B
hand	_d_	a. cut
some	____	b. where
hair	____	c. string
air	____	d. made
light	____	e. weight
jack	____	f. boat
play	____	g. chair
shoe	____	h. plane
arm	____	i. knife
life	____	j. pen

Activity B

Complete these sentences with compound words. The first part of each compound word is given. The first one is done for you.

1. Anita wears sunglasses to protect her eyes.
2. The cat licked the icing on each cup_____.
3. This week_____ we will play tennis.
4. Nicky looked for sea_____ along the beach.
5. The farmer used a pitch_____ to bail the hay.
6. Brian bites his finger_____ when he is nervous.
7. Do not lean over the guard_____.
8. Beth's note_____ is on the class_____ floor.
9. The police_____ saw the car's head_____.
10. Isn't there any_____ playing base_____?

Activity C

Add a word to each word to make a compound word.

rain   work   fire   every   grand   head

Chapter 7

Library and Dictionary Skills

Lesson 1 Dictionary Skills— Finding Words

A dictionary is a book of words in alphabetical order.

You read that your city's zoo has a baby *yak*. You want to find out what kind of animal this is. You see the word *tricycle* in a story. You want to find out how to divide this word into syllables. A dictionary can give you this information.

The dictionary is an important book. Each word listed in the dictionary is called an *entry word*. For each entry word you will find:
—the correct spelling of the word
—the way the word is divided into syllables
—the pronunciation of the word
—the meaning of the word
—the correct way to use the word in sentences

Why do you think this photograph is called a close-up? What can you notice about the egg and nest that you couldn't notice from far away?

Finding Words in the Dictionary

The dictionary can be divided into three parts according to the letters of the alphabet.

When you look up a word in the dictionary, first decide in which part of the dictionary your word can be found—*beginning*, *middle*, or *end*.

Beginning	Middle	End
a b c d e f g h i	j k l m n o p q r	s t u v w x y z

Many words begin with the same letter. To put words that begin with the same letter in alphabetical order, use the *second* letter. If the second letter is the same, then you must use the *third* letter.

Example: softball   soccer   (*c* comes before *f*)
        The word *soccer* comes before *softball*.

Activity A

On a piece of paper, make three columns with the titles *Beginning*, *Middle*, and *End*. Place each of these words in the correct column.

baseball	rowing	polo
badminton	tennis	golf
volleyball	skydiving	judo

Activity B

Put each list of words in alphabetical order.

field	sneakers	goal	net
gloves	road	penalty	foul
bats	muscles	forward	referee
score	jog	center	player
practice	exercise	kickoff	jump

Activity C

Put each list of words in alphabetical order.

acrobatics	boxing	croquet	trekking
aerobics	bowling	canoeing	track
archery	baseball	cricket	tennis

Guide Words

> **Guide words are the two words written in dark letters at the top of each dictionary page.**

The guide words tell you the *first* and *last* entry words found on that page. All the other entry words on that page come *between* the guide words in alphabetical order.
Example: cricket/croquet are guide words.
  The word *crocodile* comes between these words.

Activity D

Tell whether each of these words comes *before* or *after* the word *hiking*.

high	hilly	hinge
hearing	hire	history
hibernate	hobby	helium

Activity E

Here are the guide words on a page of the dictionary. Answer *yes* for each of these words if it comes between the guide words.

golf / gymnastics

gopher	general	gully
gerbil	gosling	gyroscope
guppy	gypsy	graphite

Lesson 2 Dictionary Skills— Understanding the Entry

For each dictionary entry, you will find information about syllables, accent marks, pronunciations, and definitions.

Dividing Words into Syllables

Look at the entry word *trombone* on the sample dictionary page. *Trombone* is divided into two parts. Each of these parts is a syllable. *Trom* is the first syllable and *bone* is the second syllable. On this dictionary page, there is a *space* between syllables. Some dictionaries place a dot between the syllables in an entry word.

el · e · phant   in · fec · tion

Some words have only one syllable, such as *yes* and *jump*. Other words have several syllables, such as *arithmetic*.

Activity A

Find each of these words in your dictionary. Divide each word into syllables. Tell how many syllables there are in each word.

Example: penguin pen guin 2

1. kangaroo
2. python
3. hedgehog
4. gorilla
5. quail

6. armadillo
7. hummingbird
8. leopard
9. orangutan
10. raccoon

trom bone (trom′bōn), a brass wind instrument with a loud tone, usually with a long sliding piece for varying the length of the tube. See picture. *noun.*

troop (trüp), **1** group or band of persons: *a troop of children.* **2** herd, flock, or swarm: *a troop of deer.* **3** unit of cavalry, usually commanded by a captain. **4 troops,** soldiers: *The government sent troops to put down the revolt.* **5** gather in troops or bands; move together: *The children trooped around the teacher.* **6** walk; go; go away: *The younger children trooped off after the older ones.* 1-4 *noun,* 5,6 *verb.*

troop er (trü′pər), **1** soldier in a troop of cavalry. **2** a mounted policeman. The state police of some states are called troopers, because they were originally organized as mounted troops. *noun.*

tro phy (trō′fē), an award, often in the form of a statue or cup, given as a sign of victory. A trophy is often awarded as a prize in a race or contest. See picture. *noun, plural* **tro phies.**

trop i cal (trop′ə kəl), of the tropics: *Bananas are tropical fruit. adjective.*

trop ics (trop′iks), regions near the equator. The hottest parts of the earth are in the tropics. *noun plural.*

trot (trot), **1** the gait of a horse between a walk and a gentle gallop. In a trot, the right forefoot and the left hind foot are lifted at the same time. **2** ride at a trot: *The riders trotted home.* **3** go or cause to go at a trot: *The pony trotted through the field. We trotted our horses through the woods.* **4** run, but not fast: *The child trotted after me.* **5** a slow running. 1,5 *noun,* 2-4 *verb,* **trot ted, trot ting.**

trou ble (trub′əl), **1** distress; worry; difficulty: *The noisy students made trouble for their teacher.* **2** cause distress or worry to; disturb: *Lack of business troubled the grocer. I am troubled by headaches.* **3** disturbance; disorder: *political troubles.* **4** extra work; bother; effort: *Take the trouble to do careful work.* **5** require extra work or effort of: *May I trouble you to pass the sugar?* **6** cause oneself inconvenience: *Don't trouble to come to the door; I can let myself in.* **7** illness; disease: *She has stomach trouble.* 1,3,4,7 *noun,* 2,5,6 *verb,* **trou bled, trou bling.**

trou ble some (trub′əl səm), causing trouble; annoying; full of trouble: *Last year we had noisy, troublesome neighbors. adjective.*

trough (trôf), **1** a long, narrow container for holding food or water: *He led the horses to the watering trough.* **2** something shaped like this: *The baker used a trough for kneading dough.* **3** a long hollow between two ridges: *the trough between two waves. noun.*

trounce (trouns), beat; thrash: *The victors trounced the losing team. verb,* **trounced, trounc ing.**

troupe (trüp), band or company, especially a group of actors, singers, or acrobats. *noun.*

trou sers (trou′zərz), a two-legged outer garment reaching from the waist to the ankles or knees. *noun plural.*

trout (trout), a freshwater food fish that is related to the salmon. *noun, plural* **trouts** or **trout.**

a hat	i it	oi oil	ch child	a in about
ā age	ī ice	ou out	ng long	e in taken
ä far	o hot	u cup	sh she	ə = i in pencil
e let	ō open	u̇ put	th thin	o in lemon
ē equal	ô order	ü rule	ᵺ then	u in circus
ėr term			zh measure	

trombone

trophy—She proudly displayed her trophy.

Using the Pronunciation Key

You can learn how to pronounce, or *say*, a word by looking at the *pronunciation* that is in parentheses *after* each entry word.

In the top right corner of the sample dictionary page, you will notice a special chart. This is called the *pronunciation key*. The pronunciation key gives *symbols* for vowel and consonant sounds. After each symbol, there is an *example word*. You can hear the vowel or consonant sound that the symbol stands for in this example word.

Try to pronounce the word *troop* (trüp) on the sample dictionary page. Look at the key for the vowel sound *ü*. Say the example word—*rule*. Now you know that the *oo* in *troop* is pronounced like the *u* in *rule*. Practice pronouncing each sound in the pronunciation key.

Activity B

Find each of these words in your dictionary. Then write the pronunciation for each.

1. giraffe
2. moth
3. squid
4. baboon
5. boar
6. gopher
7. mongoose
8. squirrel

Activity C

Match each word in column A with its pronunciation in column B. Check your dictionary.

Column A		Column B
volcano	___	a. av ə lanch
equator	___	b. vil ij
glacier	___	c. vol kā nō
avalanche	___	d. glā shər
village	___	e. i kwā tər

Accent Marks

An accent mark tells you which syllable is stressed.

When a word has more than one syllable, one of the syllables is always said more strongly than the others. An *accent mark* is given in the pronunciation of a word to tell you which syllable to say more strongly. An accent mark looks like this: '. In the word *trouble* on the sample dictionary page, the accent is on the first syllable (trub'el).

Activity D

Find each of these words in your dictionary. First divide the word into syllables. Then add the accent mark.
Example: vanilla   va nil'la

1. purple
2. yellow
3. indigo
4. coral

5. crimson
6. lavender
7. aqua
8. violet

Definitions

In a dictionary entry, the definition explains the meaning of the word.

Many words have more than one meaning. If a word has more than one meaning, each definition is given a number. Find the word *trot* on the sample dictionary page on page 143. How many meanings does this word have?

Often a definition will be followed by a sentence in *italics*. This sentence gives an example of how a word is used. When a word is used in a sentence, the meaning becomes clearer. The word *trough* on the sample page means "a long, narrow container for holding food or water." Look at the sentence in italics. How does it help make the meaning of the word clearer?

He led the horses to the watering trough.

Activity E

Answer these questions about the entry words on the sample dictionary page.
1. Which entry has seven meanings?
2. What is the meaning of the word *trout*?
3. How many entry words are on this page?
4. Name a word that has six meanings.
5. What is the definition for the word *troupe*?

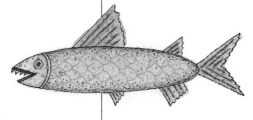

Activity F

Choose three of these words. Use your dictionary and write two meanings for each of the three words.

game	range	type
tale	season	base
plant	skip	grade

Activity G

Read each sentence. Then find each word in italics in your dictionary. Answer *yes* if the meaning of the word is correct. Answer *no* if the meaning is incorrect.

1. *Currency* means something that is up-to-date.
2. *Palette* is another name for the roof of your mouth.
3. To *squabble* means to quarrel.
4. A *tureen* is a deep covered dish for serving soup.
5. A *hedgehog* is a special kind of pig.
6. *Vapor* is steam from boiling water.
7. A *vegetarian* is a person who hates vegetables.
8. A *pagoda* is a type of building found in Japan.
9. To *grope* means to hang on to a rope.
10. A *pollywog* is a dog wagging his tail.

Lesson 3 Library Skills—
Kinds of Books

Some books tell a story. They are often read just for enjoyment. Some books contain facts about a subject. These books help you gather information about the world.

To help you find a book quickly, the library is divided into three sections:

Fiction   *Nonfiction*   *Reference*

The *fiction* section contains books that tell stories about imaginary people, places, things, and events. A fairy tale is a type of fiction book.

The *nonfiction* section contains books about real people, places, and events. A nonfiction book contains facts or ideas. A book about electricity is a type of nonfiction book.

The *reference* section contains books that give special information on many different topics. Dictionaries, encyclopedias, and atlases are reference books.

Activity A

Tell whether you would find the following books in the *fiction*, *nonfiction*, or *reference* section of the library.
1. *How to Play Field Hockey*
2. *Webster's Dictionary*
3. *The Knee-High Man and Other Tales*
4. *The Case of Princess Tomorrow*
5. *Collier's Encyclopedia*
6. *The History of Baseball*
7. *Tales the People Tell in Mexico*
8. *The Mousewife*
9. *The Land and People of Asia*
10. *The Britannica Atlas*

Kinds of Reference Books

The Encyclopedia

> **An encyclopedia is a set of books that contains facts about many topics.**

An encyclopedia is made up of articles that give information on many topics—people, places, things, and events. Articles are arranged in alphabetical order. Each book is called a *volume*. On the spine of each volume is a number and letters that tell which part of the alphabet is covered in that volume. Encyclopedias use *guide words*.

When you use an encyclopedia, remember that
—all the articles are in alphabetical order
—the guide words at the top of the page will help you locate your topics

Activity B

Use the picture of the set of encyclopedias to answer each of these questions.
1. In what volume would you find facts about *sports*.
2. Would you find facts about *fencing* in volume 4 or 5?
3. How many volumes are in this set?
4. Which of these topics would you find in volume 13?
   rugby — tobogganing — soccer
5. In which volume would you find an article on the rules for playing *tennis*?

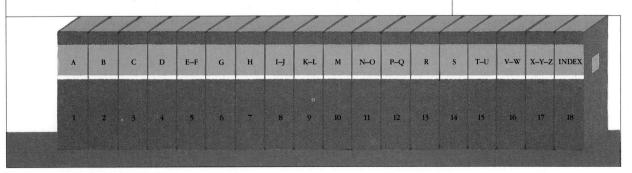

Activity C

With a partner, choose *two* of these topics. Use the encyclopedia to find four interesting facts about each topic. Write these facts and tell in what volume and on what pages you located your information.

Grandma Moses	baseball	volcano
Ty Cobb	skiing	geyser
Helen Keller	soccer	hurricane
Louis Braille	tennis	earthquake

The Atlas

> **An atlas is a book of maps.**

An atlas contains maps of continents, countries, and states. An atlas may also show you waterways, mountain ranges, or roads to travel.

Activity D

Decide whether you would use an *encyclopedia* or an *atlas* or *both* in order to answer each of these questions.

1. Where is Newfoundland?
2. How do spiders spin their webs?
3. What countries are in the Northern Hemisphere?
4. Where was baseball first played?
5. How are snowflakes formed?
6. What countries make up South America?
7. What states are on the East Coast of the United States?
8. What kinds of food do the people of Japan eat?
9. What American explored Antarctica?

Lesson 4 Library Skills—
The Card Catalog

A card catalog helps you find books in the library.

The card catalog is a cabinet filled with index cards arranged in alphabetical order. These cards give information about all the books in the library. Each card in the file is called an *entry*. In some libraries, the card catalog has been put on a computer. Look at these sample cards.

Title Card—the title of the book is on the top line.

```
                Under the sea.
   551.4    Williams, Brian
   W            Under the sea. New York, Warwick, 1978.
                    23p. illus.
                    (Explorer books)
                    Highlights undersea exploration, marine
                    animals, sunken treasures, and food from the sea.

                    1. Underwater exploration   2. Marine biology
                3. Oceanography   4. Ocean   I. Title
```

If you know just the title of a book, go to the card catalog and find the *title card*. Title cards are in alphabetical order according to the *first word* in the title. If the title begins with *The*, *An*, or *A*, however, look at the second word.
Example: *The Three Royal Monkeys*. Look for the word *Three*.

151

Author Card—the name of the author, last name first, is on the top line.

> 551.4   **Williams, Brian**
> W   Under the sea. New York, Warwick, 1978.
>   23p. illus.
>   (Explorer books)
>   Highlights undersea exploration, marine
>   animals, sunken treasures, and food from the sea.
>
>   1. Underwater exploration   2. Marine biology
>   3. Oceanography   4. Ocean   I. Title
>
>

If you know just the author of the book, look for the *author card*. Author cards are in alphabetical order according to the *last name* of the author.

Example: James Daugherty will be found under
                Daugherty, James

Subject Card—the subject is on the top line.

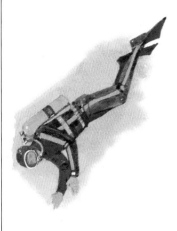

Underwater exploration.
551.4   **Williams, Brian**
W   Under the sea. New York, Warwick, 1978.
                    23p. illus.
                    (Explorer books)
                    Highlights undersea exploration, marine
                    animals, sunken treasures, and food from the sea.

                    1. Underwater exploration   2. Marine biology
               3. Oceanography   4. Ocean   I. Title

If you want to find information on a certain topic or
subject, then look for a *subject card*. The subject area is
printed at the top of a subject card. Underneath is the title
of a book that will give you information about the topic.
Subject cards are in alphabetical order according to the
first word of the subject heading.

Activity A

Look at the information below. Tell whether you would find each piece of information on the first line of a *title card*, an *author card*, or a *subject card*.

1. *The Art of Base-Stealing*
2. Cleary, Beverly
3. *The History of Football*
4. Alexander, Lloyd
5. Sports
6. *The Mouse and the Motorcycle*
7. White, E. B.
8. Cars
9. *The Lion, the Witch, and the Wardrobe*
10. Hobbies

A college football game—1890

Activity B

Look at the picture of the card catalog. Write the letter or letters of the drawer where you would find each piece of information.

Example: A book about baseball—drawer B

1. A book about inventions
2. A book by the author Maurice Sendak
3. The book *Dig to Disaster*
4. A book about whales
5. A book by the author Isaac Asimov
6. The book *Land of the Iron Dragon*
7. A book by Evaline Ness
8. A book about Christopher Columbus
9. A book by Marguerite Henry
10. The book *Daughter of the Mountains*

Activity C

Go to the card catalog in your library. Find three *title cards*, three *author cards*, and three *subject cards*. Print the first line of each card on a piece of paper. Keep the cards in order according to subject, title, and author.

Example (author card): Asimov, Isaac

Lesson 5 Library Skills— The Dewey Decimal System

The Dewey Decimal System is a special number system used to classify nonfiction books in the library.

Nonfiction books can be found by using the *Dewey Decimal System*. A man named Melvil Dewey developed this system in 1876 and we still use it today. Mr. Dewey understood that it was very important to put books in order and that all libraries should follow the same system.

Mr. Dewey arranged the nonfiction books into ten *areas* or *classes*. Each class has a special beginning and ending number. When Mr. Dewey was choosing the classes, he thought about questions that cave people might have asked about the world. Look at the Dewey Decimal Chart.

Dewey Decimal Chart

000–099	**General Reference** Encyclopedias, atlases
100–199	*Who am I?* Philosophy Books about one's mind and thoughts
200–299	*Who made me?* Religion Bible stories and mythology
300–399	*Who is the person in the next cave?* Social Sciences Books about group relations, government, careers, customs, holidays, folklore, and fairy tales
400–499	*How can I make that person understand me?* Language Grammar and spelling books
500–599	*What makes things happen in the world?* Science Books about insects, animals, flowers, birds, rocks, and stars
600–699	*How can I control nature?* Useful Arts Books about inventions, medicine, ships, cars, airplanes, business, pets, and food
700–799	*How can I enjoy my spare time?* Arts and Recreation Books about painting, music, hobbies, sports, theater, dance, and humor
800–899	*What are the stories of people's ideas and deeds?* Literature Poetry, plays, and essays
900–999	*How can I record what people have done?* History Biography, history, and geography books

Call Numbers

> **A call number is a special number given to each book in the library.**

You know that each book in the library is placed in either the nonfiction, fiction, or reference section. Within each of these sections, the books are placed on the shelves in a special order according to *call numbers*. Call numbers can be found on the cards in the card catalog.

Nonfiction Books

On the spine of each *nonfiction* book there is a Dewey decimal number and the first or first three letters of the author's last name. This is the book's *call number*. The books are placed in order by putting the smallest numbers first.

Activity A

Help the librarian put these books on the shelves. On a piece of paper, print the call numbers in order. Remember to begin with the smallest number.

796	512	607
Dag	Ast	Bon
212	945	809
Mas	Wes	Kal

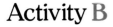

Activity B

Look at the information about each of these books. Then decide if the book would be found in the class given. Answer *yes* or *no*. Use the Dewey Decimal Chart to help you.

1. 800s   A book that describes prehistoric animals
2. 600s   A book that explains how a car is made
3. 200s   A book that tells about snowflakes
4. 500s   A book that explains our solar system
5. 900s   A book that tells about the animals in the jungle
6. 300s   A book about a real person's life
7. 700s   A book that describes the Olympic games
8. 400s   A grammar book

Activity C

Go to your library and locate the ten classes of the Dewey Decimal System. Then answer these questions on a piece of paper.

1. Which section in your library contains the largest number of books?
2. Which section contains the least number of books?
3. Which section do you use the most?
4. In which section would you find a book on spelling?
5. In which section would you find books about Greek mythology?
6. In which section would you find books about the history of our country?

Fiction Books

On the spine of each *fiction* book, you will find the letter *F* and the first or first three letters of the author's last name. This is the book's *call number*. For example, the book *The Trumpeter of Kraków* by Eric P. Kelly, has the call number F on its spine.
Kel

Activity D

Read the titles of the books below. Give the call number for each book.

Example: *The Velveteen Rabbit* by Margery Williams F/Wil

1. *The Voyages of Dr. Dolittle* by Hugh Lofting
2. *Hitty, Her First Hundred Years* by Rachel Field
3. *By the Shores of Silver Lake* by Laura Ingalls Wilder
4. *Annie and the Old One* by Miska Miles
5. *NIC of the Woods* by Lynd Ward
6. *Stuart Little* by E. B. White

Activity E

Divide a piece of paper into two columns. In the first column, print the first three letters of the author's last name. In the second column, print the sets of letters in alphabetical order.

Example: Barbara Wersba—Wer

Vera Cleaver
C. W. Anderson
Sidney Taylor
Peter Dickenson
Jeanette Eaton
Carolyn Haywood
Laurence Yep
Rumer Godden

Biographies

The call number for a *biography* is *B or 92*. Underneath this is the first or first three letters of the *subject's* last name. Biographies are placed on the shelves in alphabetical order according to the subject's last name.

Example: *The Life of Dolly Madison* $\frac{B}{Mad}$ or $\frac{92}{Mad}$

Activity F

Can you help the librarian? Read the title of each of these books. Decide whether you would find the book in the *fiction* or *biography* section. Write the *call number* for each.

Examples: *Old Yeller* by Fred Gibson $\frac{F}{Gib}$

The Story of Louis Braille $\frac{B}{Bra}$ or $\frac{92}{Bra}$

1. *The Stones* by Janet Hickman
2. *The Ghost Downstairs* by Leon Garfield
3. *The Nightingale* by Hans Christian Andersen
4. *The Story of Beatrix Potter* by Dorothy Aldis
5. *Eddie and His Big Deals* by Carolyn Haywood
6. *Abraham Lincoln* by Clara Ingram Judson
7. *The Helen Keller Story* by Catherine Owens Peace
8. *The Story of Bill Cosby* by Joel H. Cohen

Exploring Our Language

Part II

Grammar, Correct Usage, Mechanics

Chapter 1

Sentences

Rodeo

by Virginia Driving Hawk Sneve

from *Jimmy Yellow Hawk*

Today was the last day of school, but it wasn't really a school day. Today was the picnic and rodeo.

The holding corral was filled with stock. There were goats in one pen, calves in another, and two pigs in a third. The stock had been loaned by local ranchers, Big Jim among them. Mr. Russell, their white neighbor, had donated the prize stock, which the winner of each event would get to keep.

Little Jim had been down at the corral since eight o'clock making last-minute preparations. The rodeo was to be at ten and the picnic afterwards.

The first to arrive was Sha Sha, riding his pony to let Little Jim know he was going to compete in the races.

"Hi, Little Jim," Sha Sha greeted him as he tied the pony to the corral. "Is this where the race horses should be?"

"Hi, Sha Sha," Little Jim answered. "Yeah, that's okay."

"Bet I win the race this year," bragged Sha Sha. "I've been running my pony every day."

"I hope I win the calf," said Little Jim.

"I don't want one of those," said Sha Sha. "We're leaving for Pow Wows next week, and nobody'd be around to take care of it."

Sha Sha and his whole family liked to go to all the Pow Wows during the summer. Sha Sha's father was a rancher too but didn't work as hard as Big Jim did. Mr. Blue Dog's

Photographs of rodeo scenes by Steven Trimble

father had been a white man, but he had been raised by his Indian mother and given her family's name. Little Jim couldn't remember what Mr. Blue Dog's first name was. Even though Sha Sha's father was only half Indian, no one used his white first name. Everyone always called him Blue Dog, which made Little Jim resent his nickname even more.

Blue Dog liked to dance Indian and entered all the contests at the Pow Wows. He was a good dancer and many times won money or prizes of beadwork or costumes in the Pow Wow dance contests. He and his family went as far away as the Wind River Reservation in Wyoming and to the Turtle Mountains in North Dakota to compete in the Pow Wows. The only trouble was that while he was gone in the summer his ranch work never got done.

"This year," said Sha Sha, "I'm going to enter some contests, too. My Grandma has made me new moccasins and leggings."

"Gee," said Little Jim enviously, "that'll be great!" They saw Sha Sha's folks driving up in their pickup and behind them Miss Red Owl's funny little foreign car. Then came the cars of parents, relatives, and friends of the students, all coming to watch the rodeo. They parked close to the corral so that they could watch from their cars.

"Hello, boys," greeted Miss Red Owl. "Where shall I put my potato salad?"

Both boys ran up to help.

"Over here on the table," answered Little Jim as he led her and Mrs. Blue Dog, who had brought meat balls, to the long plank set on saw horses, which he had helped Big Jim fix up the night before.

Now all the parents and relatives seemed to come at once, in busy confusion, **tethering** horses, parking cars, putting the food on the plank, and calling greetings to each other. But by ten o'clock everybody was settled and the rodeo began.

Both boys and girls were contestants in all events, closely supervised by the fathers, who were stationed in different parts of the corral.

Miss Red Owl had to yell over the noise to get everyone's attention for the first event.

"Contestants for the goat tying please report to chute number one!" She made the announcements just as if she were the official master of ceremonies at the Rapid City rodeo.

"The goat tying is a timed event," she explained, "in which the contestant will ride a horse out of a chute down to the goat which you can see in the center of the corral. The contestant will jump off his or her horse, grab the goat, flip it on its back, and try to tie three of its legs together. The winner will be the one who does all of this in the shortest time."

There were cheers from the watching parents after her announcement.

"It looks easy," she went on, "but the goats put up a good fight and the goat will have to be securely tied, or it might wiggle loose and the contestant will be disqualified."

There were some sympathetic groans from the crowd, but she continued her explanation.

"The older boys in the seventh and eighth grades will be first, and they will have the biggest, strongest goat to tie. The girls will be next, and their goat will be almost as big. The youngest students will have the smallest goat. The winners will each get a goat as a prize."

The first contestant rode out of the chute to the cheers of the spectators, and the first event was underway. As Miss Red Owl had said, the goats put up a good fight and three of the older boys were disqualified, none of the girls made it, and only one proud first grader won a goat.

"All eyes on chute number two for the calf riding!" Miss Red Owl announced after the goats had been led away.

"This event is limited to fourth graders and up," she said. "Most of our entrants are boys, but we have one brave eighth-grade girl to give the boys some competition.

"The contestants will mount the calf in a chute just as a **brahma bull** is mounted in a grown-up rodeo. The gate will swing open, and out will come the bucking calf with the rider hanging on for dear life.

"If the winner can ride the calf past the line marked in the corral, he or she will get the calf as a prize. Watch them ride!"

This was the event Little Jim wanted to win. He'd feel pretty proud owning his own calf.

There were four entrants before him. They all got thrown from their calf before reaching the line. Now he felt his legs shaking as he lowered himself down on the calf's back. He'd sneaked rides on his father's calves many times, so he half knew what to expect; but this calf looked bigger than any he'd ever ridden before.

The gate opened, and he clenched his legs tightly around the calf, hanging on to the rope tied around the calf's middle. A contestant was allowed to use both hands to hang on with, and Little Jim used them.

The calf spun around in a circle, and Little Jim couldn't tell which way it was going until it was headed on a bucking

run back toward the chute. Dizzy, he was afraid he'd have to jump before the calf hit the chute, but it stopped short and, turning sharply around, ran the other way.

Little Jim could hear the crowd yelling. He heard his father, who was in the corral, yell above the others, "Hang on! Hang on!"

As the calf jumped, Little Jim was jolted from his tail bone all the way to the top of his head. He felt as if his head would snap right off his neck.

The yelling of the crowd changed to cheering, and Little Jim knew he'd crossed the line. He could get off the calf now, but the darn critter kept jumping and Little Jim didn't dare loosen his hold.

He hit the ground with a loud whlump. Face down in the dirt, he lay where he had fallen, all the wind knocked out of him.

His father rushed over, and Little Jim felt himself being lifted up by the arms. "You okay, boy?" Big Jim asked anxiously.

Little Jim leaned heavily against his father as he tried to stand. He was glad to have Big Jim's strong arms supporting him, because his legs felt like rubber. He couldn't get enough breath to breathe normally. It hurt when he attempted to talk, and suddenly everything went black.

He found himself lying on a blanket in the shade outside the corral where his mother had been watching the rodeo. He tried to sit up.

"No, you don't!" said Mama, pushing him back down on the blanket. "You just stay right where you are till the rodeo's over."

Little Jim ached in every part of his body and was glad to lie back again. "Did I win, Mama?" he asked.

"Yes, you did, you—cowboy, you," she smoothed down his hair as she answered, and Little Jim knew she'd been scared when he'd blacked out.

"I'm okay, Mama," he said and then added very proudly, "Now I own my own calf!"

He had missed the greased-pig contest—a free-for-all for students of any age. Two pigs were turned loose, and all the kids tried to catch one and hang on to it.

Little Jim had come around in time to watch the pony race. He cheered and yelled for Sha Sha to win, but his friend fell behind at the last moment, and Martin Iron, a seventh grader, won.

After the race Sha Sha came to where Little Jim was sitting. "Did you see how Martin edged me out?" Sha Sha said angrily. "Boy, he cheated and oughta be disqualified!"

Little Jim hadn't seen Sha Sha edged out and thought Martin had won fairly. He didn't want to argue with Sha Sha, so he only said, "I'm sorry you lost, Sha Sha."

To Little Jim's surprise, Sha Sha became even angrier. "I deserved to win!" Sha Sha sounded as if he was going to cry. "I suppose you think you're pretty great winning a calf. You were just lucky that you got an easy calf to ride!"

Sha Sha angrily stomped away.

Little Jim didn't know what to think. He'd been happy about winning the calf, but Sha Sha's words spoiled everything.

The Writer's Craft

1. Would you enjoy or not enjoy a rodeo ride or something like it? Explain.
2. What do you think gave Little Jim strength to stay on the bucking calf?
3. Contrast the experiences and attitudes of Little Jim and Sha Sha at the rodeo. Why do you think Sha Sha's words spoiled things for Little Jim?
4. The author uses different kinds of sentences in the story, especially in dialogue, to show how people really talk. Find examples of sentences that ask a question, state a fact, express a strong feeling, give a command.

1. A sentence expresses a complete thought. Identify the sentence: *At the corral. Little Jim won a calf.*
2. The subject of a sentence tells who or what performs the action. Name the subject in *Big Jim cheered.*
3. The predicate tells something about the subject. What is the predicate in this sentence? *Miss Red Owl smiled.*

Lesson 1 Parts of a Sentence

A sentence is a group of words expressing a complete thought.

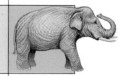

One of the contestants is not a sentence because it does not express a complete thought. *One of the contestants fell off the bucking calf* is a sentence because it expresses a complete thought.

INCOMPLETE THOUGHT	COMPLETE THOUGHT = SENTENCE
The happy boy	The happy boy won the calf.
Two hours later	The pony race began two hours later.
After animals	Native Americans were often named after animals.

Exercise 1

Tell whether each group of words is a *complete thought* or an *incomplete thought.* If it is a complete thought, it is a sentence.

1. The students celebrated the last day of school.
2. They had a picnic and a rodeo.
3. Parents, relatives, and friends of the students.
4. Little Jim held tightly to the rope.
5. The bucking calf in the gate.
6. Pain shot up and down Little Jim's back.
7. The crowd yelled and cheered.
8. Big Jim and Mama wcrc proud of their son.
9. The greased-pig contest next.
10. Martin Iron won the pony race.
11. Very early the next day.
12. Little Jim rode his pony alone on the ranch.
13. The stray horse high on the butte.
14. A rattlesnake frightened Little Jim and his pony.
15. A loud crack of thunder.
16. The rattler disappeared from sight.
17. Little Jim worried about the lost mare.
18. Great flashes of lightning across the sky.
19. The rain came in great blasting sheets.
20. A brightly colored rainbow over the butte.
21. The author is from the Sioux nation.
22. As a child in South Dakota.
23. Oren Lyons illustrated *Jimmy Yellow Hawk.*
24. He is chief of the Turtle Clan.
25. A reservation in New York.

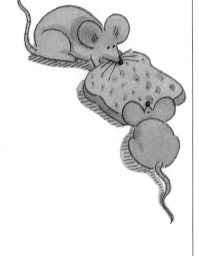

Exercise 2

Each of the groups of words in column A can be joined to those in column B to make a sentence. Match the groups of words to form sentences that make sense.

Column A

1. Our new hamster
2. Max found cookie
3. A jaguar's spots
4. A graham cracker
5. At the zoo, we
6. Lightning
7. Sherrie's dictionary
8. The puppy chased
9. The square yellow
10. Owls

Column B

A. watched porpoises.
B. its tail.
C. sometimes flashes inside clouds.
D. crumbs in his pocket.
E. fell on the floor with a bang.
F. baskets are full of blueberries.
G. squeaks at night.
H. live in the barn.
I. is good with chocolate.
J. are shaped like hearts.

Subjects and Predicates

Every sentence has two important parts. These parts are called the *subject* and the *predicate*.

SUBJECT	PREDICATE	SUBJECT	PREDICATE
Fire	burns.	Bells	jingle.
Monica	laughs.	Fireflies	glow.

The subject names the person, place, or thing talked about in the sentence.

To find the subject, ask the question *who* or *what* before the verb. In the sentence *Fire burns*, ask *who* or *what* burns. The answer is *fire*. *Fire* is the subject of this sentence. What are the subjects in the other three sentences?

The predicate tells something about the subject.

To find the predicate, ask the question *do what* or *does what* after the subject. In the sentence *Monica laughs*, ask *Monica does what*? The answer is *laughs*. *Laughs* is the predicate of this sentence. What are the predicates in the other three sentences?

Exercise 3

Find the subject in each sentence. Ask the question *who* or *what* before the predicate.
Example: Penguins waddle. *Who* waddle? Penguins.

1. Ants crawl.
2. Firecrackers popped.
3. Dishes rattled.
4. Cowboys galloped.
5. The giant balloon burst.
6. Hamburgers sizzle.
7. Striped snakes wiggle.
8. Yo-yos spin.
9. Sleds slide.
10. The green soda fizzes.
11. Excited fans yelled.
12. Noisy crickets chirp.

Exercise 4

Complete each sentence with a subject.
1. _____ ran over the bridge.
2. _____ landed the helicopter.
3. _____ have green skin.
4. _____ hoot.
5. _____ looked for an Iowa license plate.
6. _____ won a trophy.
7. _____ roasted hot dogs.
8. _____ rode on a turtle.
9. _____ bounce.
10. _____ live in that cave.

Exercise 5

Name the predicate in each of these sentences. Ask the
question *do what* or *does what* after each subject.
Example: The lion roars. The lion *does what*? Roars.

1. Jeremy dances.
2. Her eyes sparkled.
3. The door creaks.
4. Seashells clinked.
5. Taxicabs honk loudly.
6. The gorilla yawned.
7. The refrigerator hums.
8. Our eggs cracked.
9. The radio blasted.
10. Robots work in the factory.
11. Fog drifts over the city.
12. Fingers snapped to the music.

Exercise 6

Complete each sentence with a predicate.
1. A parachute _____.
2. Two clowns _____.
3. The scientist _____.
4. My elephant _____.
5. White rabbits _____.
6. The newspaper reporter_____.
7. A cannonball _____.
8. The fishing pole _____.
9. The troop leader _____.
10. The busy beavers _____.

Exercise 7

Find the subject and predicate in each sentence.

1. Kangaroos jump.
2. Teakettles whistle.
3. The shiny bubble popped.
4. Squirrels chatter in the trees.
5. The old wheel squeaks.
6. Helen twirled around.
7. Aunt Edna drives quickly.
8. The curious toddler crawled away.
9. The telephone rang often.
10. Kurt reads in the morning.
11. The juicy watermelon dripped.
12. The mushy snowpeople melted.
13. A quail travels on foot.
14. The iceberg moved slowly.
15. Hedgehogs snore loudly.

Diagraming Subjects and Predicates

A diagram is a picture that shows how the parts of a sentence are related. You have learned that name words and action words are important in a sentence. The subject word of a sentence is a name word, and the predicate is usually an action word. A diagram will help you understand better those important parts of a sentence.

In a diagram, the subject and the predicate of a sentence are shown on a horizontal (left to right) line. This line is also called the base line. A short vertical (up and down) line separates the subject from the predicate.

subject	predicate

Here is a model diagram. First, a horizontal line is drawn to represent the sentence. Then, the verb or predicate is written on the right side. A vertical line is drawn to separate the subject from the predicate, and finally the subject word is written on the left.

Fireflies	glow

Exercise 8

Diagram these sentences.

1. Bees buzz.
2. Carol sang.
3. Joey hiccuped.
4. Snow fell.
5. Clouds move.

Practice Power

Do members of your class roller-skate, swim, play football or soccer? Write four sentences about what they like to do. Underline each subject once and each predicate twice. Here is an example sentence.

Jenny rides her bike after school.

Lesson 2 Direct Objects of Sentences

The direct object is the noun or pronoun that completes the action of the verb.

Many sentences are complete with only a subject and a predicate. However, other sentences need a *direct object* to complete their meaning.

A name word can be a subject to a predicate. It can also be an *object* to a predicate.

Oscar saves *nickels*. (Oscar saves *what*? Nickels.)

Oscar is the subject of the sentence. *Saves* is the predicate. *Nickels* is the direct object. *Nickels* does not *do* the action of the predicate. It is *not* a subject. It *completes* the action of the verb. It is the *direct object* of the predicate.

To find the direct object of a sentence, ask *whom* or *what* after the predicate.

Mark cracked a peanut. (Cracked *what*?—a peanut)
Paula pulled dandelions. (Pulled *what*?—dandelions)
Priscilla helped the carpenter. (Helped *whom*?—the carpenter)

Exercise 1

Find the direct object in each sentence. Ask the question *whom* or *what* after the predicate.

Example: Uncle Floyd builds bridges. Uncle Floyd builds *what*? Bridges.

1. George will flip pancakes.
2. The Boy Scouts collected cans.
3. Jessica solved the problem in two minutes.
4. Yolanda delivers newspapers.
5. Ralph salted the warm pretzels.
6. Ms. Waldorf trains seals.
7. We lost the toothpaste near that tree.
8. Marvin put them into the box.
9. John invented a toy with a motor.
10. My dog loves pickles.
11. A dragon attacked the castle.
12. Phyllis popped the baseball over the fence.
13. I'll peel the oranges.
14. Marcy chose him to play the hero.
15. I collect books on the solar system.

Exercise 2

Complete each sentence with a direct object.

1. The ships carried _____.
2. Jugglers threw _____.
3. Mr. Turner bought a _____.
4. We'll watch the _____.
5. Tammy painted the _____.
6. My mother likes _____.
7. Yesterday I saw a _____.
8. Mrs. Thompson repairs _____.
9. Dave cooked _____.
10. Twelve horses ate the _____.

Exercise 3

Find the subject, predicate, and object in each sentence.

1. The pony gobbled the apples.
2. Sally built it.
3. Dad bakes brownies.
4. Kara wrote a haiku.
5. Hans explored the cave.
6. Octopuses squirt ink.
7. Joanie waxes cars.
8. Anna cracked an egg.
9. Victor touched the caterpillar!
10. I dislike oatmeal.

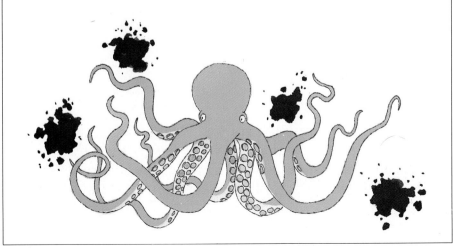

Diagraming Direct Objects

Ask these questions to find the subject, the predicate, and the direct object of a sentence:

SUBJECT	PREDICATE	OBJECT
Who or what?	Did what?	Whom or what?
	Does what?	
	Do what?	

In a diagram, the subject, the predicate, and the direct object are all written on the horizontal line, or the base line.

Example: Mario plays checkers.

	Does	
Who?	What?	What?
SUBJECT	PREDICATE	DIRECT OBJECT
Mario	plays	checkers

The line between the subject and the predicate cuts through the base line. The line between the predicate and the direct object stops at the base line.

Exercise 4

Diagram these sentences.
1. Spiders spin webs.
2. Julia wrote messages.
3. George digs tunnels.
4. Yoshi chased dragonflies.
5. Courtney likes olives.

Practice Power

Write five sentences of your own. Describe animals and other things you saw during a visit to the zoo. Each sentence should have a subject, predicate, and direct object. Use these verbs in your sentences: ate, saw, drank, took, watched.

Lesson 3 Compound Parts of a Sentence

Compound Subjects

A compound subject has two subjects.

Elephants take mud baths. *Rhinoceroses* take mud baths.

Elephants is the subject of the first sentence. *Rhinoceroses* is the subject of the second sentence. Notice that elephants and rhinoceroses do the same action—they both take mud baths. Both sentences have the same predicate.

Imagine that you read these sentences in a paragraph. They repeat the same information. Since the sentences share the same predicate, you can *combine* the subjects to make one sentence.

Elephants and *rhinoceroses* take mud baths.

Elephants and *rhinoceroses* are the two subjects in the above sentence. The word *and* is used to combine, or join, the two subjects into one *compound subject.*

Exercise 1

Find the compound subject in each sentence.
1. Basketball and football are popular sports.
2. Polar bears and penguins like cold weather.
3. Saturdays and Sundays are my favorite days in the week.
4. Joanne and Joseph share the same birthday.
5. The sky and the lake in that picture are green!
6. Raisins and peanuts are healthy snacks.
7. A dictionary and a notebook are under my desk.
8. Daniel and his collie go everywhere together.
9. Yesterday, Alex and Brian climbed the hill.
10. Aardvarks and gophers like to dig.

"Polar Bear"
Beth Van Hoesen

Exercise 2

Combine each pair of sentences into one sentence with a compound subject.

Example: Carrots crunch when you eat them.
Pretzels crunch when you eat them.
Carrots and *pretzels* crunch when you eat them.

1. My sisters write with their left hands.
   My brothers write with their left hands.
2. Monkeys eat bananas.
   People eat bananas.
3. Bison roam around Canada.
   Elk roam around Canada.
4. Skateboards have four wheels.
   Cars have four wheels.
5. Fifth-graders know how to multiply numbers.
   Fourth-graders know how to multiply numbers.
6. Scarecrows frighten crows.
   Loud noises frighten crows.
7. Shoppers walk down the busy street.
   Tourists walk down the busy street.
8. On Saturdays, Sarah took piano lessons.
   On Saturdays, Monica took piano lessons.
9. Seaweed floated near the shore.
   Jellyfish floated near the shore.
10. When they are afraid, cats lay their ears back.
    When they are afraid, zebras lay their ears back.

Compound Predicates

> **A compound predicate has two predicates.**

Hornets *chew* wood.   Hornets *build* nests.

Hornets is the subject of the first sentence. *Hornets* is also the subject of the second sentence. Both of these sentences give information about the same subject. They tell that hornets chew wood *and* build nests.

Since the sentences share the same subject, you can *combine* the predicates to make one sentence.

Hornets *chew wood* and *build nests*.

Chew wood and *build nests* are the two predicates in the above sentence. The word *and* is used to combine, or join, the two predicates into one *compound predicate*.

Exercise 3

Find the compound predicate in each sentence.
1. The snake slithers and hisses.
2. Sheila cracked and beat the eggs.
3. Mac kicked sand and splashed water everywhere.
4. The star shot across the sky and disappeared.
5. Stan carefully mows and trims the tall grass.
6. The bull pawed the ground and snorted.
7. The ice cream melted and dripped on my hand.
8. Jeannette licked the envelope and stamped it.
9. Brigid sneezed and hiccuped during class.
10. Carefully, we lifted the cover and looked in the box.

Exercise 4

Combine each pair of sentences into one sentence with a compound predicate. Look at the example.

> The sun rises in the east.
> The sun sets in the west.
> The sun *rises* in the east and *sets* in the west.

1. Sea lions throw stones.
   Sea lions fetch them back.
2. Molly walks on her hands.
   Molly stands on her head.
3. Greg opened the refrigerator.
   Greg took out a jar of pickles.
4. The lynx jumps into the air.
   The lynx catches birds.
5. During the winter, we shovel snow.
   We build snow forts.
6. Every morning I eat cereal.
   I drink orange juice.
7. Sandra filled the bicycle tires with air.
   Sandra oiled the chain.
8. William read the book.
   William wrote a report.
9. Suddenly, the goose honked.
   The goose bit my finger.
10. Carl and Ann swept the floor.
    Carl and Ann washed the windows.

Practice Power

Write a sentence for each group of words below. In the first column are compound subjects. In the second column are compound predicates.

crocodiles and alligators	chomp and chew
hot dogs and hamburgers	walked and ran
slide and swing	climbed and jumped

Lesson 4 Kinds of Sentences

Every sentence you speak or write has a special job. There are four kinds of sentences: *declarative, interrogative, imperative,* and *exclamatory*. These sentences end with special marks of punctuation. All sentences begin with capital letters.

> A *declarative sentence* states a fact. It begins with a capital letter and ends with a *period*.

The Earth revolves around the Sun.
We made a canoe from the tree trunk.
Six dolphins swam by our ship.

> An *interrogative sentence* asks a question. It begins with a capital letter and ends with a *question mark*.

Have you ever taken a mud bath?
Did you see that flying frog?
Where is my purple notebook paper?

> An *imperative sentence* gives a command or makes a request. It begins with a capital letter and ends with a *period*.

Check your bag at the museum.
Please save some popcorn for me.
Feed the goldfish, Henry.

An *exclamatory sentence* expresses a strong feeling. It begins with a capital letter and ends with an *exclamation point*.

I can't believe my eyes!
This echo is so loud!
That was an exciting movie!

Exercise 1

Tell whether each sentence is *declarative* or *interrogative*. Use the correct punctuation mark at the end of each sentence.

1. Where is my skateboard
2. Tigers like to swim
3. The humpback whale can sing beautifully
4. Can you tell me that joke again
5. A tugboat pushes and pulls big ships
6. Chalk is a soft, white rock
7. Is there water on the moon
8. Do you know which Indian tribe lived in Delaware
9. What is this bubbly purple liquid
10. Backgammon is one of the oldest games
11. Blue whales migrate to the equator in the fall
12. Did you ever visit Idaho

Exercise 2

Change these declarative sentences to interrogative sentences. Use the correct punctuation mark at the end of each sentence.

Example: There are thirty-seven kinds of cats.
        Are there thirty-seven kinds of cats?

1. Kim earned a black belt in karate.
2. The history book was very interesting.
3. Our hockey team will practice after school.
4. Bert saw a ghost on the stairs.
5. The cowhand's name is Betsy.
6. Braille is an alphabet for the blind.
7. The cupcakes are ready to eat.
8. Carlos can use a computer.
9. The umbrella turned inside out.
10. The donkey is a cousin of the horse.

Exercise 3

Tell whether each sentence is *declarative* or *imperative*.

1. The giant icicle was five feet long.
2. The Declaration of Independence was signed on July 4, 1776.
3. Bring a racquet with you, please.
4. Plant the turnip seeds today.
5. Help your sister make a pinwheel.
6. Draw a picture of your favorite animal.
7. Sean, show me how to somersault.
8. Helicopters can hover over the ground.
9. My class worked on the antipollution project.
10. Shanna followed the directions.
11. A blue whale weighs more than two thousand people.
12. Climb down from the tree right now.

Exercise 4

Tell whether each sentence is *interrogative* or *exclamatory*.
Use the correct punctuation mark at the end of each
sentence.

1. How many questions David asks every day
2. Do you understand the problem
3. What a great adventure story that was
4. What a big block of ice the swimming pool became
5. How long is a giraffe's neck
6. What a big pizza that was
7. Have you ever played a drum
8. How loud the thunder is
9. Did you look over the edge of the cliff
10. Will the rabbit eat this spinach
11. How high the kite is
12. What flavor is that bubble gum

Exercise 5

Change these declarative sentences to exclamatory
sentences. Use the word *how* or *what* to begin each
sentence. Use the correct punctuation mark at the end
of each sentence.

Example: This bus is crowded. (declarative)
How crowded this bus is! (exclamatory)
What a crowded bus this is! (exclamatory)

1. These doughnuts are heavy.
2. A car engine is complicated.
3. Jason quickly dashed up the stairs.
4. Andrea draws funny cartoons.
5. That superball bounces high.
6. The chimpanzee looks sad.
7. This tunnel is long and dark.
8. The dinosaur looks fierce.
9. This is an old tree.
10. Windshield wipers are useful.

Exercise 6

Tell whether each sentence is *declarative*, *interrogative*, *imperative*, or *exclamatory*. Add the correct punctuation mark at the end of each sentence.

1. We made a swing out of an old tire.
2. Leave your frog at home.
3. Give me my paste and scissors.
4. Will Carl get a sleeping bag for his birthday?
5. Fish cannot close their eyes.
6. A sunflower grew through a crack in the sidewalk.
7. Do you know how to predict the weather?
8. What a scary cave this is!
9. Can you stand on your head?
10. My sneakers are getting holes in them.

You Are the Author

Your class is having a party to celebrate Native American Heritage Week. You have been chosen to direct the party.

1. Write two imperative sentences telling your classmates what to do to get ready for the party.
2. Write two interrogative sentences asking your classmates questions about the party.
3. Write two declarative sentences about the party.
4. Write two exclamatory sentences about what a great party it is.

Chapter Challenge

Read this paragraph carefully, and then answer the questions.

¹Strange forms moved quietly from house to house. ²Scary sounds drifted through the air. ³Children walked carefully past the dark corners. ⁴Was this the same street where they had played a few hours ago? ⁵How frightening it was! ⁶Witches walked beside skeletons, and monsters laughed loudly. ⁷People wore odd costumes. ⁸Jack-o'-lanterns flashed smiles at the trick-or-treaters. ⁹Both children and adults shivered and giggled with excitement. ¹⁰How thrilling Halloween night is!

1. What kind of sentence is sentence 2?
2. What is the subject of sentence 3?
3. What kind of sentence is sentence 4?
4. Change sentence 4 to a declarative sentence.
5. What kind of sentence is sentence 5?
6. Copy sentence 7. Write S over the subject, P over the predicate, and DO over the direct object.
7. In sentence 8, what is the direct object of the predicate *flashed*?
8. What are the two predicates in sentence 9?
9. What punctuation mark is used at the end of sentence 10?
10. What punctuation mark is used at the end of an interrogative sentence?
11. What punctuation mark is used at the end of an imperative sentence?
12. What kind of sentence is *not* found in this paragraph?

The Box

I've taken it down
From the shelf;
The box marked OLD TOYS:
    A silly stuffed chicken with a missing eye,
    A farmhouse painted red with a spotted cow,
    A set of blocks and a ball made of fuzz,
    A puzzle with only five pieces,
    A giraffe with a bent neck.

Why did I play with those old things, anyway?

Myra Cohn Livingston

Exploring the Poem...

When the speaker in the poem says, "Why did I play with those old things, anyway?," it sounds as if he or she doesn't care about the old toys. But think: Does the speaker look at each toy carefully? How can you tell? How do you think this speaker felt as she or he looked at the old toys?

★ Can you remember a few of your favorite toys? What was special about each toy?

Write a poem about your old toys. First think of three or four toys. Then think of a specific detail that describes each one. Try to paint pictures of your old toys in your reader's mind.

Before you begin your poem, read this poem written by a student.

In the garage
I found a box
Of old toys:
    A blond doll whose hair is almost gone,
    A toy clock with only one yellow hand,
    A plastic monster which bends into any
       shape,
    A coloring book with many faces colored
       blue.

It seems long ago that they were mine.

Chapter 2

Nouns

Henry's Summer Vacation

by Keith Robertson

from *Henry Reed's Think Tank*

My name is Henry Harris Reed and this is my private journal. I am staying with my aunt and uncle in Grover's Corner, New Jersey. Grover's Corner isn't a real town, just a cluster of ten houses near Princeton, New Jersey. My address is c/o Mr. J. Alfred Harris, R.D. 1, Grover's Corner, Princeton, NJ 08540. If I should lose this journal, and anyone finds it, please mail it back to me. I will pay you back for the postage.

The reason I am spending the summer with my aunt and uncle is that my father is in the **diplomatic** service and we have lived abroad most of my life. Two years ago my dad and mom decided it would be a good idea if I spent my summers in the United States.

"You are being **culturally deprived**," my father said. "I'm not a bit worried that you are missing all those silly so-called comedies on TV, or the cartoons, or the advertising. But a normal American boy ought to see a few big-league baseball games and occasionally eat a real American hamburger and drink a genuine milk shake. And I've noticed that quite a few foreign words have crept into your speech. That's okay, but you are probably way out of touch with current American slang. You won't be able to understand what the average American kid is saying unless we do something."

Detail from *Country Girl Diner* by Ralph Goings

I think Dad was wrong about the slang because American slang gets all over the world pretty fast. But he was certainly right about the hamburgers and milk shakes. We were living in Italy when I came over to New Jersey the first time. You can't get a really good hamburger with relish and ketchup and onions and everything in Italy or anyplace else in Europe. As for a good thick milk shake—forget it! For that matter you can't get a pizza in Rome that is nearly as good as the pizzas you can get almost anywhere in the United States.

My father is now at the **embassy** in Manila. This is my third summer here. Spending the summer out in the country is fun even if there aren't many kids to play with. There is really only one person anywhere near my age in Grover's Corner and that is a girl named Margaret Glass. Her nickname is Midge. Midge acts crazy at times but she is smart and you can depend on her. She is not the giggly sort that some girls are or else she's past that stage. She and I have been partners in several things and have become good friends. We had a research business, we ran a baby-sitting service, and we just put on a big rodeo. Midge isn't here now because she is visiting an aunt in Washington, D.C., for a few days.

I also have a dog named Agony. Agony is a beagle who sort of adopted me the first summer I came here. I don't really know if he's my dog now or Uncle Al and Aunt Mabel's, since they have become very fond of him. He spends a lot more of the year with them than he does with me. However, he always knows me and carries on like crazy when I come back for the summer.

It has been raining all day and everybody has been cooped up in the house. Aunt Mabel wanted to go outside and work in her flower garden, Uncle Al wanted to do something with his tomatoes, and I guess Agony wanted to go chase a rabbit. Instead Aunt Mabel puttered around in the kitchen, Uncle Al did something in his workshop, and Agony slept. I found a good book.

About seven in the evening the telephone rang. It was my mother calling from Manila. Of course it was seven in the morning out there. It was great to hear her voice. I told her all about what I had been doing and she told me what had been happening there. The most important news was about school. It is going to start late, maybe not until the first of October. We don't have a very big American school in Manila and a missing teacher is really missed. One of our teachers broke his leg while he was back in the United States for the summer. Now it seems another one has a very sick mother and doesn't know when she will be able to go back. They have to find one temporary replacement and one permanent one, so school will start late.

"What would you like to do?" Mom asked. "Come back September 3, or stay two or three weeks longer?"

I didn't want to hurt her feelings, but I like Grover's Corner better than I like Manila. "Well, I'd like to see you and Dad but there won't be much happening out there," I said. I looked outside and there wasn't much happening in Grover's Corner either, except a steady drizzle. But things change fast around here. "I'd just as soon stay here a while."

Her feelings weren't hurt a bit. "Well, if that is what you prefer, we'll see if your Aunt Mabel is willing to put up with you a bit longer. I will probably go to India with your father. They have a special project there and they would like his help for a few weeks. Let me speak to Mabel for a few minutes, Henry."

Detail from *Country Girl Diner* by Ralph Goings

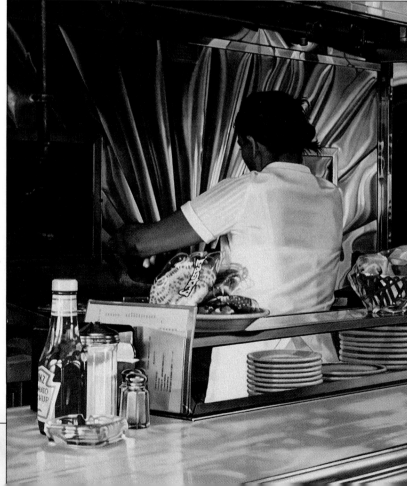

She talked to Aunt Mabel, who said she would be delighted to have me stay several weeks longer. Then Mom talked to Uncle Al, who is her older brother.

"Well, he seems to find things to do," Uncle Al said in answer to some question. "And Grover's Corner isn't such a quiet place these days. It's more like it used to be when you were a kid—stirring everything to a boil." There was a pause while he listened to something Mom said. "Yes, I suppose school will start here at the usual time and his partner Midge will be gone during the day. But don't worry about it. The schoolhouse will blow up or there will be a flood or something to liven things a bit."

Uncle Al talks in riddles a lot of the time, but Mom seems to understand him. Anyhow, it was settled that I would stay on several weeks longer than originally planned.

The Writer's Craft

1. Because his father works for the State Department, Henry Reed is not an average American child. How is his life different from yours? Discuss what you think are some good and bad points of his life-style.
2. Henry has been creative about finding things to do. What were some of his projects? What other activities do you think he might enjoy in the summer?
3. Have you ever kept a journal or a diary or known someone who did? These notebooks are similar records of what someone thinks and does. Why do some diaries you can buy have locks on them?
4. When authors wish to present a great deal of information quickly and plainly, they sometimes write a paragraph that contains many nouns. Reread the first and third paragraphs of this selection. Which paragraph has more facts? Which has more nouns?

Recalling What You Know

1. A common noun is a *general* name and a proper noun is a *specific* name for a person, place, or thing. Give examples of proper nouns for *city, lake, actress.*
2. Nouns can show possession. What was done to make the following nouns possessive? *Grover's, parents', children's, dog's*

Lesson 1 Identifying Nouns

A noun is a name word.

In stories and poems that you read, you find the names of many persons, places, and things. Here are the opening paragraphs from *Henry Reed's Think Tank* by Keith Robertson. Notice that the words in italics are name words, which are called *nouns.*

> My name is *Henry Harris Reed* and this is my private *journal.* I am staying with my *aunt* and *uncle* in *Grover's Corner, New Jersey. Grover's Corner* isn't a real *town*, just a cluster of ten *houses* near *Princeton, New Jersey.* If I should lose this *journal*, and anyone finds it, please mail it back to me. I will pay you back for the *postage.*
>
> The *reason* I am spending the *summer* with my *aunt* and *uncle* is that my *father* is in the diplomatic *service* and we have lived abroad most of my *life.* Two *years* ago my *dad* and *mom* decided it would be a good *idea* if I spent my *summers* in the *United States.*

NAME WORDS IN THESE PARAGRAPHS

PERSONS	PLACES	THINGS
Henry Harris Reed	Grover's Corner	journal
aunt	New Jersey	houses
uncle	town	postage
father	Princeton	reason
dad	United States	summer
mom		service
		life
		years
		idea

Exercise 1

Find the nouns in these sentences.

1. Mr. Reed wanted Henry to eat an American hamburger.
2. Their family once lived in Italy.
3. Henry likes American pizza better than pizza in Rome!
4. Manila is now the Reeds' home.
5. Henry's school won't open until October.
6. His father works for the State Department.
7. Why did Uncle Al suggest opening a think tank?
8. Soon Henry and Midge will concentrate on problems.
9. The author lives on a farm in New Jersey.
10. He has written a series of books about Henry Reed.

Exercise 2

Complete each sentence with a noun or nouns.

1. Andy built a _____ in the snow.
2. My family went to _____ this summer.
3. Is the _____ your favorite animal?
4. Joey ate _____ and _____ for lunch.
5. This book about _____ is very interesting.
6. Margaret drew a _____ in the wet cement.
7. Tiny _____ crawled along the sidewalk.
8. I was surprised to find a _____ in the box.
9. Jackie went bowling with _____ and _____.
10. We heard loud bangs coming from the _____.

Practice Power

The "Name Game" is a fun way to practice using name words.

First, divide the class into two teams. Choose a captain for each team. To begin, the captain of Team One asks a member of Team Two to name three things found in a certain place. If that player cannot name three things, he or she is out of the game. Then the captain of Team Two asks someone on Team One to name three things from another place. Continue playing until every player has had a turn. The team with more players left in the game at the end wins.

The captain of Team One can begin like this: "Name three things found in a kitchen."

Lesson 2 Proper and Common Nouns

A proper noun names a particular person, place, or thing.

A common noun is a general name for a person, place, or thing.

Some words—such as Molly, Mexico, and Monday—are *proper nouns*. A proper noun names a specific person, place, or thing. Proper nouns begin with capital letters. These name words are proper nouns:

PERSON	PLACE	THING
William Schmidt	Toronto	Statue of Liberty
Suzanne Lopez	Yellowstone National Park	*New York Times*

Some words—such as daughter, parks, and trees—are *common nouns*. A common noun is a general name that many persons, places, and things share. Common nouns do not begin with a capital letter except when they are the first word of a sentence.

A common noun becomes a proper noun when a specific person, place, or thing is named. Proper nouns are often made up of two or more words.

COMMON NOUNS	PROPER NOUNS
girl	Janice
president	Abraham Lincoln
continent	Europe
day	Tuesday
city	Montreal
astronaut	Sally Ride
month	November
poet	Robert Frost
country	China
river	Nile
club	4-H Club
scientist	Marie Curie
inventor	Thomas Edison
gulf	Gulf of Mexico
park	Fairmount Park
lake	Lake Erie
ocean	Pacific Ocean

Exercise 1

Find the nouns in these sentences. Tell if each is a *proper* or a *common* noun.

1. Cecile lives in Quebec.
2. The boys made lanterns out of yellow paper.
3. Some people think Bigfoot lives in Oregon.
4. Freddie likes books about cameras.
5. Diane took the train to Cloverleaf Farm.
6. Luke wants to join the Boy Scouts.
7. Rico followed the raccoon to the corner.
8. Many whales live near Mexico in the winter.
9. Michael watched a movie about Babe Ruth.
10. Mercury is the smallest planet.
11. Tokyo is a city in Japan.
12. How did this raisin get into my pocket?
13. Count the scales on a fish to find out its age.
14. Erie is a city in Pennsylvania on Lake Erie.
15. Trees in a forest are like big umbrellas.

Exercise 2

Give a common noun for each proper noun.

1. Saturday
2. Independence Day
3. Mississippi River
4. Iowa
5. Arctic Ocean
6. August
7. General Lee
8. Rocky Mountains
9. Lake Huron
10. London

Exercise 3

Give a proper noun for each common noun.

1. country
2. boy
3. scientist
4. continent
5. monument
6. school
7. book
8. musician
9. friend
10. teacher

Practice Power

Name two places to visit and two people in your city or town. Write a sentence about each place and each person. Be sure to capitalize each proper noun.

Lesson 3 Singular and Plural Nouns

A singular noun names one person, place, or thing.
A plural noun names more than one person, place, or thing.

The *horse* galloped away. (*Singular—one horse*)
The *horses* galloped away. (*Plural—more than one horse*)

Horse is a singular noun because it names one horse. *Horses* is a plural noun because it names more than one horse. The letter *s* is added to *horse* to form the plural.

Some nouns form the plural by adding *s* to the singular.

SINGULAR	PLURAL
(one)	(more than one)
river	rivers
pillow	pillows
frog	frogs
letter	letters
wagon	wagons
doctor	doctors
star	stars
bug	bugs
cake	cakes
Indian	Indians

Some singular nouns form the plural by adding *es*. Add *es* when the singular ends in *ch*, *s*, *sh*, *x*, or *z*.

SINGULAR	PLURAL
(one)	(more than one)
tax	taxes
witch	witches
box	boxes
wish	wishes
beach	beaches
inch	inches
six	sixes
guess	guesses

Some singular nouns form the plural by a change of spelling within the word or by adding a suffix.

SINGULAR	PLURAL
(one)	(more than one)
man	men
goose	geese
tooth	teeth
child	children
woman	women

Nouns ending in a consonant followed by *y* form the plural by changing the *y* to *i* and adding *es*.

SINGULAR	PLURAL
(one)	(more than one)
story	stories
baby	babies
country	countries
city	cities

Exercise 1

Tell whether each noun is *singular* or *plural*.

guppy	planets	man	astronaut
oxen	tooth	satellite	comb
buses	drums	geese	radio
roses	paws	tents	robots
carrot	moon	bell	candies

Exercise 2

Give the plural noun for each singular noun.

1. book
2. woman
3. brush
4. bunny
5. peach
6. daisy
7. car
8. mountain
9. fox
10. television

Exercise 3

Find the nouns in each sentence. Tell if each is *singular* or *plural*.

1. Detectives looked for the diamonds.
2. Pedro skied down the hill.
3. Sissy traced her foot on a box.
4. Five balloons all popped at once.
5. A turtle was eating our cabbages!
6. Two jeeps were stuck in the swamp.
7. Children touched the smooth fossils.
8. Jenny blinked her eyelids.
9. The new pool was closed.
10. Puppies try to catch their own tails.
11. A submarine is a sandwich.
12. Cindy and Matthew will race around the track.
13. An octopus has eight arms.
14. Some Indians made marbles from clay.
15. Stay away from crocodiles!

Exercise 4

Complete each sentence with the plural of the noun in parentheses.

1. Some people can predict rain without _____. (instrument)
2. They watch nature's _____. (sign)
3. Leaves on _____ may turn upside down. (tree)
4. Curly _____ will curl tighter. (hair)
5. _____ fly lower. (Goose)
6. _____ bite more often. (Fly)
7. Morning _____ are red. (sky)
8. _____ will stampede. (Pony)
9. Some older people say their _____ ache. (joint)
10. _____ will close their blooms. (Dandelion)
11. _____ chirp more loudly. (Goldfinch)
12. Cats may clean their _____ more often. (foot)
13. _____ and calves stand close together. (Cow)
14. The sound of bells from _____ carries farther. (church)
15. Do you know other _____ to predict rain? (way)

Practice Power

Choose one of these lists of name words. Write a paragraph using the words. Make a word plural when you need to.

clown	watermelon	spaceship
acrobat	garden	star
elephant	daisy	orbit
tent	shovel	experiment

Lesson 4 Singular Possessive Nouns

The possessive form of a noun shows possession or ownership. Singular nouns can show possession.

Kevin's tuba   Sarah's watch

Kevin's tuba means the tuba belongs to Kevin. *Sarah's* watch means the watch belongs to Sarah.

To form the singular possessive, add an apostrophe (') and the letter *s* after the name of the owner.

SINGULAR (one)	POSSESSIVE FORM
child	child's tooth
Maria	Maria's backpack
pilot	pilot's uniform
father	father's tools
Joe	Joe's gerbils
lion	lion's cage

Exercise 1

Find the possessive noun in each sentence.
1. Ellen's purple toothbrush is in the sink.
2. Toni's violin is very old.
3. Russell's boat was built from popsicle sticks.
4. Carmen's book about dinosaurs has entertaining pictures in it.
5. The puppy's squeaky toy scared me when I stepped on it.
6. My brother's baseball was left in the rain.
7. A zebra's stripes are black and white.
8. Have you ever seen Jupiter's giant red spot?
9. Watch out for that cat's claws.
10. The hiker's heavy boots left giant footprints.

Exercise 2

Give the possessive form of each italicized singular noun.
Example: *Kenny* bicycle had a flat tire. *Kenny's*

1. That *robin* nest has an egg in it.
2. The *reporter* story was in the newspaper.
3. Did you see *Alex* new digital watch?
4. A *dinosaur* egg is as big as a football.
5. *Hilary* feet are bigger than mine.
6. The *bear* paw is injured.
7. *Carrie* pet frogs escaped.
8. The *carpenter* saw buzzed.
9. The *engineer* son blows the train whistle.
10. My little *sister* crayons are under the couch.

Exercise 3

Find the noun that should be in singular possessive form.
Then give the possessive form for each of these nouns.

1. The dog tail was wagging quickly.
2. Jeanette cereal is getting soggy.
3. The ballerina shoe fell off.
4. Did you read Tanya poem?
5. Color this cardinal feathers red.
6. Bob returned his uncle fishing rod.
7. Don't eat Connie chocolate chip cookie!
8. Larry puppet looks like a parrot.
9. An Eskimo canoe was made from animal skins.
10. He held Terry paper crane.

Practice Power

What are five interesting things that your friends or family
own? Write a sentence naming each object and the person
who owns it. Tell something about the object. Use the
singular possessive form of each person's name.

John's pet anteater sleeps in the kitchen.
My cousin's tree house has three rooms.

Lesson 5 Plural Possessive Nouns

The possessive form of a noun shows possession or ownership. Plural nouns can show possession.

girls' bicycles   bears' den

The *girls'* bicycles means the bicycles belong to more than one girl. The *bears'* den means the den belongs to more than one bear.

To form the plural of most nouns, add *s*. To form the plural possessive, add an apostrophe (') after the *s*.

SINGULAR	PLURAL	POSSESSIVE FORM
brother	brothers	brothers' aquarium
bird	birds	birds' nests
leopard	leopards	leopards' spots
artist	artists	artists' studio
sister	sisters	sisters' garden
baby	babies	babies' rattles

When a plural noun does not end in *s*, add an apostrophe (') and *s* to show possession.

SINGULAR	PLURAL	POSSESSIVE FORM
child	children	children's pool
goose	geese	geese's eggs
woman	women	women's teams

Exercise 1

Complete this chart with the plural form and the plural possessive form for each word.

SINGULAR	PLURAL	POSSESSIVE
1. cat	_____	the _____ toys
2. guard	_____	the _____ keys
3. fox	_____	the _____ dens
4. ox	_____	the _____ horns
5. mouse	_____	the _____ cheese
6. artist	_____	the _____ paintings
7. daisy	_____	the _____ petals
8. firefighter	_____	the _____ red truck
9. child	_____	the _____ giggles
10. tiger	_____	the _____ food

Exercise 2

Give the possessive form of each italicized plural noun.
1. The *pilgrims* first Thanksgiving meal was breakfast.
2. The *camels* grain is in a big sack.
3. Where are the *childrens* skates?
4. The *students* parents came to the play.
5. The ballet *dancers* costumes were bright orange.
6. *Womens* gloves are on sale today.
7. The *players* jerseys are in this closet.
8. The wild *geeses* cries warned of a long winter.
9. Two *birds* nests are in the old oak tree.
10. The *teachers* meeting is at 3:00 P.M.

Exercise 3

Find the noun that should be in plural possessive form in each sentence. Then give its possessive form.

1. Eagles nests can weigh almost 4000 pounds!
2. Here are the musicians instruments.
3. The campers tents have patches on them.
4. Students projects are on display.
5. Put the scouts knapsacks away.
6. Opossums tails are completely bare.
7. Some swimmers towels are in the locker room.
8. The divers goggles were filled with water.
9. Turtles eggs have tough shells.
10. The bees home is a center of much activity.

Practice Power

Write the plural and the plural possessive forms for each of these nouns. Then write a sentence using each noun in its plural possessive form.

1. mouse
2. astronaut
3. baby
4. ox
5. boy

Lesson 6 Uses of Nouns– Subject

A noun may be used as the subject word in a sentence.

Swimmers splashed.

The person, place, or thing talked about is the subject. In this sentence, the persons talked about are *swimmers*. What is said about the swimmers? They *splashed*. Therefore, *swimmers* is the subject and *splashed* is the predicate.

If you know the predicate, you can find the subject by asking *who* or *what* before the predicate, and then answering the question. *Splashed* is the predicate. Who splashed? *Swimmers* splashed. Swimmers is the subject of the sentence.

Exercise 1

Find the subject word by answering the question beside each sentence.

1. Anita sings.   Who sings?
2. Three mice squeak.   What squeak?
3. A bucket tumbled.   What tumbled?
4. Green grapes squirted. What squirted?
5. Basketballs bounce.   What bounce?
6. Keys jingled.   What jingled?
7. David studies.   Who studies?
8. Papers ripped.   What ripped?
9. Young fairies danced.   Who danced?
10. The snow melted.   What melted?

Exercise 2

Find the subject word in each sentence. Ask *who* or *what* before the predicate.

1. Stan returned my book.
2. Crows can learn to speak.
3. Sherman listens carefully.
4. The bicycle skidded.
5. A conductor called loudly.
6. The robot will mop the floor.
7. The logs burned.
8. The diamonds sparkled.
9. Two snakes moved slowly.
10. That volcano might erupt soon.
11. Wolves howl.
12. Elaine picked strawberries.
13. Mr. Scott put up a basketball hoop.
14. Lucy has the measles.
15. A giraffe has escaped!

Exercise 3

Complete each sentence with a subject word.

1. _____ will take photographs.
2. _____ plays the drums.
3. Our _____ is blue.
4. _____ swims.
5. _____ shelled the peanuts.
6. The antique _____ ticks loudly.
7. _____ surprised me.
8. _____ was broken.
9. _____ stared out the window.
10. _____ likes crossword puzzles.
11. My little _____ ate the whole coconut pie!
12. _____ jumped over the fence.
13. _____ shook his umbrella.
14. _____ grabbed the rolling pin.
15. _____ listened to the tape.

Diagraming Subjects and Predicates

Here is a diagram of a *subject* and a *predicate*.

Boats sail.

What sail? Boats do what?

Boats | sail

Exercise 4

Diagram these sentences. Use the form shown above.
1. Rabbits hop.
2. Soap bubbled.
3. Eagles circle.
4. Computers buzzed.
5. Julia skates.

Practice Power

Choose one of the following places. Write five sentences
describing what happens in this place. Underline the
subject word in each of your sentences.

Your school's gym
A busy supermarket
The monkey house at the zoo

219

Lesson 7 Uses of Nouns—
Direct Object

A noun may be used as a direct object in a sentence.

The polar bear threw *ice*.

A noun that names the receiver of the action is a direct object. The object word answers the question *whom* or *what* after the predicate. In this sentence, the predicate is *threw*. The polar bear threw what? The polar bear threw *ice*. Ice is the direct object.

Exercise 1

Find the direct object by answering the question beside each sentence.

1. Kelly ate the sardines.	Kelly ate what?
2. Joshua lost a tooth.	Joshua lost what?
3. He helped Julianna.	He helped whom?
4. Lightning struck the tree.	Lightning struck what?
5. Pete peeled an avocado.	Pete peeled what?
6. Chris painted the garage.	Chris painted what?
7. Emily dribbled the basketball.	Emily dribbled what?
8. The snowball missed Maria.	The snowball missed whom?
9. George stubbed his toe.	George stubbed what?
10. Jody made a bookmark.	Jody made what?

Exercise 2

Find the object word in each sentence. Ask *whom* or *what* after the predicate.

1. Jeremy flipped the pancakes.
2. Betsy pushed the red button.
3. My brother climbed the ladder.
4. The elephant sprayed water.
5. Randy hurdled the fence.
6. We found a dark cave.
7. I need a calendar for my wall.
8. The chimpanzee jiggled the stick.
9. Jill cracked the eggs into the bowl.
10. Stewart rolled his eyes.
11. We spotted four helicopters.
12. Anne climbed the mountain.
13. Skipper buried the bone under the porch.
14. Pioneers built their own cabins.
15. Patrick cautiously petted the pig.

Exercise 3

Complete each sentence with an object word.

1. We baked two _____.
2. Beth will wrap the new _____.
3. Rita found _____ on the map.
4. Tony threw a _____ at me!
5. My parakeet likes _____.
6. Kevin and Brian ride _____.
7. Mr. Perez pulled a _____ from the closet.
8. Marsha collects _____.
9. A dog chased the _____.
10. Gina constructed a _____ from toothpicks.
11. Astronomers watched for _____.
12. Mrs. Milliken washed the _____.
13. My friend caught a _____.
14. The two clowns wore _____.
15. Rose discovered many _____ in the sand.

Diagraming Subjects, Predicates, and Direct Objects

Here is a diagram of a *subject*, a *predicate*, and a *direct object*.

Birds build nests.

What build?	Birds do what?	Build what?
Birds	build	nests

Exercise 4

Diagram these sentences. Use the form shown above.
1. Peter shoveled snow.
2. Moles dig holes.
3. Henry fixes bicycles.
4. Kara tames burros.
5. Rita cleaned oysters.

You Are the Author

Choose one.
1. Keith Robertson has described Henry and Midge's adventures in his books *Henry Reed, Inc.; Henry Reed's Big Journey; Henry Reed's Babysitting Service; Henry Reed's Big Show;* and *Henry Reed's Think Tank.* Write a letter to the author suggesting that he write about Henry and Midge doing an activity you suggested in The Writer's Craft. Select your nouns carefully.
2. In a small group make a "photo album" that shows Henry and Midge engaging in various summertime activities. Different students can draw the pictures, write short captions, and make the cover.

Chapter Challenge

Read this paragraph carefully, and then answer the questions.

¹Yesterday Sue's father drove my friends and me to the new swimming pool in Greenwood Park. ²We thought it was going to be just another swimming pool. ³We were really surprised. ⁴This pool is very unusual. ⁵It has many special features. ⁶My favorite is the twisting slide that shoots you into the water with a splash. ⁷Becky likes the fountain that sprays everyone who swims near it. ⁸The pool has a fence that divides the deep end from the shallow end. ⁹Giant plastic geese float calmly on the surface of the water. ¹⁰The geese's backs are great places to sit and rest. ¹¹I think this pool is the most exciting place in our city!

1. Name the simple predicate in sentence 1.
2. Is the word *friends* in sentence 1 singular or plural?
3. Name the possessive noun in sentence 1.
4. Name the subject word in sentence 4.
5. What is the plural of *slide* in sentence 6?
6. Name the direct object of the verb *likes* in sentence 7.
7. Name the proper noun and the common noun in sentence 7.
8. Name another proper noun in this paragraph.
9. Name the subject word in sentence 9.
10. Name the plural possessive noun in sentence 10. What is the singular form of this noun?

Creative Space 2

The Park

I'm glad that I
    Live near a park

For in the winter
    After dark

The park lights shine
    As bright and still

As dandelions
    On a hill.

James S. Tippett

Exploring the Poem...

Many poets try to paint pictures in their readers' minds. When you read this poem, can you picture the bright, still park lights after dark? Can you picture dandelions on a green hillside?

Why do you think the speaker says the park lights shine like dandelions? What do lights and dandelions have in common?

Poets often use *rhyme*. In this poem, the words *park* and *dark* rhyme. Words that rhyme have the same ending sound. Can you find two other words that rhyme in this poem?

★ Write a poem about something you can see near your house. Your poem should also have eight lines. Try to rhyme line 2 with line 4 and line 6 with line 8.

Before you begin your poem, read these poems written by students.

I'm glad that I
    Live near a tree
For in the winter
    I can see
Snow stick on its limbs
    So bare
But in the springtime
    Leaves are there.

I'm glad that I
    Live near a bus
Although its motor
    Makes a fuss
Yet I can go
    Just anywhere
The friendly bus
    Will take me there.

Chapter 3

Pronouns

Electricity

by Robert Lawson

from *Ben and Me*

Ben never thereafter mentioned my little adventure in printing, so I tried to be somewhat more lenient about his **maxims.**

Trying though they were, however, they were nothing compared to an enthusiasm which beset him about this time. This was the study of what he called "electricity."

It all started with some glass tubes and a book of instructions sent him by a London friend. These tubes he would rub with a piece of silk or fur, thereby producing many strange and, to me, unpleasant effects. When a tube was sufficiently rubbed, small bits of paper would spring from the table and cling to it, or crackling sparks leap from it to the finger of anyone foolish enough to approach.

Ben derived great amusement from rubbing a tube and touching it to the tip of my tail. Thereupon a terrible shock would run through my body, every hair and whisker would stand on end, and a convulsive contraction of all my muscles would throw me several inches in the air.

This was bad enough, but my final rebellion did not come until he, in his enthusiasm, used the fur cap to rub the tube. And I was in the cap.

"Ben," said I, "this has gone far enough. From now on, kindly omit me from these experiments. To me they seem a perfectly senseless waste of time, but if they amuse you, all right, go ahead with them. Just leave me out."

Benjamin Franklin by Charles Wilson Peale

"I fear that you are not a person of vision, Amos," said he. "You fail to grasp the worldwide, the **epoch**-making, importance of these experiments. You do not realize the force—"

"Oh, don't I?" I replied. "My tail is still tingling."

"I shall tear the lightning from the skies," he went on, "and harness it to do the bidding of man."

"Personally," said I, "I think the sky's an excellent place for it."

Nothing I could say, though, served to dampen Ben's enthusiasm.

Soon he received an elaborate machine that could produce much greater currents than the glass tubes. It was worked by a crank which he ground at happily for hours. Our room became **cumbered** with rods, wires, tubes, copper plates, and glass jars filled with evil-smelling liquids. It was so difficult to move about without touching something likely to produce one of those hair-stiffening shocks.

Ben even went so far as to organize a group of similarly obsessed people, calling it "the Philosophical Society." They gathered once a week, armed with their glass tubes, bits of silk and wires. They spent whole evenings fiddling with these things or listening to long speeches about the wonders of "electricity," mostly by Ben. I napped.

After he had played with the new apparatus for a few weeks and had it working well, Ben decided to give an exhibition of his achievements in this field.

A large hall having been secured for the occasion by the Philosophical Society, Ben spent several busy days arranging and testing his apparatus, planning various experiments, writing a speech and inviting prominent people.

Frankly, I was bored by the whole affair, but since Ben seemed rather hurt by my attitude I tried to take a little interest. I read his speech and the descriptions of all the various experiments. By noon I understood everything quite thoroughly.

While we ate a light lunch of bread and cheese, I told Ben of my studies. He was delighted and quite touched by my interest.

In the afternoon he went to have his hair curled, leaving me in the hall, where I went on with my research. Determined that no errors should mar this performance, since it meant so much to Ben, I carefully went over each wire and piece of apparatus, comparing them with his diagrams and descriptions.

I discovered that he had apparently made several grave mistakes, for not a few of the wires were connected in a manner that seemed to me obviously incorrect. There were so many of these errors to rectify that I was kept quite busy all afternoon. My corrected arrangements seemed to leave several loose wires and copper plates with no place to go, so I just left them in one of the chairs on the stage. I was barely able to finish before Ben arrived from the hairdresser's.

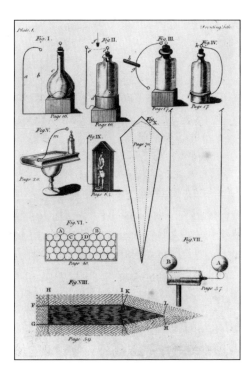

Machine for Producing Electricity,
engraver unknown

As we hurried home for supper, he was so filled with pride and excitement that I had no opportunity to tell him how narrowly he had escaped ruining the exhibition by his carelessness.

When we arrived back at the hall in the evening, the brilliantly lit auditorium was crowded. Seated in chairs on the stage were the Governor and his Lady; the Mayor; several of the clergy; and the Chief of the Volunteer Fire Brigade holding his silver trumpet.

Ben made his speech and performed several simple experiments with the glass tubes. They were watched with great interest by the audience and generously applauded.

He then stepped to the new apparatus and signaled to a young **apprentice** from the print shop who was stationed at the crank. The lad turned with a will, and a loud humming sound came from the whirling wheel while blue sparks crackled about it.

"And now, my friends," said Ben proudly, "when I turn this knob you shall see, if my calculations are correct, a manifestation of electrical force never before witnessed on this continent."

They did.

As Ben turned the knob, the Governor rose straight in the air in much the same manner that I used to when Ben applied the spark to my tail. His hair stood out just as my fur did. His second leap was higher and his hair even straighter. There was a noticeable odor of burning cloth.

On his third rising the copper plate flew from the chair, landing, unfortunately, in his Lady's lap. Her shriek, while slightly muffled by her wig, was, nevertheless, noteworthy.

The Fire Chief, gallantly advancing to their aid, **inadvertently** touched one of the wires with his silver trumpet. This at once became enveloped in a most unusual blue flame and gave off a strange clanging sound.

Ben leaped toward them, but I clamped on his ear. I had felt those shocks before.

"The boy—" I hissed. "Stop the machine!"

He sprang at the apprentice, who was still grinding

merrily. The lad, not an admirer of the Governor, ceased his efforts with some reluctance.

The Governor was stiff and white in his chair, his Lady moaned faintly under her wig, the Fire Chief stared dazedly at his tarnished trumpet, and the audience was in an uproar.

Roadside advertisement of Franklin's experiments, engraving

"Never mind, Ben," I consoled him as we walked home, "I feel certain that we'll succeed next time."

"Succeed!" shouted Ben. "SUCCEED! Why, Amos, don't you realize that I have just made the most successful, the most momentous, experiment of the century? I have discovered the effects produced by applying strong electric shocks to human beings."

"Granted the Governor is one," I said, "we surely did."

The Writer's Craft

1. *Ben and Me* is an example of historical fiction. Robert Lawson tells about the life and experiments of Benjamin Franklin through the eyes of a fictional character, Amos, a mouse. What events in this story do you think really happened?

2. Why do you think Lawson used the character Amos to tell the story?

3. In the first paragraph, the author used the pronouns *I* and *my* for Amos and *his* for Ben. Why do you think he chose to use *I* for Amos instead of *he?*

4. In the third paragraph, the author used the pronouns *him* and *he* for Ben, *me* for Amos, and *it* for tube. Why do you think he chose to replace these nouns with pronouns?

EXPERIMENTS
AND
OBSERVATIONS
ON
ELECTRICITY,
MADE AT
Philadelphia in *America,*
BY
Mr. BENJAMIN FRANKLIN,
AND
Communicated in several Letters to Mr. P. COLLINSON
of *London,* F. R. S.

L O N D O N :
Printed and sold by E. CAVE, at *St. John's Gate.* 1751.
(Price 2s. 6d.)

Book title page, 1751

Recalling What You Know

1. Pronouns may be subjects or direct objects of sentences. In *I connected it to the apparatus,* which pronoun is the subject? Which is the direct object?
2. Possessive pronouns show ownership. Choose possessive pronouns to complete this sentence: *Aleta's book is heavier than _____ or _____.*

Lesson 1   Identifying Personal Pronouns

A personal pronoun is a word used in place of a noun.

Ben and Amos liked to relax and fly a kite on spring days. One day, Ben and Amos had a surprising experience with their kite. While Amos was riding near the top of the kite, a storm came. Amos was surprised because the lightning came so close, but Ben did not pull Amos out of the storm. Amos realized that Ben was experimenting again!

The nouns *Ben, Amos,* and *kite* are repeated many times in this paragraph. Other words can be used in place of nouns. These words are called *pronouns.* In the paragraph below, pronouns replace some of the nouns.

Ben and Amos liked to relax and fly a kite on spring days. One day, *they* had a shocking experience with their kite. While Amos was riding near the top of *it,* a storm came. *He* was surprised because the lightning seemed so close, but Ben did not pull *him* out of the storm. *He* realized that Ben was experimenting again!

233

Which paragraph sounds better? The first paragraph does not sound natural because the nouns *Ben, Amos,* and *kite* are repeated too often. In the second paragraph, what words take the place of *Ben* and *Amos?* What word takes the place of *kite?*

Study this list of pronouns.

I	we	he	she	you	it	they
me	us	him	her			them

Notice how pronouns replace nouns in these sets of sentences:

Rosa jumped over *a puddle*.
Rosa jumped over *it*.

Luis invited *the team*.
Luis invited *them*.

Margie won a stuffed panda bear.
She won a stuffed panda bear.

Exercise 1

Find the personal pronoun(s) in each sentence.
1. He put bricks under the stove.
2. Glasses helped him to read much better.
3. They enjoyed *Poor Richard's Almanack*.
4. He printed it in Philadelphia.
5. I saw Franklin's generator at the museum.
6. We marvel at Franklin's inventions.
7. Did he sign the Declaration of Independence?
8. It has great meaning for us.
9. She gave me other books by Robert Lawson.
10. He illustrated them too.

Exercise 2

Complete each sentence with a personal pronoun.
1. Where did you meet _____?
2. _____ roared loudly.
3. Which color do _____ want, Simon?
4. _____ slid down the hill together.
5. Give _____ three guesses.
6. Borrow a pencil from _____.
7. The box you want has a red stripe on _____.
8. Debby's sister took _____ to the zoo.
9. That jacket looks nice on _____.
10. _____ called down the street after Geof.

Practice Power

Imagine that you and your friends are playing your
favorite game or sport. Write five sentences that describe
what happens as you play. Use as many pronouns as you
can in your sentences. Before you begin, look at these
sentences:

Larry and *I* are playing our favorite game.
I throw *him* the Frisbee.
He tosses *it* back to *me*.

Lesson 2 Three Kinds of Personal Pronouns

A personal pronoun names the *speaker*, the person *spoken to*, or the person or thing *spoken about*.

The Speaker

> The personal pronouns that name the speaker are *I, me, we,* and *us.*

When you speak about yourself, use the pronoun *I* or *me.*

> *I* found a four-leaf clover.
> Clara gave *me* a blue daisy.

When you speak about yourself as part of a group, use *we* or *us.*

> *We* put marshmallows between the crackers.
> A squirrel followed *us* down the path.

Exercise 1

Find the pronoun that names the *speaker* in each sentence.
1. I will wax the new truck.
2. The lambs followed us.
3. Two crows flew toward us.
4. The mountain climber helped me.
5. We played the guitars.
6. I will bake the eggplants.
7. We held the old quilt carefully.
8. That alligator winked at me!
9. I should give the old diary to the library.
10. We expect Carlos soon.

Complete each sentence with a pronoun that names the speaker.
11. _____ saw a chameleon change colors.
12. The elevator took _____ 100 stories high.
13. _____ won first prize at the book fair.
14. _____ like to run backward.
15. Marty invited _____ to a pig roast.

The Person Spoken To

> **The personal pronoun that names the person or persons spoken to is *you*.**

When you speak to a person without using his or her name, use the pronoun *you*. When you speak to more than one person, use the same pronoun, *you*.

> Can *you* do a cartwheel, Tony?
> Class, *you* shouldn't wear shoes on the trampoline.

Exercise 2

Find the pronoun that names the person or persons *spoken to* in each sentence.

1. Why didn't you win the pie-eating contest?
2. These spiders are for you!
3. Can you name the tenth president?
4. You draw the giant panda.
5. Team, do you need help?
6. I'll hold a place in line for you.
7. Are you the owner of this sports car?
8. When did you go to the science museum?
9. Margo will tell you about the tornado.
10. Where did you put my telescope?

The Person or Thing Spoken About

> The personal pronouns that name the person or thing spoken about are *he, him, she, her, it, they,* and *them*.

When you speak about another person without using his or her name, use the pronoun *he, she, him,* or *her*. When you speak about a thing, use the pronoun *it*.

He sneezed three times.
The puppy licked *him*.
She jumped off the swing.
The noise gave *her* the shivers.
It is the capital of the state.
Andy fixed *it* with his tools.

When you speak about more than one person or thing, use *they* or *them*.

They went to the grocery store.
Ronny hasn't seen *them*.

Exercise 3

Find the pronoun that names the person or thing *spoken about* in each sentence.

1. He couldn't catch any bullfrogs.
2. Sixty snowballs rolled toward it!
3. They barely escaped the blizzard.
4. Give the colored pencils to them.
5. She is playing croquet.
6. The lizards crawled away from him.
7. Mother asked him to sweep the stairs.
8. The teacher sent for her.
9. They will listen to the whale's song.
10. She watches for dark clouds.

Complete each sentence with a pronoun that names the person or thing spoken about.

11. The captain asked _____ to sail the ship.
12. _____ crumbled the cookies in his hand.
13. Give _____ away.
14. _____ captured the aardvark in a sack.
15. Sheila's Seeing-Eye dog helps _____ cross the street.

Exercise 4

Find the personal pronoun in each sentence. Tell whether it names the *speaker*, the *person spoken to*, or the *person or thing spoken about*.

1. Trace it on a piece of paper.
2. Do you and Cassie eat a banana every day?
3. Last year we discovered a cave.
4. They built a dinosaur in the sand.
5. That lemon made me pucker my lips.
6. Take them from under the chickens.
7. It was the best trip of all!
8. She entered the blue frog in the contest.
9. Don't disturb us.
10. You can't catch a mouse by the tail.

Practice Power

Write six sentences of your own, using these personal pronouns. Underline each pronoun. Tell if it names the *speaker*, the *person spoken to*, or the *person or thing spoken about*.

we	she	them
you	me	him

Lesson 3 Singular and Plural Pronouns

A singular pronoun names one person or thing. A plural pronoun names more than one person or thing.

Like nouns, pronouns are *singular* or *plural*. Look at each set of sentences below and notice how the pronouns are used.

> *Tracy* likes to ride escalators. (*Singular noun—one*)
> *She* likes to ride escalators. (*Singular pronoun—one*)

> *Tracy and Roxanne* like to ride escalators.
>   (*Two nouns—more than one*)
> *They* like to ride escalators.
>   (*Plural pronoun—more than one*)

> The *jungle* is very dark. (*Singular noun—one*)
> *It* is very dark. (*Singular pronoun—one*)

> *Plants* grow very large. (*Plural noun—more than one*)
> *They* grow very large. (*Plural pronoun—more than one*)

Singular pronouns take the place of singular nouns. *Plural pronouns* take the place of plural nouns. Study the lists of singular and plural pronouns below. Notice that the pronoun *you* can be singular or plural.

SINGULAR	PLURAL
I, me	we, us
you	you
he, him	they, them
she, her	
it	

Exercise 1

Find the pronoun in each sentence. Tell whether it is *singular* or *plural*.

1. She can write funny stories.
2. It is an old Spanish coin.
3. That flashlight is for him.
4. We will find the missing stamps.
5. Can you walk with snowshoes on your feet?
6. They baked the biscuits too long.
7. He will climb into the boat.
8. Uncle Gene gave him the harmonica.
9. Didn't it ever hatch?
10. The kangaroo leaped over them.

Exercise 2

Use a pronoun in place of the italicized word or words. Tell whether the pronoun is *singular* or *plural*.

1. *Judy and Steve* watched for the comet.
2. The elephant turned toward *Anita*.
3. *Walter* flipped a coin.
4. The *eagles* wait to catch salmon.
5. *Bobbie and Barbie* are twin sisters.
6. The waves splashed around *Margie*.
7. This saddle doesn't fit *Ringo*.
8. The *mongoose* grabbed the cobra.
9. *Elizabeth* moved away from the camp fire.
10. One wolf follows the *rabbits*.

Complete each sentence with a pronoun. Tell whether it is *singular* or *plural*. The pronoun is used in place of the italicized noun.

11. The *plane* is going to Seattle. ____ will take off soon.
12. *Hal* likes volleyball. ____ plays almost every day.
13. The *amusement park* is closed. ____ will reopen next week.
14. Roberta bought *hamsters*. She put ____ in a cage.
15. *Winston and Clyde* won the race. ____ received a bronze trophy.

Practice Power

Imagine that you are at the park with your class. Write five sentences that describe what happens as you play. Use pronouns in your sentences. Underline each pronoun and tell whether it is singular or plural. Before you begin, look at these sentences:

Jen and Jim like to run in the park.
They race around the track as soon as they arrive.

Lesson 4 Uses of Pronouns—Subject and Direct Object

Subject

A pronoun may be used as the subject in a sentence.

The person, place, or thing talked about is the subject. To find the subject of a sentence, ask the question *who* or *what* before the predicate.

She plays the flute.

Who plays? The answer is *she*. *She* is the subject of the sentence.

Pronouns that can be subjects are

	SINGULAR	PLURAL
SPEAKER	I	we
PERSON SPOKEN TO	you	you
PERSON SPOKEN ABOUT	hc, she, it	they

Study these sentences.

SENTENCE	QUESTION	SUBJECT
I write haiku.	Who writes?	I
He practices every day.	Who practices?	He
We visited Quebec.	Who visited?	We
They belong there.	Who belong?	They
It is large.	What is large?	It

Exercise 1

Find the subject pronoun in each sentence. Ask the question *who* or *what* before the predicate.

1. He photographed the whole class.
2. They like raspberry ice cream.
3. We will tour the submarine.
4. Sing softly.
5. It is a very noisy pet!
6. Does he make model rockets?
7. You saw the falling star.
8. It snores loudly.
9. She watched the computer screen.
10. What hobbies do you have?

Exercise 2

Complete each sentence with a subject pronoun. Use different pronouns.

1. _____ saved their own money to buy a pony.
2. _____ will write his own report about weasels.
3. _____ took us on the roller coaster.
4. _____ tried to climb the pine tree.
5. _____ gave her map to the detective.
6. _____ looked through their telescopes.
7. _____ should plant spinach in the spring.
8. _____ am watching the pelicans.
9. _____ want to make their own paper airplanes.
10. _____ makes up her own jokes.

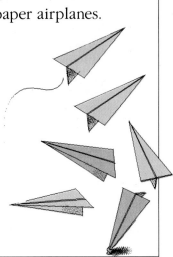

Diagraming Subject Pronouns

A subject pronoun is diagramed in the same way a subject noun is diagramed.

They like pancakes.

Who likes?	They do what?	Like what?

They	like	pancakes

Exercise 3

Diagram these sentences.
1. She telephoned Mary.
2. We roasted marshmallows.
3. He repairs radios.
4. They raked leaves.
5. I planted flowers.

Direct Object

A pronoun may be used as the direct object in a sentence.

The word that answers the question *whom* or *what* after the predicate is the direct object.

Jean invited *them*.

Jean invited whom? The answer is *them*. *Them* is the direct object of the verb.

Pronouns that can be direct objects are

	SINGULAR	PLURAL
SPEAKER	me	us
PERSON SPOKEN TO	you	you
PERSON SPOKEN ABOUT	him, her, it	them

Study these sentences.

SENTENCE	QUESTION	DIRECT OBJECT
James built it.	Built what?	it
The doctor saw her.	Saw whom?	her
Monkeys eat them.	Eat what?	them
Sam chose him.	Chose whom?	him

Exercise 4

Find the direct object pronoun in each sentence. Ask the question *whom* or *what* after the predicate.

1. Ramon repaired it today.
2. The storm damaged them.
3. The sun will dry it quickly.
4. Gerri took him to the launching pad.
5. Janet helped me with the sundial.
6. Why did the coach call you?
7. That loud noise scared her.
8. Four boys collected them.
9. The pitcher caught it.
10. I saw her in the hardware store.

Exercise 5

Complete each sentence with a direct object pronoun. Use different pronouns.

1. Mary's lamb followed _____ to school.
2. Rich will cook _____ tomorrow.
3. The net trapped _____.
4. Sally sliced _____.
5. I saw _____ carrying the pies.
6. That alarm surprised _____.
7. The choir sang _____.
8. Carmine will invite _____.
9. The carpenter helped _____.
10. The cows were chasing _____.

248

Diagraming Direct Object Pronouns

A direct object pronoun is diagramed in the same way a noun used as the direct object is diagramed.

Scott collects them.

Who collects?	Scott does what?	Collects what?
Scott	collects	them

Exercise 6

Diagram these sentences.
1. Jody invited us.
2. Sam carved it.
3. Sheila called her.
4. Hector caught it.
5. I believe you.

Practice Power

You and a friend have found a cave to explore. Write five sentences about your discoveries in this cave. Use at least three subject pronouns and two direct object pronouns. Before you begin, look at these sentences:

Jeff and *I* discovered many bones in the cave.
We knew *they* were from prehistoric animals.

Lesson 5 Correct Use of Personal Pronouns

I and *Me*

> **Use the word *I* to talk about yourself. *I* is used as the subject in a sentence.**

I rode a camel at the zoo.

I is a subject pronoun and names the person who is speaking. It answers the question *who* before the predicate *rode*.

> **Use the word *me* to talk about yourself. *Me* is used as the direct object in a sentence.**

The ride thrilled *me*.

Me is a direct object pronoun. It answers the question *whom* after the predicate *thrilled*.

Exercise 1

Complete each sentence with the personal pronoun *I* or *me*.

1. ___ play the clarinet.
2. Mr. Henderson taught ___ last year.
3. That spotted puppy followed ___.
4. ___ will build a ship in a bottle.
5. ___ took French lessons.
6. The rain soaked ___.
7. ___ flew to Florida.
8. Elaine and David visited ___.
9. ___ cooked hamburgers on the grill.
10. Tomorrow ___ will join the science club.

Exercise 2

These sentences do not have to begin with the word *I*.
Rewrite them and place the italicized words first.

1. I deliver newspapers *every Sunday*.
2. I like to pick blueberries *in the summertime*.
3. I walked onto the diving board *slowly*.
4. I tied my shoelaces *quickly*.
5. I reached into the box *carefully*.
6. I saw the lightning *when I opened the curtains*.
7. I made the pancakes *this morning*.
8. I will be nine years old *in October*.
9. I watched the snow fall *all day*.
10. I held onto the reins *tightly*.

We and Us

Use the word *we* to talk about yourself and at least one other person. *We* is used as the subject in a sentence.

We visited the planetarium with our teacher.

We is a subject pronoun and names the persons who are speaking. It answers the question *who* before the predicate *visited*.

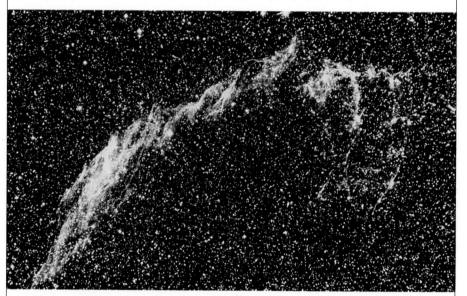

Section of the Milky Way

Use the word *us* to talk about yourself and at least one other person. *Us* is used as the direct object in a sentence.

The guard helped *us*.

Us is a direct object pronoun. It answers the question *whom* after the predicate *helped*.

Exercise 3

Complete each sentence with the personal pronoun *we* or
us.

1. You'll never catch ___.
2. Natasha called ___ for dinner.
3. ___ hiked until noon.
4. Did you see ___ on the Ferris wheel?
5. ___ raced toward the river.
6. No one helped ___ paddle the canoe.
7. ___ will rake leaves into a pile.
8. On Saturday, ___ have to get haircuts.
9. Our band teacher helped ___.
10. Each day ___ threw peanuts to the pigeons.

Practice Power

Write four sentences. In each, tell something you did with
your friends or family over the weekend. Use these
pronouns: I, me, we, us.

Lesson 6 Possessive Pronouns

A pronoun used to show ownership or possession is a possessive pronoun.

The possessive pronouns are

	SINGULAR	PLURAL
SPEAKER	mine	ours
PERSON SPOKEN TO	yours	yours
PERSON SPOKEN ABOUT	his, hers, its	theirs

A possessive pronoun also takes the place of a noun in a sentence. Look at these sentences. Notice how the possessive pronoun in column B takes the place of the italicized words in column A.

<u>A</u>	<u>B</u>
This is *my bat*.	This is *mine*.
Our lizard slid away.	*Ours* slid away.
Your dinner is ready.	*Yours* is ready.
His tooth is lost.	*His* is lost.
I have *her book*.	I have *hers*.
Don't eat *their apples*.	Don't eat *theirs*.

254

Exercise 1

Find the possessive pronoun in each sentence.

1. Ours is purple and orange.
2. That pet alligator is his.
3. They keep theirs in the refrigerator.
4. Yours must be the green one.
5. Theirs has two collars on it.
6. Ours arrived yesterday.
7. I have hers in a paper bag.
8. His was washed today.
9. I like mine better than that one.
10. Hers has spots on it.

Exercise 2

Complete each sentence with the correct possessive pronoun. The words in parentheses tell you which one to use.

1. Rory carries his books in a schoolbag. I carry _____ in my arms. (speaker, singular)
2. The prince left his pony in the field. The princess put _____ in the barn. (spoken about, singular)
3. Mrs. Needham plants squash in her garden. We plant okra in _____. (speaker, plural)
4. I'll wash my dog today. You can wash _____ tomorrow. (spoken to, singular)
5. Our geraniums are red. Ted and Carla think _____ will be pink. (spoken about, plural)
6. A robin builds its nest in a tree. A bluebird will build _____ in a box. (spoken about, singular)
7. I brought my sneakers inside. My brother left _____ in the rain. (spoken about, singular)
8. You work your math problem on paper. I'll work _____ on the board. (speaker, singular)
9. Sal's drawing is finished. Michelle needs to work on _____. (spoken about, singular)
10. These are my rings. What did Sara and Kim do with _____? (spoken about, plural)

You Are the Author

1. Imagine yourself as a newspaper reporter present at Benjamin Franklin's first demonstration of electrical force. Write a headline and a short article describing the event. Choose your pronouns carefully.
2. Using the letters of the name *Franklin,* write eight sentences about Benjamin Franklin. Begin the first sentence with *F,* the second with *R,* and so forth. You may want to mention his character traits, inventions, or famous deeds. Illustrate one of your sentences.

Chapter Challenge

Read this paragraph carefully, and then answer the questions.

¹We hurried off the school bus. ²For a day, the zoo was ours. ³As we walked through the tall gates, lions' roars greeted us. ⁴We faced wild animals that some of us had met only in books! ⁵Bears growled and clawed at their cages. ⁶Ostriches strutted beside a pond. ⁷Monkeys amused us with their tricks. ⁸We were disappointed when our teacher called us to leave. ⁹Don't you think that field trips always end too soon?

1. In sentence 1, what is the subject of the predicate *hurried*?
2. Is this subject pronoun singular or plural?
3. In sentence 2, name a possessive pronoun.
4. In sentence 3, name the direct object of the predicate *greeted*.
5. Is this direct object pronoun the speaker, the one spoken to, or the one spoken about?
6. In sentence 4, what is the subject?
7. In sentence 4, name all the personal pronouns.
8. In sentence 8, name the direct object pronoun.
9. Is this direct object pronoun singular or plural?
10. In sentence 9, name the subject pronoun.

E Is the Escalator

E is the Escalator
    That gives an elegant ride.
You step on the stair
With an easy air
    And up and up you glide.
It's nicer than scaling ladders
    Or scrambling 'round a hill,
For you climb and climb
But all the time
    You're really standing still.

Phyllis McGinley

Exploring the Poem...

When you read this poem aloud, you will hear words that rhyme. Which line rhymes with "That gives an elegant ride"? Which line rhymes with "You step on the stair"?

What are you doing when you are "scaling ladders"? How can you climb and climb and stand still at the same time?

★ Pick a letter of the alphabet. You might even want to use the first letter of your name. Think of something that begins with that letter and describe it in a poem that has five lines. Try to rhyme line 2 with line 5 and line 3 with line 4.

Before you begin your poem, read these poems written by students.

F is the little Fish
    In her bowl she swims all day.
She seems to know
There are places to go
    If she can find a way.

M is the shopping Mall
    A place where people meet.
They shop and shop
And when they stop
    They go somewhere to eat.

Chapter 4

Adjectives

Honoring America's Birth

by James Cross Giblin

from *Fireworks, Picnics, and Flags: The Story of the Fourth of July Symbols*

The Spirit of '76

On the Fourth of July, **patriotic** paintings and drawings are often published on the front pages of newspapers. The painting that probably appears more frequently than any other is called *The Spirit of '76.*

There are three main figures in the painting, all of them playing musical instruments. A white-haired old man beats a drum, a middle-aged man with a bandaged head plays a **fife,** and a young drummer boy looks admiringly at the old drummer. Behind them marches a company of Revolutionary soldiers. One of the soldiers is carrying the first American flag.

Archibald Willard, the man who painted *The Spirit of '76,* lived in the small town of Wellington, Ohio, and worked in a carriage factory. In his spare time he painted landscapes and humorous pictures. On July 4, 1871, he got the idea for the painting that was to bring him fame.

Early that morning, Willard saw three boys—two drummers and a fife player—getting ready to march in the Wellington holiday parade. One drummer was juggling his sticks, and all three were good-humoredly bumping into one another. Willard made a quick pencil sketch of the boys and meant to do a painting of them later.

A friend who saw the sketch gave Willard a different idea. Instead of a comic scene, the friend suggested that

The Spirit of '76 by Archibald Willard

Willard paint a serious picture with a patriotic theme. The artist was intrigued. It would be unlike anything he had ever done.

As he planned the painting, Willard remembered stories told him by his grandfather, who had fought in the Revolutionary War. They helped him decide what figures to include. Willard's own father posed as the old drummer, and a Civil War **comrade** of Willard's posed as the fife player. Thirteen-year-old Henry Devereaux was the model for the drummer boy.

The large painting, eight-by-ten feet, was completed early in 1876. That year marked the **centennial** of the Declaration of Independence. Willard heard there would be an exhibit of paintings at the grand Centennial **Exhibition** in Philadelphia. He decided to submit *The Spirit of '76*.

The Centennial Commission had said that only classical paintings from the major art centers of Europe and America would be **eligible** for the exhibit. But when the Commission members saw Willard's painting, they were so moved that they accepted it at once. *The Spirit of '76* quickly became one of the most popular pictures in the entire exhibit. It attracted such large crowds that special guards were assigned to protect it.

After the Centennial Exhibition closed, General Devereaux, the father of the model for the drummer boy, bought the painting from Archibald Willard. It finally came to rest in Marblehead, Massachusetts, General Devereaux's birthplace. There it can be seen today.

Over the past one hundred years, *The Spirit of '76* has been reproduced on china plates, towels, and napkins, as well as on posters and greeting cards. It has come to symbolize the courage of Revolutionary War soldiers, who were willing to fight for America's right to govern itself. And it reminds people everywhere of why we celebrate Independence Day.

The Centennial Exhibition of 1876

Philadelphia's Centennial celebration in 1876 lasted six months. That was how long the Centennial International Exhibition, the first such exhibition in the United States, was open to the public. All the states and thirty-nine foreign countries had displays at the exhibition, which covered 236 acres in Philadelphia's Fairmount Park.

President Ulysses S. Grant opened the exhibition on May 10, 1876, by pulling a lever that started a fifteen-hundred-horsepower Corliss steam engine. This huge engine provided power for all the displays in Machinery Hall, the main building at the fair. It quickly became one of the most popular items in the entire exhibition. Another machine that always drew a crowd was Alexander Graham Bell's new invention, the telephone.

Other buildings at the exhibition focused on agriculture, education, architecture, and the achievements of American women. European countries lent famous art works. There were also arts and crafts on display from Latin America, Africa, and the Far East. One of the most popular paintings at the exhibition was Archibald Willard's *The Spirit of '76*.

View of the grounds and buildings, 1876 Centennial International Exhibition, Fairmount Park, Philadelphia, engraver unknown

France had intended to give the Statue of Liberty to the United States as a centennial present. Construction was delayed because all the money for the statue had not been raised. However, Liberty's right arm holding the torch was completed in time for the Centennial Exhibition. Visitors excitedly climbed up a flight of stairs inside the giant arm and had their pictures taken on the balcony surrounding the torch.

By the time the Centennial Exhibition closed on November 10, 1876, it had been seen by almost ten million people. That was one-fifth of the total population of the United States at the time.

Torch of the Statue of Liberty on display at the 1876 Centennial International Exhibition, archival photograph

The Bicentennial of 1976

One hundred years later, more than twenty-five million Americans helped to get the country ready for its **bicentennial**.

The nation's celebrations officially began atop Mars Hill in northeastern Maine. There the rising sun first struck U.S. soil at 4:31 A.M. While more than five hundred tourists and local farmers cheered, National Guardsmen fired a fifty-gun salute and raised the American flag.

In Philadelphia, 25,000 people crowded into the square behind Independence Hall where the Declaration of Independence was first read publicly in 1776.

The main event in New York was a parade up the Hudson River of 212 sailing ships from thirty-four nations. The parade began at 11:00 A.M. and lasted until late in the afternoon. Millions of people lined both sides of the river. Thousands more watched from the windows of high-rise apartment and office buildings as the tall-masted ships sailed upstream. Among the highlights were the schooner *Sir Winston Churchill* with its all-female crew, an exact replica of a Viking ship with a striped sail, and a full-scale model of Christopher Columbus's flagship, the *Santa Maria*.

President Ford reviewed the parade from the aircraft carrier *U.S.S. Forrestal*. At 2:00 P.M. he rang the ship's bells thirteen times to honor the thirteen original colonies.

At the same moment, the Liberty Bell in Philadelphia was tapped with a rubber mallet. The Ceremonial Bell in the steeple of Independence Hall rang out loud and clear. And hundreds of other bells all across the country pealed in a joyful national chorus.

More than 400,000 people crowded onto the **esplanade** along the Charles River in Boston to hear the Boston Pops give an outdoor concert. The highlight of the concert was Tchaikovsky's *1812 Overture,* during which **howitzers** boomed, church bells rang, and fireworks lit up the scene.

In New York City, fireworks were fired from barges in the harbor and fell in showers of light around the Statue of Liberty. At the end of the spectacle a helicopter flew over the statue, towing behind it a flag made of red, white, and blue lights. Loudspeakers played "The Star-Spangled Banner," and the crowds along the shore burst into song.

Three thousand miles away in San Francisco, fireworks shot up above Candlestick Park and Alcatraz Island.

The biggest fireworks display of all was staged in Washington, D.C. More than thirty-three tons of fireworks rose into the sky above the Mall near the Washington Monument and exploded in light patterns of all sizes, shapes, and colors. At the close, a battery of laser guns spelled out on the clouds, "1776–1976, Happy Birthday, U.S.A."

Each new July Fourth gives us a chance to show our love for our country. It also offers us an opportunity to examine ourselves as Americans. We can look back at the road we have traveled and decide what direction we want to take in the future.

The Writer's Craft

1. What are some of our country's historic sites and monuments? Which would you most like to visit? Explain your choice.
2. If you could attend either celebration—the American centennial or bicentennial—which would you choose? Explain your answer.
3. In the first sentence, author James Cross Giblin uses the adjective *patriotic* to describe paintings and drawings that appear in newspapers on the Fourth of July. In what ways do you think that *The Spirit of '76* is a patriotic painting?
4. The author uses the adjectives *huge* and *giant* to describe the steam engine and the arm of the Statue of Liberty. Do you think these exhibits were popular because of their size? Why or why not?

Recalling What You Know

1. Articles are adjectives that tell you a noun will follow. Identify the article in *The fireworks were exciting.*
2. In the sentence *The white-haired man was older than the drummer boy,* does the adjective *older* compare persons, places, or things?

Lesson 1 Descriptive Adjectives

An adjective is a word that describes or limits a noun or a pronoun.

Have you ever seen fireworks on the Fourth of July? If you were going to write a paragraph about them, you would try to paint a clear picture with words. You might use these words to describe the fireworks: *beautiful, loud, colorful.*

Notice how the words in italics help you create lively pictures in your mind.

> Across our country on the Fourth of July, many *spectacular* displays of fireworks brighten the *dark* sky. Experts create *colorful* patterns of shooting stars, the flag, and even the Liberty Bell to celebrate the birth of our nation. Sometimes the fireworks cause *loud* bangs, which are not to everyone's liking. More often, however, hearts fill with pride when *beautiful red, white,* and *blue* sparkles soar into the sky.

Here are adjectives from this paragraph and the nouns they describe.

spectacular displays	*dark* sky	*colorful* patterns
loud bangs	*beautiful, red, white, blue* sparkles	

> **A descriptive adjective describes a noun or a pronoun.**

A descriptive adjective usually tells *what kind*. Look at these three lists of adjectives that can be used to describe the nouns *peanut butter*, *balloons*, and *squirrel*.

sticky	bright	alert
tasty	colorful	brown
healthy *peanut*	delicate *balloons*	curious *squirrel*
smooth *butter*	light	speedy
nutty	big	clever

Look at these sentences. The descriptive adjectives answer the question *what kind* about each of the nouns.

		NOUN	ADJECTIVE
The *juicy* melon burst.	What kind of	melon?	juicy
We walked into the *dark* cave.	What kind of	cave?	dark
The *noisy birds* woke me up.	What kind of	birds?	noisy
This is an *interesting* story.	What kind of	story?	interesting
Don't step on that *tiny* bug!	What kind of	bug?	tiny

Exercise 1

Find the descriptive adjective in each sentence. Name the noun it describes.

1. On July 4, 1776, a new nation was born.
2. The American colonies declared independence from Great Britain.
3. They did so by creating a historic document, the Declaration of Independence.
4. Its main author, Thomas Jefferson, later became president of the United States.
5. Is John Hancock known for his bold signature?
6. The Declaration states that everyone has basic rights—life, liberty, and the pursuit of happiness.
7. Washington read the important paper to his troops.
8. View the original Declaration of Independence at the National Archives in Washington, D.C.
9. It is kept in a special case filled with helium.
10. Americans are proud of this priceless treasure!

Exercise 2

Add a descriptive adjective before each noun. Then use the adjectives and nouns in sentences of your own.

1. _____ grass
2. _____ house
3. _____ spaghetti
4. _____ bicycles
5. _____ vegetables

Add two descriptive adjectives before each noun. Then use the adjectives and nouns in sentences of your own.

6. _____ hair
7. _____ friend
8. _____ mountain
9. _____ sweater
10. _____ breakfast

Exercise 3

Add a noun that could follow each pair of descriptive adjectives.

1. big, friendly
2. large, noisy
3. energetic, green
4. sharp, pointy
5. delicate, graceful
6. dark, gloomy
7. bright, colorful
8. soft, gentle
9. crisp, crunchy
10. creaking, haunted

Exercise 4

Find the adjective in each sentence. Tell whether it refers to the sense of *touch*, *taste*, *sight*, *smell*, or *sound*.

1. An orange leaf landed on my head.
2. Hissing steam escaped from the kettle.
3. I often chew grape bubblegum.
4. The hot sand burned our feet.
5. I like sour pickles on hamburgers.
6. Jason grabbed the smooth snake.
7. Shari rubbed her hand over the rough paper.
8. Mr. Chapman makes delicious cheesecakes.
9. A thumping noise is coming from the washer!
10. That sweet perfume smells like roses.

Diagraming with Descriptive Adjectives

Here is how a descriptive adjective is placed in a diagram.

Hungry lions ate lunch.

Who ate? Lions did what? Lions ate what?

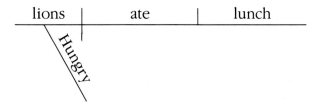

The word *hungry* describes lions. It tells *what kind* of lions ate lunch. It is placed on a slanted line under the word it describes. *Hungry* modifies the noun *lions* and is a *descriptive adjective*.

Exercise 5

Diagram each of these sentences.
1. Sturdy Eskimos train dogs.
2. Zookeepers feed hungry animals.
3. Jerri picked wild strawberries.
4. Trained archaeologists study fossils.
5. Andrea received loud applause.

Proper Adjectives

Some descriptive adjectives come from proper nouns. These adjectives are called proper adjectives.

You have learned that a proper noun names a particular person, place, or thing, and that it begins with a capital letter. Sometimes an adjective can be formed from a proper noun. When it is, it is called a *proper adjective*. A proper adjective describes a noun. It always begins with a capital letter.

PROPER NOUNS	PROPER ADJECTIVES
America	American
Canada	Canadian
India	Indian
Japan	Japanese
Mexico	Mexican

Look at these sentences. Notice how proper adjectives describe nouns by telling *what kind*.

> *Chinese* lanterns are made from colorful paper.
> (*what kind of* lanterns? *Chinese*)
> Have you ever eaten *Greek* meatballs?
> (*what kind of* meatballs? *Greek*)

Exercise 6

Find the proper adjective in each sentence. Name the noun it describes.

1. Can you write your name with Arabic letters?
2. At the zoo, I like to watch the African animals.
3. *Pippi Longstocking* was written by a Swedish woman.
4. Siberian tigers are very rare.
5. The Italian flag is red, green, and white.

Complete each sentence with a proper adjective formed from the proper noun in parentheses.

6. Is the hot dog an _____ invention? (America)
7. Do you like this _____ green tea? (Japan)
8. The _____ elephant drinks 24 gallons of water a day. (Africa)
9. I bought an _____ sweater. (Ireland)
10. Have you ever tasted _____ chocolate? (France)

Practice Power

Think of four gifts you have received for your birthday. Use a descriptive adjective to tell about each gift. The adjective should answer the question *what kind*. Then use the adjectives and nouns in sentences.

Lesson 2 Limiting Adjectives

A limiting adjective *points out* a noun or tells *how many*.

The purple popsicle melted.
This puddle is frozen.
Two icicles hang from *the* thin branch.

The adjectives *the, this*, and *two* are *limiting adjectives*. *The* and *this* point out nouns. *Two* tells how many.

Limiting adjectives are often used with descriptive adjectives. A limiting adjective comes before a descriptive adjective in a sentence.

Adjectives That Point Out Nouns

A, An, The

> *A*, *an*, and *the* are limiting adjectives. Each of them tells you that a noun will follow. *A*, *an*, and *the* are called *articles*.

A and *an* are used before singular nouns. Use *a* before words that begin with a *consonant sound*.

> *A* small boy rode past on *a* donkey.

Use *an* before words that begin with a *vowel sound*.

> *An* elephant ate for *an* hour.

The is used before singular nouns and plural nouns.

> *The* hikers followed *the* long trail.

Exercise 1

Find the articles in these sentences. Name the noun each points out.

1. A monkey peeled the banana.
2. An aardvark is in the box.
3. The race was exciting.
4. The new mitt belongs to Frankie.
5. Eve has the measles.
6. Oliver looked at the giant footprints.
7. A hungry bear ate the blackberries.
8. Did you see the game?
9. Look! A helicopter is landing.
10. An umbrella was left in the hall.

Exercise 2

Complete each sentence with *a* or *an*.

1. ___ sleepy piglet refused to move.
2. It's good luck to find ___ penny.
3. Nicole picked ___ armful of daisies.
4. ___ dolphin performed for us.
5. Farmers rise at ___ early hour.
6. There is ___ lemon under the table.
7. Each child wrote ___ invitation.
8. Marty dropped ___ ice cube in the glass.
9. Suzanne made ___ pillow for her armadillo.
10. Draw ___ straight line on your paper.

This, That, These, Those

> ***This***, *that*, *these*, and *those* are limiting adjectives
> that point out persons, places, or things.

This and *that* are singular. They point out one person,
place, or thing.

> *This* park has a swimming pool. (*One place*)
> *That* boy is my brother. (*One person*)

These and *those* are plural. They point out more than one
person, place, or thing.

> I like *these* puzzles. (*More than one thing*)
> *Those* flags are new. (*More than one thing*)

This and *these* point out persons, places, or things that are
near.

> *This* letter is for you. (*Near*)
> *These* pens are magic. (*Near*)

That and *those* point out persons, places, or things that are
far away.

> *That* lion is sleeping. (*Far away*)
> *Those* sharks look hungry. (*Far away*)

Exercise 3

Find the limiting adjective in each sentence. Tell whether it points out *one* or *more than one* person, place, or thing.

1. I wear these shoes to school every day.
2. Did you make these paper flowers?
3. Those clouds look like cotton candy.
4. That giraffe's neck is the longest.
5. Where did you find this old photograph?
6. I don't know how to solve this problem.
7. Please bring me that chair.
8. I found this pink stone in your garden.
9. Who carried those books here?
10. Did C. S. Lewis write these stories?

Exercise 4

Complete each sentence with the correct adjective. Tell whether it points out persons, places, or things that are *near* or *far away*.

1. (This, These) sandwiches are peanut butter and jelly.
2. Is (that, those) girl in fifth grade?
3. (Those, That) monkeys play tag.
4. Rake (these, this) leaves into a big pile.
5. Who brought (those, that) caterpillar to class?
6. (This, These) hot dog needs mustard.
7. Let's play with (this, these) cards.
8. (That, Those) funny animal is called a zonkey.
9. (These, This) sock has a big hole.
10. Nancy painted (those, that) pictures with watercolors.

Complete each sentence with *this, that, these,* or *those.* The words in parentheses will help you choose the adjective.

11. _____ paintings were made by early cave dwellers. (more than one, near)
12. Did you see _____ wild horses? (more than one, far away)
13. _____ kangaroo hopped onto the bus. (one, far away)
14. Did Cheri write _____ adventure story? (one, near)
15. A robot repaired _____ machine. (one, far away)

Adjectives That Tell How Many

> Some limiting adjectives tell *how many* or *about how many*.

Numbers are limiting adjectives when they come before a noun. Numbers tell exactly *how many*.

    one shovel   *four* dancers
    fifteen kittens   *nine* tall players

Some, *few*, and *many* are limiting adjectives that tell *about how many*. They come before the noun.

    many baseballs   *many* old socks
    few clouds   *few* coins
    some nests   *some* shiny gold

Exercise 5

Find the limiting adjectives in these sentences. Tell whether each adjective *points out* or tells *how many* or *about how many*.

1. A frog lives in that tree.
2. Who made those taffy apples?
3. Many trucks use this wide road.
4. There are twelve inches in one foot.
5. That snake has fourteen red stripes.
6. The oak tree in the yard has few red leaves.
7. Some lions sleep twelve hours every day.
8. Jenny found these pretty rocks in that closet.
9. Steven ran a mile in twenty minutes.
10. This book was written by a young girl.

Exercise 6

Complete each sentence with an adjective that tells *how many* or *about how many*.

1. _____ birds were sitting on the telephone wire.
2. Please pour me _____ milk, Larry.
3. There were _____ chocolate-covered raisins left in the dish.
4. There are _____ boys in our classroom.
5. _____ giant loads of dirt filled up the hole.
6. I would like to have _____ new clothes.
7. Steve went on a vacation for _____ days.
8. _____ fans were disappointed when the game was canceled.
9. I can see _____ windsurfers on the lake.
10. Julie had to take _____ buses to get home.

Diagraming with Limiting Adjectives

In a diagram, a limiting adjective is put on a slanted line under the noun it modifies.

> Joel received a prize.

Who received? Joel did what? Received what?

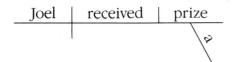

Practice Power

Imagine that you are giving a tour of your room at home. Write five sentences that tell about the things in your room. In your sentences, use adjectives that point out and adjectives that tell how many. Here are two examples.

> *That* guitar in *the* corner has *two* broken strings.
> *These* books are from *the* library.

Lesson 3 Using Adjectives to Compare

Adjectives can be used to compare two or more persons or things.

A rhinoceros is *large*.
An elephant is *larger* than a rhinoceros.
A blue whale is the *largest* animal in the world.

In the first sentence, the adjective *large* describes the size of a rhinoceros. In the second sentence, the largeness of an elephant is compared with that of a rhinoceros. In the third sentence, the largeness of the blue whale is compared with the largeness of all other animals.

When you compare, you tell how people, places, or things are similar or different. To compare two persons, places, or things, add *er* to the adjective. To compare three or more persons, places, or things, add *est.*

When you use longer adjectives, use the words *more* and *most.* To compare two persons, places, or things, use *more* before the adjective. To compare three or more persons, places, or things, use *most* before the adjective.

Dolphins are *intelligent*.
Dolphins are *more intelligent* than sharks.
Scientists think the blue whale is the *most intelligent* animal.

Exercise 1

Name the adjective that compares in each sentence. Then tell what is being compared.

1. Polar bears live in the coldest place on earth.
2. The sloth takes longer naps than the hedgehog.
3. Crocodiles have sharper teeth than people.
4. A snake has more powerful jaws than a frog.
5. That chimpanzee is the most playful monkey at the zoo.
6. A cat is a safer pet than a tiger.
7. Woodpeckers are the noisiest birds.
8. The hammerhead bird builds the biggest nest of all birds.
9. The skunk is the smelliest animal.
10. My dog is more playful than my cat.

Here are some spelling rules you should remember when you add *er* and *est* to adjectives.

If the adjective ends in a single consonant following a single vowel, double the final consonant and add *er* or *est*.

big	bigger	biggest
sad	sadder	saddest

If the adjective ends in a silent *e*, drop the *e* and add *er* or *est*.

safe	safer	safest
brave	braver	bravest

If the adjective ends in *y* following a consonant, change the *y* to *i* and add *er* or *est*.

happy	happier	happiest
sunny	sunnier	sunniest

Exercise 2

Complete each sentence with the correct form of the adjective in parentheses.

1. My sister's hair is _____ (curly) than mine.
2. This math problem is the _____ (difficult) of all the problems.
3. Yellow is the _____ (bright) color in my crayon box.
4. The red pepper is _____ (hot) than the yellow pepper.
5. An ocean is _____(wide) than a lake.
6. This is the _____ (exciting) story I've ever read!
7. Chocolate ice cream is _____ (delicious) than vanilla ice cream.
8. Your joke was _____ (silly) than Jeremy's joke.
9. The dictionary is the _____ (heavy) book on the shelf.
10. Joanie's whistle is _____ (loud) than Sam's.

Forms of *Good* and *Bad*

> *Good* and *bad* are adjectives that can be used to compare two or more persons, places, or things.

Good is a descriptive adjective that changes forms when it is used to compare persons, places, or things. To compare two things, use the word *better*. To compare three or more things, use the word *best*.

> That was a *good* movie.
> We watched a *better* movie last night.
> It's the *best* movie I've seen.

The descriptive adjective *bad* also changes forms when it is used to compare persons, places, or things. To compare two things, use the word *worse*. To compare three or more things, use the word *worst*.

> Jim has a *bad* mosquito bite on his arm.
> It's a *worse* bite than the one on his leg.
> That bite has the *worst* itch of all his bites.

Exercise 3

Choose the correct adjective to complete each sentence.

1. I have a (good, best) idea.
2. This is the (worse, worst) snowstorm of the year.
3. Of all my paintings, this one is the (best, better).
4. Which is (best, better)—the strawberry pie or the blueberry pie?
5. Lisa is (better, best) at shortstop than Larry.
6. Did you think of a (best, good) name for your puppy?
7. Last winter I had a (bad, worst) cold.
8. In our club, Brian tells the (worse, worst) jokes.
9. Andrea's ice-skating is (worse, worst) than mine.
10. Beth is my (better, best) friend.

Complete each sentence with the correct form of *good* or *bad*.

11. Mark is _____ at math than Matt. (good)
12. This is the _____ desk in the room. (bad)
13. Which poster is the _____ of all? (good)
14. Sally's cut looks _____ than Alan's. (bad)
15. Some people say walking is _____ than jogging. (good)

You Are the Author

Choose one.

1. Recall a Fourth of July celebration that you especially enjoyed. Write a paragraph about it. Be sure to use at least four descriptive adjectives.
2. Write a paragraph explaining why you are proud to be an American. Make your reasons come alive by choosing good descriptive adjectives. Illustrate your paragraph. Then have your teacher help combine the paragraphs and drawings of everyone in your class into a book. With your classmates make a list on the chalkboard of possible titles. Choose one and then have a member of the class illustrate the cover. You may wish to present your book to the school library.

Chapter Challenge

Read this paragraph carefully, and then answer the questions.

¹Some places on the earth are very cold, and some are very hot. ²The North Pole is one of the coldest spots on earth. ³This freezing weather is the best weather for polar bears. ⁴As you move south toward the equator, the weather becomes warmer. ⁵You will begin to see many trees, green grass, and colorful flowers. ⁶Once you pass the equator, the weather gets cooler. ⁷It gets cooler until you reach the South Pole. ⁸These spots, the North and South Poles, are the coldest places on earth.

1. In sentence 1, find a limiting adjective that tells about how many.
2. In sentence 2, find an adjective that compares the cold spots on earth.
3. In sentence 3, find an adjective that compares three or more things.
4. In sentence 3, does the limiting adjective *this* refer to one or more than one?
5. In sentence 4, find an adjective that compares.
6. In sentence 5, find an adjective that tells about how many.
7. In sentence 5, find two descriptive adjectives.
8. In sentence 6, find an article.
9. In sentence 8, does the adjective *coldest* compare two things or three or more things?
10. In sentence 8, does the adjective *these* refer to one or more than one?

Creative Space 4

Butterflies dancing through falling snow!
What a wonderful sight it would be.

Oemaru

Exploring the Poem...

Would you be surprised to see the wonderful sight that the speaker describes in this poem? By picturing butterflies and snow together, the poet can open the door of our imagination. What is so unusual about seeing butterflies and snow together?

★ Can you think of two objects that can be seen together only in the world of imagination? What about roller skates on a cat? A polar bear at the equator?

Write a short poem about two objects that can be seen together only in your imagination.

Before you begin your poem, read this poem written by a student.

> A soft white cloud
> Spread out on my living room floor.
> I can lie on it and watch TV.
> How comfortable!

Chapter 5

Verbs

The Most Worthy and Most Beautiful Daughter

by John Steptoe

from *Mufaro's Beautiful Daughters*   1988 Caldecott Honor Book

A long time ago, in a certain place in Africa, lived a man named Mufaro with his two daughters, who were called Manyara and Nyasha. Everyone agreed that Manyara and Nyasha were very beautiful.

Manyara was almost always in a bad temper. She teased her sister whenever their father's back was turned, and she had been heard to say, "Someday, Nyasha, I will be a queen, and you will be a servant in my household."

Nyasha kept a small plot of land on which she grew **millet**, sunflowers, yams, and vegetables. One day Nyasha noticed a small garden snake resting beneath a yam vine. "Good day, little Nyoka," she called to him. "You are welcome here." From that day on, Nyoka was always at Nyasha's side when she tended her garden.

Early one morning, a messenger from the city arrived. The Great King wanted a wife. "The Most **Worthy** and Beautiful Daughters in the Land are invited to appear before the King, and he will choose one to become Queen!" the messenger proclaimed.

Mufaro called Manyara and Nyasha to him. "It would be a great honor to have one of you chosen," he said. "Prepare yourselves to journey to the city."

Illustrations by author John Steptoe

That night, when everyone was asleep, Manyara stole quietly out of the village. She had never been in the forest at night before, and she was frightened, but her greed to be the first to appear before the king drove her on. In her hurry, she almost stumbled over a small boy who suddenly appeared, standing in the path.

"Please," said the boy. "I am hungry. Will you give me something to eat?"

"I have brought only enough for myself," Manyara replied.

After traveling for what seemed to be a great distance, Manyara came to a small clearing. There, **silhouetted** against the moonlight, was an old woman seated on a large stone.

The old woman spoke. "I will give you some advice, Manyara. Soon after you pass the place where two paths cross, you will see a grove of trees. They will laugh at you. You must not laugh in return. Later, you will meet a man with his head under his arm. You must be polite to him."

"How dare you advise your future queen? Stand aside, you ugly old woman!" Manyara scolded.

Just as the old woman had foretold, Manyara came to a grove of trees, and they did indeed seem to be laughing at her.

"I must be calm," Manyara thought. "I will *not* be frightened." She looked up at the trees and laughed out loud. "I laugh at you, trees!" she shouted, and she hurried on.

It was not yet dawn when Manyara heard the sound of rushing water. "The river must be up ahead," she thought. "The great city is just on the other side."

But there, on the rise, she saw a man with his head tucked under his arm. Manyara ran past him without speaking. "A queen acknowledges only those who please her," she said to herself.

Nyasha woke at the first light of dawn. Her thoughts were interrupted by loud shouts and a commotion from the wedding party assembled outside. Manyara was missing! When they found her footprints on the path that led to the city, they decided to go on as planned.

They were deep in the forest when Nyasha saw the small boy standing by the side of the path.

"You must be hungry," Nyasha said and handed him a yam she had brought for her lunch.

Later, as they were approaching the place where the two paths crossed, the old woman appeared and silently pointed the way to the city. Nyasha thanked her and gave her a small pouch filled with sunflower seeds.

The sun was high in the sky when the party came to the grove of towering trees. Their uppermost branches seemed to bow down to Nyasha as she passed beneath them.

At last, arm in arm, Nyasha and her father approached the city gate. Just as they entered, the air was **rent** by piercing cries, and Manyara ran wildly out of a **chamber** at the center of the **enclosure**.

"Do not go to the king, my sister. Oh, please, Father, do not let her go!" she cried hysterically. "There's a great monster there, a snake with five heads! He said that he knew all my faults and that I displeased him."

But Nyasha bravely made her way to the chamber and opened the door.

On the seat of the great chief's stool lay the little garden snake.

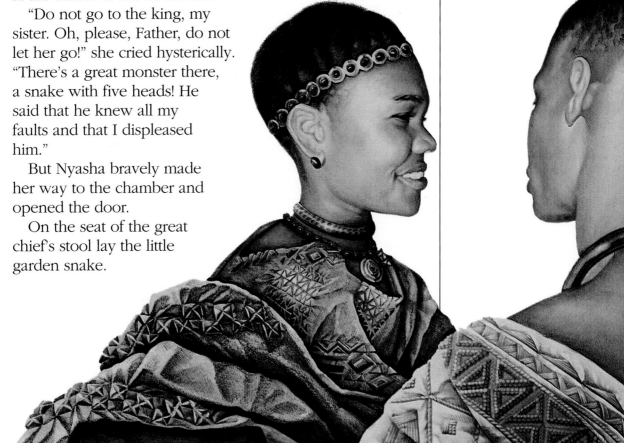

"My little friend!" she exclaimed. "It's such a pleasure to see you, but why are you here?"

"I am the king, " Nyoka replied.

And there, before Nyasha's eyes, the garden snake changed shape.

"I am the king. I am also the hungry boy with whom you shared a yam in the forest and the old woman to whom you made a gift of sunflower seeds. But you know me best as Nyoka. Because I have been all of these, I know you to be the Most Worthy and Most Beautiful Daughter in the Land. It would make me very happy if you would be my wife."

And so it was that, a long time ago, Nyasha agreed to be married. Mufaro proclaimed to all who would hear him that he was the happiest father in all the land, for he was blessed with two beautiful and worthy daughters—Nyasha, the queen; and Manyara, a servant in the queen's household.

The Writer's Craft

1. From what you have learned about Nyasha, do you think she will be a good queen? Why or why not?
2. This story has been called an African Cinderella tale. What are some differences and some similarities between this story and "Cinderclla"?
3. What is the big surprise in the story?
4. Some of the action verbs that the author used to tell what Nyasha did while she journeyed to the city are *saw, handed, thanked, gave, passed,* and *entered.* How are such simple verbs suited to a folktale?

Recalling What You Know

1. Verbs express action or being. Identify the verbs and tell whether each expresses action or being.
   a. *Mufaro called Manyara and Nyasha to him.*
   b. *Brightly plumed birds darted about in the shadows.*
   c. *Manyara was almost always in a bad temper.*
2. Regular verbs form their past by adding *-d* or *-ed*. Spell the past of *tease, pass, laugh, change.*

Lesson 1 Action Verbs

Many verbs express action.

The author, John Steptoe, chose names from the Shona language for the characters of this African tale. Mufaro means "happy man," Nyasha means "mercy or kindness," and Manyara means "ashamed." Read these sentences about the characters.

Mufaro lived with his daughters, Manyara and Nyasha.
Everyone agreed on the girls' beauty.
Manyara teased Nyasha about her goodness.
Manyara often showed a bad temper.
Mufaro knew nothing of this behavior.
Nyasha ignored Manyara's hurtful words.
She was kind and always treated everyone well.
Mufaro beamed with pride at his daughters.

Almost all of the verbs in these sentences are *action verbs.* They tell what someone *does.* Can you find the action verbs in these sentences?

Did you name these words: *lived, agreed, teased, showed, knew, ignored, treated, beamed*?

Here are other action verbs. They tell what a *horse does*
and what *water does*.

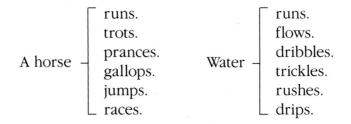

A horse
- runs.
- trots.
- prances.
- gallops.
- jumps.
- races.

Water
- runs.
- flows.
- dribbles.
- trickles.
- rushes.
- drips.

Exercise 1

Find the action verb in each sentence.
1. A few years ago John Steptoe traveled to Africa.
2. He searched for an African Cinderella tale.
3. For several months Steptoe read many folktales.
4. One day he discovered a special book of old stories.
5. G. M. Theal collected these folktales in 1895.
6. From these stories, Steptoe found a Cinderella tale.
7. The people of Zimbabwe told the original story.
8. Steptoe based his book on ideas in this story.
9. With pen, ink, and vivid colors, he illustrated it.
10. John Steptoe won many awards for his book!

Exercise 2

Complete each sentence with an action verb.
1. The shaggy dog _____ when he sees a stranger.
2. Who _____ the homework?
3. We often _____ the subway to Chestnut Street.
4. A tap-dancer _____ across the stage.
5. Two bears and a monkey _____ in the circus ring.
6. A woolly worm _____ up my arm.
7. Who _____ the salad?
8. We watched the herons _____ over the beach.
9. Jerome _____ the paper dragon.
10. Terrell _____ the cellar door with a gasp.

Exercise 3

Name two action verbs for each of these nouns. The first one is done for you.

planes *soar, zoom*   wind
babies   astronauts
trucks   trees

Diagraming Action Verbs

Notice how an action verb is diagramed in this sentence.

Tammy unlocked the mysterious trunk.

Who unlocked? Tammy did what? Unlocked what?

| Tammy | unlocked | trunk |

the   *mysterious*

Exercise 4

Diagram these sentences.
1. An outfielder caught the ball.
2. The prince solved the riddle.
3. The sheriff wore a gold badge.
4. Dragons scare the villagers.
5. The wind howls.

Practice Power

Name a person, an animal, or a thing that can perform each of these actions. Write a sentence for each action verb. Here is an example.

rumbles   A train *rumbles* down the tracks.

1. chirps   5. screeches
2. gathers   6. flies
3. kneels   7. teaches
4. scampers   8. purrs

Lesson 2 Being Verbs

A being verb shows that someone or something *is*.

There is a difference between an *action verb* and a *being verb*. Look at these sentences:

COLUMN A

Taffy *purrs* quietly.
They *slide* on the ice.
Greg *hit* a home run.
Eric and I *read* the script.

COLUMN B

Taffy *is* gentle.
They *are* ice skaters.
Greg *was* a baseball player.
Eric and I *were* two clowns.

The action verbs are in column A. The being verbs are in column B. Being verbs do *not* express any action. They show that someone or something simply *is*.

Here is a list of being verbs:

am	was	(has) been	(will) be
is	were	(have) been	(shall) be
are		(had) been	

Exercise 1

Find the being verb in each sentence.
1. An elephant is a pachyderm.
2. I will be the referee.
3. Lewis and Clark were explorers.
4. This is an old butter churn.
5. Frédéric Chopin was a composer.
6. Joe has been a lifeguard for two summers.
7. The lion is the king of beasts.
8. This winter has been the coldest in history.
9. Yesterday was my tenth birthday.
10. We are triplets.
11. I am the babysitter.
12. This caterpillar will be a butterfly soon.

Exercise 2

Find the predicate verb in each sentence. Tell whether it expresses *action* or *being*.
1. Students studied the French words.
2. Cathy is the editor of the magazine.
3. Gorillas are vegetarians.
4. What was the monster of the Black Lagoon?
5. The cream pie fell to the floor.
6. Many termites gnawed on the giant log.
7. Peru is a country in South America.
8. Mr. Adams paints merry-go-round ponies.
9. She tasted the seaweed cookies.
10. Do yaks yawn?
11. Jake will be six years old on Friday.
12. The loop-the-loop has been my favorite ride.

Verbs and Sentences

The verb is the most important word in a sentence. Without a verb, there is no sentence. Sometimes a sentence may be only one word.

Read.   Dig.
Listen.   Jump.
Chat.   Whistle.

In each of the above sentences, there is a verb, but you do not see a subject. The pronoun *you* is the subject. *You* is not always seen or expressed in a sentence. Read each of the sentences above with the word *you* in front of it.

What is the subject in each of these sentences?

Collect as many beetles as you can.
Sift two cups of flour.
Call the repairman tomorrow.

Which of these groups of words is a sentence?
A. Over the meadow and through the woods to Darcy's house.
B. Sing.

B is a sentence. A has more words, but it is not a sentence. It does not have a verb.

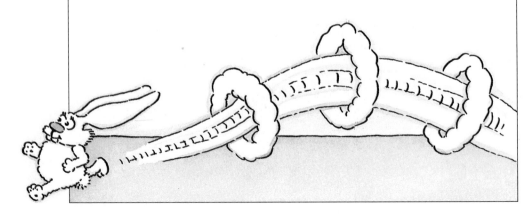

298

Exercise 3

Read each group of words. Tell whether it is a *sentence* or *not a sentence*.

1. I saw a terrific magic act.
2. Rabbit in the hat.
3. All the doves escaped.
4. Those white birds.
5. We will see the rocket launch.
6. A report from the weather station.
7. A police car raced through town.
8. Stand quietly.
9. Sneeze.
10. At the corner for ten minutes.
11. A monkey in the tree.
12. Go.

Practice Power

Go back to exercise 3. Use a being verb to make every nonsentence a sentence. Change the words around if necessary. Here is an example sentence.

There *was* a rabbit in the hat.

Lesson 3 Verb Phrases

A verb phrase is made up of one or more helping verbs and a main verb.

The verbs in these sentences are italicized. Can you tell what makes them different?

  A. The astronaut *helped* his friend into the spaceship.
  B. The explorer *has found* the hidden treasure.
  C. Tracey *might be coming* to my Halloween party.
  D. *Catch* the Frisbee!

Sentences A and D have only one verb. Sentences B and C have more than one verb. Whenever there is more than one verb, the group of words is called a *verb phrase*.

A verb phrase has two parts—a *helping verb* and a *main verb*.

In sentence B, *found* is the main verb and *has* is the helping verb.

In sentence C, *coming* is the main verb and *might* and *be* are the helping verbs. There may be more than one helping verb in a verb phrase.

Here is a list of helping verbs:

am, is, are	shall, will	do, does, did
was, were	may, can	should, would
be, being, been	has, have, had	might, could, must

Exercise 1

The verb phrase is italicized in each sentence. For each verb in the phrase, tell if it is a *main verb* or a *helping verb*.

1. Patty *must be making* a sardine sandwich.
2. *Do put* ice cream on my pie, please.
3. The signal *was given* by Chief Running Horse.
4. I *have found* my missing sock.
5. You *should have smelled* those onions.
6. Owls *must catch* their prey quickly.
7. Josh *can say* the alphabet backwards.
8. We *shall enter* the jump rope contest.
9. The hamburgers *were sizzling*.
10. The dog *has hidden* its bone.
11. Chris *can play* soccer today.
12. Rachel *should know* her way to the park.

Exercise 2

Find the verb phrase in each sentence. For each verb in the phrase, tell if it is a main verb or a helping verb.

1. She is skating around the rink.
2. The sand castle was disappearing with each wave.
3. Jan will watch for the taxi.
4. I have read three library books this weekend.
5. The bells are calling everyone to church.
6. The gas station was closed.
7. The duck was quacking down the street.
8. A robot was bouncing on a trampoline.
9. Comets have been named after the people who discover them.
10. You might catch poison ivy.

Exercise 3

Complete these sentences with helping verbs.

1. Tara _____ searching for a safety pin.
2. It _____ _____ raining for three days.
3. Mr. Costello _____ _____ chasing the mice with a broom.
4. My aunt and uncle _____ living in the apartment next door.
5. We _____ walk the dogs down Atlantic Avenue.
6. Chan _____ made a terrarium.
7. Sherry _____ _____ playing the clarinet.
8. _____ Ellen go tomorrow?
9. I _____ complete my story today.
10. Clowns _____ tumbling in the circus ring.
11. My brother _____ sailing his ship to China.
12. I _____ _____ waiting for you to come home.

Practice Power

Write five sentences about some of the things that have happened or will happen in your school today. Use verb phrases in your sentences. Here is an example sentence.

Mr. Nutley *will make* school announcements after lunch.

Lesson 4 Regular and Irregular Verbs

There are three principal parts of a verb—present, past, and past participle.

A regular verb forms its past and past participle by adding *d* or *ed* to the present form.

Read these sentences carefully. Can you tell the difference in the form of each verb?
  A. Laura and Ben *glue* very carefully.
  B. Laura *glued* the cotton to the paper.
  C. Ben *has glued* the buttons to the paper.

—In sentence A, *glue* is the *present form* of the verb.

—In sentence B, *glued* is the *past form* of the verb. The letter *d* has been added to *glue* to form the past.

—In sentence C, *glued* is the *past participle form*. The letter *d* has been added to *glue* to form the past participle. Helping verbs such as *has*, *have*, or *had* must be used with the past participle form.

The verb *glue* is a *regular verb*. It forms its past and past participle by adding *d* or *ed* to the present form.

Study this short list of regular verbs.

PRESENT	PAST	PAST PARTICIPLE (used with a helping verb such as *has, have, had*)
bake	bak*ed*	bak*ed*
call	call*ed*	call*ed*
learn	learn*ed*	learn*ed*
like	lik*ed*	lik*ed*
play	play*ed*	play*ed*

Exercise 1

Tell the form of the italicized verb in each sentence—
present, *past*, or *past participle*.

1. The musicians *played* for three hours.
2. Jennie *has named* her turtle Slow Poke.
3. They *talk* every day on the telephone.
4. Andy *learned* to play chess.
5. The cheese *had melted* in the sun.
6. Even in cold weather, our neighbors *walk* their chimp.
7. Each day Chuck and Cindy *help* with the dishes.
8. Julie *has learned* to swim.
9. She *looked* at her mask in the mirror.
10. *Listen* carefully to these directions.
11. The chipmunks *have joined* in the fun.
12. We *like* crushed pretzels on our pudding.

Irregular Verbs

An irregular verb does *not* form its past and past
participle by adding *d* or *ed* to the present form.

Read these sentences carefully. Can you tell the difference
in the form of each verb?
A. The kings *sing* for their supper.
B. The kings *sang* for their supper.
C. The kings *have sung* for their supper.

—In sentence A, *sing* is the present form of the verb.

—In sentence B, *sang* is the past form of the verb. The
letters *d* or *ed* are not added to *sing* to form the past.

—In sentence C, *sung* is the past participle form. The
letters *d* or *ed* are not added to *sing* to form the past
participle. Helping verbs such as *has*, *have*, or *had* must
be used with the past participle form.

The verb *sing* is an *irregular verb*. It does *not* form its past
and past participle by adding *d* or *ed* to the present form.

Study this list of irregular verbs. Notice how the past and past participle are formed.

PRESENT	PAST	PAST PARTICIPLE
		(used with a helping verb such as *has*, *have*, *had*)
am (is, be, are)	was (were)	been
begin	began	begun
blow	blew	blown
break	broke	broken
burst	burst	burst
choose	chose	chosen
come	came	come
do	did	done
draw	drew	drawn
eat	ate	eaten
fall	fell	fallen
fly	flew	flown
give	gave	given
go	went	gone
grow	grew	grown
know	knew	known
make	made	made
see	saw	seen
sing	sang	sung
take	took	taken
teach	taught	taught
throw	threw	thrown
write	wrote	written

Exercise 2

Choose the correct verb form to complete each sentence.
1. Joan has (wrote, written) a report about Sir Francis Drake.
2. She (drew, drawn) pictures, too.
3. Lonnie (ate, eaten) almost all the raisin cookies.
4. He has (gave, given) me only two of them.
5. I (threw, thrown) the ball to Mr. Gibson.
6. He has (gave, given) me lessons on aiming.
7. Lucy (chose, chosen) to go to the library.
8. Has she (went, gone) yet?
9. We have (took, taken) the radio to be repaired.
10. It (broke, broken) yesterday.
11. Brigid has (sang, sung) to her parakeet every day.
12. Today it (sang, sung) back to her.

Exercise 3

Complete each sentence with the *past* or *past participle* form of the irregular verb in parentheses. Remember to use the past participle form if a helping verb is given. Use the list of irregular verbs to help you.
1. My dog, Sauerkraut, _____ (eat) three dog biscuits.
2. Chris has _____ (take) the pictures of the carnival.
3. I _____ (know) the name of one Spanish explorer.
4. Pinocchio's nose _____ (grow) very long.
5. The birds have _____ (fly) south for the winter.
6. Erin had _____ (write) her name in Chinese.
7. I _____ (see) the Pueblo Indians weave blankets.
8. Mrs. Peterson _____ (teach) us to make fudge.
9. Our train ride has _____ (take) too long.
10. My family _____ (go) to the pumpkin farm.
11. Margie had _____ (do) her homework by noon.
12. I have _____ (am) here for a long time.

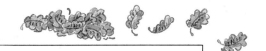

More Practice with Irregular Verbs

Begin, Began, Begun

Begin is the present form.

> The leaves *begin* to change colors in autumn.

Began is the past form.

> The leaves *began* to change colors.

Begun is the past participle form. It is always used with a helping verb such as *has*, *have*, or *had*.

> The leaves *have begun* to change colors.

Exercise 4

Complete each sentence with the correct verb form—*begin*, *began*, or *begun*.

1. Have you _____ to feel better?
2. The rodeo _____ at eight o'clock.
3. Has Susanna _____ collecting stamps?
4. The molasses had _____ to boil over.
5. _____ to clean up the paint.
6. Has it _____ to rain yet?
7. Suddenly it _____ to move!
8. Go ahead and _____ without me.
9. We all _____ to laugh.
10. Has Katrina _____ her karate lesson?

Break, Broke, Broken

Break is the present form.

> *Break* the piñata.

Broke is the past form.

> Ana *broke* the piñata.

Broken is the past participle form. It is always used with a helping verb such as *has*, *have*, or *had*.

> Ana *has broken* the piñata.

Exercise 5

Complete each sentence with the correct verb form—*break*, *broke*, or *broken*.

1. Has that track record been _____?
2. Ms. Schumacher _____ her doorbell.
3. The telephone fell on the floor and _____.
4. They have _____ their radio.
5. _____ the peanut brittle into small pieces.
6. Andy _____ the bicycle spokes when he fell.
7. I have _____ the badminton racket.
8. Do not _____ the antique toys.
9. Who _____ the alarm clock?
10. The zipper on my jacket has _____.

Choose, Chose, Chosen

Choose is the present form.

> I *choose* Jill for my team.

Chose is the past form.

> I *chose* Jill for my team.

Chosen is the past participle form. It is always used with a helping verb such as *has*, *have*, or *had*.

> I *have chosen* Jill for my team.

Exercise 6

Complete each sentence with the correct verb form—*choose*, *chose*, or *chosen*.

1. The director _____ Laura to play the part of the witch.
2. I _____ a computer game as my prize.
3. We have _____ chicken chow mein.
4. They _____ blue and green for the new baseball uniforms.
5. _____ a photograph of the rock star you like.
6. He has _____ the red motorcycle.
7. My brother has _____ to drive the stagecoach.
8. Have you _____ your favorite television program?
9. Daniella has _____ to do finger painting.
10. She _____ to ride the roller coaster first.

Do, Did, Done

Do is the present form.

> Kelly and Ken *do* push-ups every night.

Did is the past form.

> Kelly and Ken *did* push-ups every night.

Done is the past participle form. It is always used with a helping verb such as *has*, *have*, or *had*.

> Kelly and Ken *have done* push-ups every night.

Exercise 7

Complete each sentence with the correct verb form—*do*, *did*, or *done*.

1. Julian has ＿＿＿ his science project.
2. ＿＿＿ you wear a vampire costume?
3. We ＿＿＿ a report on extinct animals.
4. What have you ＿＿＿ with my camera?
5. The sky divers ＿＿＿ stunts in the air yesterday.
6. Please ＿＿＿ this laundry.
7. Has Mark ＿＿＿ the crossword puzzle?
8. I ＿＿＿ a book report on *Little Women*.
9. Have you ＿＿＿ the assignment yet?
10. Everyone has ＿＿＿ a share of the weeding.

Exercise 8

Find the verb or verb phrase in each sentence. Tell whether the main verb is *regular* or *irregular*.

1. Every balloon at the party burst.
2. Some people live in mud huts.
3. Theresita made a tadpole from a carrot.
4. My baby brother has grown three inches.
5. I visited a mushroom factory on Monday.
6. Pablo planned the perfect picnic.
7. Marc and Mike have missed the last bus home.
8. I ate too many tortillas.
9. Elly wished she could fly.
10. Her wish came true.
11. Living in the city has been exciting.
12. She has traveled to the North Pole.

Practice Power

Make up the name of an animal that is now extinct. Write four imaginary facts about this animal. Use only past and past participle forms in your sentences. Tell whether each verb is regular or irregular. Here is an example sentence.

The monkfox once lived in the Sahara Desert.

Lesson 5 Simple Tenses

A verb can be in present, past, or future tense.

Present Tense

A verb in the present tense tells about action that is happening now or that happens again and again. The present form of the verb is used for forming the present tense.

A. Alex and Fred *play* the bagpipes every day.
B. They *play* the bagpipes every day.
C. Alex *plays* the bagpipes every day.
D. He *plays* the bagpipes every day.

Did you notice that the verbs in sentences A and B do *not* end in *s*, but the verbs in sentences C and D do end in *s*?

If the subject noun or pronoun is *plural*, the verb does not end in *s*.

Mules *carry* heavy loads.
They *carry* heavy loads.

If the subject noun or pronoun is *singular*, the verb ends in *s*.

The mule *carries* a heavy load.
It *carries* a heavy load.

Exercise 1

Choose the correct verb for each sentence. If the subject is singular, the verb will end in *s*. If the subject is plural, the verb will not end in *s*.

1. Seals (perform, performs) every day at Sea World.
2. One seal (balance, balances) a ball on his nose.
3. Another seal (flap, flaps) her flippers.
4. It (scurry, scurries) across the platform.
5. The whales (play, plays) with a beach ball.
6. The trainer (feed, feeds) fish to the dolphins.
7. He (like, likes) to make them jump for their food.
8. Starfish (cling, clings) to the rocks for safety.
9. A clam (open, opens) its shell slightly.
10. The oysters (make, makes) pearls.
11. A grain of sand (start, starts) the pearl.
12. Crabs (inch, inches) their way under the rocks.

Past Tense

A verb in the past tense tells about action that has already happened. The past form of the verb is used for forming the past tense.

> Jack *attended* the book fair.
> Lee *went* to the book fair.

Future Tense

A verb in the future tense tells about action that will happen at a future time. The present form of the verb and the helping verbs *shall* or *will* are used for forming the future tense. *Will* and *shall* are the helping verbs of the future tense.

> Chang *will close* the door with a skeleton key.
> I *shall open* the door with a skeleton key.

Exercise 2

Tell whether the italicized verb in each sentence is in the *present, past,* or *future* tense.

1. My brother *raises* pigs in a "pig parlor."
2. Long ago, people *believed* that the world was square.
3. Jody *took* third place at the music fair.
4. The fur on the polar bear *protects* it from the cold.
5. I *will begin* figure-skating lessons next week.
6. Most people *blink* twenty-five times a minute.
7. Kris *will wear* his sunglasses on the boat.
8. We *taught* Dave the rules of the game.
9. Chip *painted* a picture of the panda at the zoo.
10. The heart of a whale *beats* only nine times a minute.
11. A plastic unicorn *appeared* on my desk.
12. Kim *will serve* tea as the Japanese do.

Exercise 3

Complete each sentence with the correct verb form. The words in parentheses will tell you the verb and the tense to use.

1. The planes _____ every three minutes. (land—present)
2. Jonathan _____ his marbles. (sell—future)
3. Carl _____ six balls at one time. (juggle—present)
4. The captain _____ at the huge shark. (look—past)
5. That carrot cake _____ spicy. (taste—past)
6. The parade _____ immediately. (begin—future)
7. Jeff _____ on the giant foam pillow. (bounce—past)
8. Some bees _____ more honey than others. (make—present)
9. The gorilla _____ to rock music. (listen—present)
10. Doug _____ his social studies project. (explain—past)
11. The electric eel _____ its victim. (shock—future)
12. Twelve inches of snow _____ the ground. (cover—past)

Practice Power

There is a new science building in your town. When you enter, there are three windows. In the first window, you see things that happened in the past. In the second window, you see things that are happening in the present. In the third window, you see things that will happen in the future. Write two sentences about what you see in each window. Here are some example sentences.

First window: Columbus sailed to the New World.
Second window: Astronauts travel in spaceships.
Third window: I will live on another planet.

Lesson 6 Linking Verbs

A linking verb is a being verb. A linking verb joins the subject to a noun or an adjective.

Many verbs show action, but some do not. Being verbs sometimes *link* or join the subject to a noun or an adjective. These verbs are called *linking verbs*.

Study these sentences:
  A. These kittens *are* lively.
  B. This kitten *is* my friend.

In sentence A, the linking verb *are* links the subject *kittens* with the adjective *lively*. In sentence B, the linking verb *is* links the subject *kitten* with the noun *friend*.

Can you tell what words the linking verb links in these sentences?
  A. Those buildings *are* tall.
  B. That building *is* a skyscraper.

In sentence A, *are* links the subject *buildings* with the adjective *tall*. In sentence B, *is* links the subject *building* with the noun *skyscraper*.

Here is a list of linking verbs:

am	was	(has) been	(will) be
is	were	(have) been	(shall) be
are		(had) been	

316

Exercise 1

Find the linking verb in each sentence.
1. I am a scientist.
2. This book about the earth will be interesting.
3. A hole in a volcano is a crater.
4. A moon is a ball of rock.
5. Earthquakes are moving rocks.
6. The movie about the galaxies was fascinating.
7. Galaxies are groups of stars.
8. That star is a ball of gas.
9. Desert lands are dry.
10. A geyser is a fountain of hot water.
11. Some pieces of marble were rough.
12. This earth show has been exciting.

Exercise 2

A linking verb links the subject with a noun or an adjective. Tell whether the italicized word is a *noun* or an *adjective*.
1. A subway is an underground *train*.
2. That giant butterfly was *colorful*.
3. These sponges are *animals*.
4. Seaweed can be *food* for some people.
5. Paul has been *helpful*.
6. Hens are female *chickens*.
7. I am *generous* with my time.
8. These peanuts are *salty*.
9. German food is *delicious*.
10. Those lines in the drawing were *straight*.

Complete each sentence with a linking verb.
11. Black pearls _____ valuable.
12. Mr. Kenny _____ my grandfather.
13. The sixteenth president _____ Abraham Lincoln.
14. These trucks _____ bright orange.
15. The sunset _____ pink and red.

Helping Verbs

> **A being verb may be a linking verb or a helping verb.**

In this sentence, the verb *was* links the subject *pudding* with the adjective *creamy*. *Was* is a linking verb.

> Mom's rice pudding *was* creamy.

In this sentence, the verb *was* helps the main verb *eaten*. *Was* is a helping verb.

> Mom's rice pudding *was eaten* in ten minutes.

Exercise 3

The verb or verb phrase is italicized in each sentence. Tell whether the being verb is a *linking verb* or a *helping verb*.

1. I *am joining* the math club.
2. Matt *is practicing* the French horn.
3. Steven *was* an elf in the play.
4. Diana *is* an usher for the school play.
5. The hut *is made* of grass.
6. These gems *are* valuable.
7. The crickets *were chirping* all night.
8. Hippos *have been wading* in the mud.
9. The Easter eggs *are* hard-boiled.
10. The paper clip *was* a clever invention.
11. The boy's voices *were* strong.
12. Rain *was coming* in the window.

Diagraming Linking Verbs

Notice how a linking verb is diagramed in this sentence.

Kangaroos are mammals.

What are?   Are what?

| Kangaroos | are \ mammals |

The line following the linking verb is slanted. This line is slanted to show that the noun *mammals* is linked to the subject *Kangaroos*.

Exercise 4

Diagram these sentences.
1. The goat is funny.
2. Harry is a fisherman.
3. These girls are friends.
4. The days were short.
5. Jessica will be secretary.

Practice Power

Think about the foods you like. Write five sentences about your favorite ones. Make sure you use a linking verb in each sentence. Here is an example sentence.

This fried chicken is juicy.

Lesson 7 Subject and Verb Agreement

A subject and a verb must always agree.

A singular subject must have a singular verb. A plural subject must have a plural verb. This is called *subject and verb agreement.*

Is, Am, and *Are*

> *Is* and *am* are singular verbs. *Are* is a plural verb.

Look carefully at this chart. Notice how *is* and *are* are used with pronouns. *Is* is usually used with singular pronouns. *Are* is used with plural pronouns. *Am* is used only with the pronoun *I. Are* is always used with the pronoun *you.*

SINGULAR	PLURAL
I am	We are
You are	You are
He is	They are
She is	
It is	

The verb *is* is used with singular nouns. The verb *are* is used with plural nouns.

> That daffodil *is* bright yellow.
> The daisies *are* in a vase.

Exercise 1

Complete each sentence with the correct verb—*is, am,*
or *are.*

 1. Vegetables _____ good for you.
 2. The carrots _____ very hot.
 3. Spinach _____ a green leaf.
 4. It _____ very nutritious.
 5. The string beans _____ in a sauce.
 6. They _____ in a bowl on the table.
 7. This cucumber _____ crunchy.
 8. It _____ in the salad with the mushrooms.
 9. Now we _____ ready to eat.
10. I _____ ready, too.

Was and Were

> **Was** is a singular verb. **Were** is a plural verb.

Look carefully at this chart. Notice how *was* and *were* are used with pronouns. *Was* is used with singular pronouns. *Were* is used with plural pronouns. *Were* is always used with the pronoun *you*.

SINGULAR	PLURAL
I was	We were
You were	You were
He was	They were
She was	
It was	

The verb *was* is used with singular nouns. The verb *were* is used with plural nouns.

> The sleeping bag *was* soft and warm.
> The sleeping bags *were* on the ground.

Exercise 2

Complete each sentence with the correct verb—*was* or *were*.

1. Joey's birthday _____ yesterday.
2. It _____ a fun day.
3. Gifts _____ on the table.
4. Ice cream _____ in the refrigerator.
5. Candles _____ on the cake.
6. They _____ blue, yellow, and pink.
7. His friends _____ happy to come.
8. His sister _____ eager to play the game.
9. His aunt and uncle _____ there.
10. I _____ there, too.

Does and Do

Does is a singular verb. *Do* is a plural verb.

Look carefully at this chart. Notice that *does* is usually used with singular pronouns and *do* is used with plural pronouns. *Do* is always used with the pronouns *I* and *you*.

SINGULAR	PLURAL
I do	We do
You do	You do
He does	They do
She does	
It does	

The verb *does* is used with singular nouns. The verb *do* is used with plural nouns.

What animal licks its paws?   A lion *does*.
What animals have humps?   Camels *do*.

Exercise 3

Complete each sentence with the correct verb—*does* or *do*.

1. Dad ＿＿ the lawn.
2. He always ＿＿ it on Saturday morning.
3. Kevin and Bobby ＿＿ the dishes.
4. They ＿＿ them carefully.
5. Mom ＿＿ the gardening.
6. She ＿＿ it in the afternoon.
7. I ＿＿ my homework on Sunday.
8. On Sunday evening, my sister ＿＿ the crossword puzzle.
9. We ＿＿ many chores together.
10. Who ＿＿ the chores in your family?

Practice Power

Your job is to make up questions for a popular quiz show.
Write two questions that require *is* or *are* in the answer.
Example: Question: What fruit *is* yellow and sour?
          Answer: A lemon *is* yellow and sour.

Write two questions that require *was* or *were* in the
answer.
Example: Question: What day *was* yesterday?
          Answer: Yesterday *was* "spirit" day.

Write two questions that require *does* or *do* in the answer.
Example: Question: Who *does* the school newspaper?
          Answer: The fourth graders *do*.

Lesson 8 There Is and There Are

Sometimes the subject will follow the predicate in a sentence.

There is a toy on the floor.
There was a toy on the floor.

There are ten crayons in the box.
There were ten crayons in the box.

There is NOT a subject. To find the subject, ask

What *is* or *was* on the floor?   *a toy*
  Toy is the subject of *is* and *was. There is* or *there are*
  is used when the subject is *singular*.

What *are* or *were* in the box?   *crayons*
  Crayons is the subject of *are* and *were. There are* or
  there were is used when the subject is *plural.*

Toy and *crayons* come AFTER the predicate.

Exercise 1

Name the subject that follows the predicate *is* or *are*. Tell
whether the subject and predicate are *singular* or *plural*.

1. There are two elephants outside.
2. There are three cookies in the jar.
3. There are twenty-six letters in the alphabet.
4. There are two broken eggs in this carton.
5. There is a little girl at the door.
6. There is one chicken in the pen.
7. There are twelve months in the year.
8. There are some watermelons in the field.
9. There is a letter for you on the table.
10. There is an actor on the stage.

Exercise 2

Name the subject that follows the predicate in each sentence. Then choose the correct predicate to match it.

1. There (was, were) a funny clown at the circus.
2. There (was, were) pretty fireworks over the river.
3. There (was, were) many colors on the quilt.
4. There (was, were) only one parrot at the store.
5. There (was, were) one small candle in the dark castle.
6. There (was, were) a kind queen in the land of Awe.
7. There (was, were) thick rugs on the floor.
8. There (was, were) many people in the apartment.
9. There (was, were) a large cave on the hillside.
10. There (was, were) two tennis players on the court.

Exercise 3

Write sentences using the subjects from exercise 2. Choose *was* or *were*. Do not include the word *there*. The first one is done for you.

1. A funny clown *was at the circus.*
2. Some pretty fireworks
3. Many colors
4. Only one parrot
5. One small candle
6. A kind queen
7. Thick rugs
8. Many people
9. A large cave
10. Two tennis players

You Are the Author

When John Steptoe created *Mufaro's Beautiful Daughters,* he wanted to write a Cinderella tale. Write your own Cinderella tale—perhaps about brothers instead of sisters. Create your characters and describe their kind or selfish acts. Write about where the story takes place, what the characters want, and what they do.

Chapter Challenge

Read this paragraph carefully, and then answer the questions.

¹Tina and Tim were excited about their space trip. ²Their first stop was Jupiter, the largest planet. ³They discovered that Jupiter is so big that all the other planets can fit inside it. ⁴Next, they went to Mars. ⁵There were many craters on this planet. ⁶The next stop was Pluto. ⁷They dressed warmly for their visit there. ⁸Finally, they traveled to Venus, the planet nearest Earth. ⁹Before long they landed in their own backyard. ¹⁰Tina and Tim will plan their next trip after they enjoy a little bit of home.

1. In sentence 1, name the verb phrase.
2. In sentence 2, name the linking verb.
3. In sentence 3, is *discovered* regular or irregular? Name the present, past, and past participle forms of this verb.
4. In sentence 3, name the helping verb in the verb phrase *can fit*.
5. In sentence 4, is *went* regular or irregular?
6. In sentence 5, what is the subject?
7. In sentence 6, *was* links the subject *stop* with what other word? Is that word a noun or an adjective?
8. In sentence 7, what tense is the verb *dressed*?
9. Is the verb *dressed* regular or irregular?
10. In sentence 8, is the predicate an action verb or a being verb?
11. In sentence 9, give the present tense of the verb *landed*.
12. In sentence 10, what tense is the verb *will plan*?

Creative Space 5

Leavetaking

Vacation is over;
It's time to depart.
I must leave behind
(although it breaks my heart)

Tadpoles in the pond,
A can of eels,
A leaky rowboat,
Abandoned car wheels;

For I'm packing only
Necessities:
A month of sunsets
And two apple trees.

Eve Merriam

Exploring the Poem...

This poem has three *stanzas*. A stanza is a group of lines. How many lines are there in each stanza in this poem?

In the second stanza, what four things does the speaker leave behind when vacation is over? Do you think the speaker is happy to leave these things behind?

In the third stanza, what two things does the speaker pack? How can someone pack sunsets and trees?

★ Have you ever taken a vacation? What things did you have to leave behind when your vacation ended?

Write a poem that begins with the same first stanza as "Leavetaking." Write your own list for the second stanza. Finally, think of two things for the third stanza that can only be packed in your memory. Before you begin, read this poem written by a student.

> Vacation is over;
> It's time to depart.
> I must leave behind
> (although it breaks my heart)
>
> Two sandy shoes,
> A bike in the shed,
> A faded beach towel,
> A cot as my bed;
>
> For I'm packing only
> Necessities:
> The ocean's breeze,
> The place where sky meets sea.

Chapter 6

Adverbs

Dorothy's Greatest Wish

by L. Frank Baum

from *The Wonderful Wizard of Oz*

Before they went to see Glinda, however, they were taken to a room of the castle, where Dorothy washed her face and combed her hair, and the Lion shook the dust out of his mane, and the Scarecrow patted himself into his best shape, and the Woodman polished his tin and oiled his joints.

When they were all quite presentable, they followed the soldier girl into a big room where the Witch Glinda sat upon a throne of rubies.

She was both beautiful and young to their eyes. Her hair was a rich red in color and fell in flowing ringlets over her shoulders. Her dress was pure white, but her eyes were blue, and they looked kindly upon the little girl.

"What can I do for you, my child?" she asked.

Dorothy told the Witch all her story: how the cyclone had brought her to the Land of Oz, how she had found her companions, and of the wonderful adventures they had met with.

"My greatest wish now," she added, "is to get back to Kansas, for Aunt Em will surely think something dreadful has happened to me, and that will make her put on **mourning**. And unless the crops are better this year than they were last, I am sure Uncle Henry cannot afford it."

Glinda leaned forward and kissed the sweet, upturned face of the loving little girl.

Illustrations by Mary Lynn Blasutta

"Bless your dear heart," she said, "I am sure I can tell you of a way to get back to Kansas." Then she added, "But if I do, you must give me the Golden Cap."

"Willingly!" exclaimed Dorothy. "Indeed, it is of no use to me now, and when you have it you can command the Winged Monkeys three times."

"And I think I shall need their service just those three times," answered Glinda, smiling.

Dorothy then gave her the Golden Cap, and the Witch said to the Scarecrow, "What will you do when Dorothy has left us?"

"I will return to the Emerald City," he replied, "for Oz has made me its ruler and the people like me. The only thing that worries me is how to cross the hill of the Hammer-Heads."

"By means of the Golden Cap I shall command the Winged Monkeys to carry you to the gates of the Emerald City," said Glinda, "for it would be a shame to deprive the people of so wonderful a ruler."

"Am I really wonderful?" asked the Scarecrow.

"You are unusual," replied Glinda.

Turning to the Tin Woodman, she asked, "What will become of you when Dorothy leaves this country?"

He leaned on his ax and thought a moment. Then he said, "The Winkies were very kind to me and wanted me to rule over them after the Wicked Witch died. I am fond of the Winkies. If I could get back again to the Country of the West, I should like nothing better than to rule over them forever."

"My second command to the Winged Monkeys," said Glinda, "will be that they carry you safely to the land of the Winkies. Your brains may not be so large to look at as those of the Scarecrow, but you are really brighter than he is—when you are well polished—and I am sure you will rule the Winkies wisely and well."

Then the Witch looked at the big, shaggy Lion and asked, "When Dorothy has returned to her own home, what will become of you?"

"Over the hill of the Hammer-Heads," he answered, "lies a grand old forest, and all the beasts that live there have made me their king. If I could only get back to this forest, I would pass my life very happily there."

"My third command to the Winged Monkeys," said Glinda, "shall be to carry you to your forest. Then, having used up the powers of the Golden Cap, I shall give it to the King of the Monkeys, that he and his band may thereafter be free for evermore."

The Scarecrow and the Tin Woodman and the Lion now thanked the Good Witch earnestly for her kindness.

Then Dorothy exclaimed, "You are certainly as good as you are beautiful! But you have not yet told me how to get back to Kansas."

"Your Silver Shoes will carry you over the desert," replied Glinda. "If you had known their power, you could have gone back to your Aunt Em the very first day you came to this country."

"But then I should not have had my wonderful brains!" cried the Scarecrow. "I might have passed my whole life in the farmer's cornfield."

"And I should not have had my lovely heart," said the Tin Woodman. "I might have stood and rusted in the forest till the end of the world."

"And I should have lived a coward forever," declared the Lion, "and no beast in all the forest would have had a good word to say to me."

"This is all true," said Dorothy, "and I am glad I was of use to these friends. But now that each of them has had what he most desired, and each is happy in having a kingdom to rule, I think I should like to go back to Kansas."

"The Silver Shoes," said the Good Witch, "have wonderful powers. And one of the most curious things about them is that they can carry you to any place in the world in three steps, and each step will be made in the wink of an eye. All you have to do is to knock the heels together three times and command the shoes to carry you wherever you wish to go."

"If that is so," said the child joyfully, "I will ask them to carry me back to Kansas at once."

She threw her arms around the Lion's neck and kissed him, patting his big head tenderly. Then she kissed the Tin Woodman, who was weeping in a way most dangerous to his joints. But she hugged the soft, stuffed body of the Scarecrow in her arms instead of kissing his painted face and found she was crying herself at this sorrowful parting from her loving **comrades**.

Glinda the Good stepped down from her ruby throne to give the little girl a good-bye kiss, and Dorothy thanked her for all the kindness she had shown to her friends and herself.

Dorothy now took Toto up **solemnly** in her arms, and having said one last good-bye she clapped the heels of her shoes together three times.

"Take me home to Aunt Em!"

Instantly she was whirling through the air so swiftly that all she could see or feel was the wind whistling past her ears.

The Silver Shoes took but three steps, and then she stopped so suddenly that she rolled over upon the grass several times before she knew where she was.

At length, however, she sat up and looked about her. "Good gracious!" she cried.

For she was sitting on the broad Kansas **prairie**, and just before her was the new farmhouse Uncle Henry had built after the cyclone had carried away the old one. Uncle Henry was milking the cows in the barnyard, and Toto had

jumped out of her arms and was running toward the barn, barking joyously.

Dorothy stood up and found she was in her stocking feet, for the Silver Shoes had fallen off in her flight through the air and were lost forever in the desert.

You may enjoy reading more about Dorothy's adventures in the book *The Wonderful Wizard of Oz*.

The Writer's Craft

1. The Scarecrow desired a brain, the Tin Woodman wanted a heart, and the Cowardly Lion asked for courage. If you could ask the Wizard of Oz for one gift, what would it be?
2. Think about the character Dorothy. Is she someone you would like to know in real life? Why or why not?
3. How do you know that this story is a fantasy? Give examples of some imaginary characters and events.
4. Adverbs of time, such as *then* and *now*, are not always essential to the meaning of a sentence. They convey a sense of time, however, and often make the sentence read more smoothly. Find sentences in the story that contain adverbs of time and read them first without and then with the adverbs. Choose a sentence in which you think the adverb is well used and read it to the class.

An adverb answers the question *when, where,* or *how.* Read these sentences. Identify the adverbs and tell what question each adverb answers.

1. Dorothy looked anxiously at the sky.
2. Her uncle said that a cyclone was coming soon.
3. The house, with Dorothy in it, rose up into the sky.

Lesson 1 Kinds of Adverbs

An adverb modifies a verb, an adjective, or another adverb. An adverb tells *when, where,* or *how.*

Look at the sentence below.

The Wizard of Oz speaks.

In this sentence, the action verb is *speaks.* It tells what the Wizard *does.*

The Wizard of Oz speaks *sometimes.*

In this sentence, the word *sometimes* describes the action of the verb. It tells *when* or *how often* the Wizard speaks.

The Wizard of Oz speaks *here.*

In this sentence, the word *here* describes the action of the verb. It tells *where* the Wizard speaks.

The Wizard of Oz speaks *loudly.*

In this sentence, the word *loudly* describes the action of the verb. It tells *how* the Wizard speaks.

Adverbs *modify,* or give information about, verbs. They answer the question *when, where,* or *how.* Adverbs tell *time, place,* or *manner.*

Adverbs of Time

> **Adverbs of time answer the question *when* or *how often*.**

Dorothy *soon* closed her eyes.
The Scarecrow *then* stumbled over the yellow bricks.
"I've *always* been a coward," said the Lion.

Words that tell *when* or *how often* an action is performed are adverbs of time. Here are some adverbs of time.

again	sometimes
always	soon
early	then
immediately	today
now	tomorrow
often	yesterday

Exercise 1

Find the adverb that tells *when* or *how often* in each sentence.

1. A cyclone slammed into Dorothy's house yesterday!
2. On top of the Wicked Witch the house soon landed.
3. The happy Munchkins then celebrated their freedom.
4. Dorothy met the Scarecrow early in the day.
5. The Tin Woodman often longed for a heart.
6. Would the Cowardly Lion ever get the gift of courage?
7. They finally arrived at the Emerald City.
8. Dorothy now wished to return to Aunt Em in Kansas.
9. Do you think that Dorothy will go home today?
10. Dorothy will never forget her adventures.

Exercise 2

Complete each sentence with an adverb of time.

1. We went to the parade _____.
2. I _____ eat oatmeal for breakfast.
3. These caterpillars will _____ turn into butterflies.
4. My cousin came _____ to the cookout.
5. I _____ chew grape sugarless gum.
6. Julie hit a home run _____.
7. The newspaper is delivered _____ in the morning.
8. I _____ know what time it is.
9. _____ he'll go spelunking.
10. Miles _____ ice-skates in the winter.

Adverbs of Place

> **Adverbs of place answer the question *where*.**

Read this poem and then answer the questions that follow.

> The colorful carnival came to town;
> Lights went *up* as the sun went *down*.
> Fast rides *here* and slow ones *there*,
> Fun and excitement *everywhere*.
>
> *Where* did the lights go?
> *Where* did the sun go?
> *Where* were the rides?
> *Where* was the fun and excitement?

Words that tell *where* an action is performed are adverbs of place. Here are some adverbs of place.

above	down	here	outside
away	everywhere	in	there
back	far	inside	up
below	forward	near	within

Exercise 3

Find the adverb that tells *where* in each sentence.
1. Put your muddy boots there.
2. I looked everywhere for a stamp.
3. The snail crawled inside.
4. We took the elevator up to the third floor.
5. Come here and open the door.
6. The chocolate chips scattered everywhere.
7. Joanne went outside to play in the tent.
8. I put my favorite pencil away.
9. The worm inched forward on the sidewalk.
10. From the treetop, the koala bears looked down.

Exercise 4

Complete each sentence with an adverb of place.
1. Jack and Jill fell _____.
2. Mike hunted _____ for his snowshoes.
3. The bus stops _____.
4. The Chinese kite soared _____.
5. After you make a sandwich, put the bread _____.
6. A fox lives _____.
7. Some ponies on the merry-go-round go _____.
8. Run to the big tree and _____.
9. Take a giant step _____.
10. When he heard the beep, Ben ran _____.

Adverbs of Manner

Adverbs of manner answer the question *how*.

If you went to a circus, you might see and hear

a crowd applauding *loudly*
a lion roaring *ferociously*
elephants stomping *heavily*
a band playing *confidently*

Words that tell *how* an action is performed are adverbs of manner. Here are some adverbs of manner.

carefully	happily
clearly	kindly
easily	quickly
fast	slowly
gracefully	stubbornly

Exercise 5

Find the adverb that tells *how* in each sentence.
1. Julie petted the lamb gently.
2. Harry stood proudly on the stage.
3. The eagle soared swiftly across the sky.
4. The train pulled noisily into the station.
5. Joanne cleverly discovered the answer to the mystery.
6. Aunt Susan skillfully dabbed paint on my face.
7. The kindergarten students nap peacefully after their snack.
8. The North Star shines brightly.
9. The tiger growled angrily at the mosquito.
10. In this game, you must run fast.

Exercise 6

Find an adverb of manner in column 2 that best answers
the question in column 1. Write your answer in a sentence.
Example: How does the secretary write? *neatly*
The secretary writes neatly.

COLUMN 1

How does the tightrope walker walk?
How does a ballerina dance?
How does a jet plane fly?
How should you speak on the telephone?
How do turtles walk?
How does the marching band play?

COLUMN 2

clearly
loudly
gracefully
speedily
slowly
carefully

Exercise 7

Complete each sentence with an adverb of manner.

1. _____ write your name on the line.
2. Alfredo _____ petted the lion cub.
3. Barbie _____ joined the basketball team.
4. Right before lunch, my stomach always growls _____.
5. Lynn _____ chewed the licorice.
6. Joey _____ threw the softball to me.
7. A buffalo charged _____ through the fence.
8. We climbed the icy steps _____.
9. The troop shouted _____ when they won the prize.
10. Our dog lies on the rug and yawns _____.

Exercise 8

Find the adverbs in these sentences. Tell whether each adverb is an adverb of *time*, *place*, or *manner*.

1. People were everywhere in the airport.
2. They were walking up and down.
3. Soon we would board the plane.
4. We waited nervously for our seats to be called.
5. Now we headed for home.
6. Eagerly, the school cheerleaders began to practice.
7. All of them shouted loudly.
8. Some cheerleaders jumped forward.
9. Others jumped backward.
10. To win the championship, they must practice daily.
11. My robot, Robby, carefully picked up my books.
12. Slowly, we walked to school together.
13. Sometimes Robby would wait for me.
14. Often he would go to an amusement park.
15. After school, I would wait outside for Robby to return.

Diagraming Adverbs

Notice how an adverb is diagramed in this sentence.

The thunder boomed loudly.

What boomed? Thunder did what?

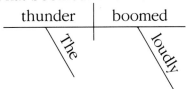

The thunder boomed *how*? The answer is *loudly*. *Loudly* is an adverb of manner.

An adverb modifies a verb and is placed on a slanted line under the verb.

Exercise 9

Diagram these sentences.
1. Juan hummed softly.
2. The pink flowers wilted quickly.
3. This street ends here.
4. Our vacation begins tomorrow.
5. Patrick rises early.

Practice Power

Can you find the adverbs in the poem? Tell whether each one is an adverb of time, place, or manner. Try writing a poem like the one below. First, think of an animal. Then use adverbs to help describe the action of this animal.

Mischievous monkey,
You always swing up and down
    Happily
    Noisily.

Lesson 2 Comparison of Adverbs

Like adjectives, many adverbs can be used to make comparisons. Adverbs can compare the actions of two or more persons, places, or things.

Many adverbs can be used to make *comparisons*. They can tell how the actions of people, places, or things are similar or different. To compare the actions of two persons, places, or things, *er* is added to short adverbs. To compare the actions of three or more persons, places, or things, *est* is added to short adverbs.

> Maria arrived *early*.
> Maria arrived *earlier* than Tom.
> Maria arrived *earliest* of all the students.

To make comparisons with longer adverbs that end in *ly*, use the words *more* or *most*. To compare the actions of two persons, places, or things, use *more* before the adverb. To compare the actions of three or more persons, places, or things, use *most* before the adverb.

> The kitten pounced *playfully*.
> The kitten pounced *more playfully* than the puppy.
> The kitten pounced *most playfully* of all the animals.

Exercise 1

Name the adverb that compares in each sentence. Then tell if the adverb is an adverb of *time*, *place*, or *manner*.
1. The blue car stopped more quickly than the red car.
2. It rains more heavily in spring than in winter.
3. The trombone played louder than the flute.
4. Of the three rolling balls, the large one stopped soonest.

5. The brown spider crawled highest of all the spiders.
6. If you pull harder, the door will open.
7. Of all the children, Ben listened to the story most eagerly.
8. Andy plays tennis more frequently than Carl does.
9. The brownies were finished sooner than the cookies.
10. The sun shone more brightly today than yesterday.

Exercise 2

Complete each sentence with the correct form of the adverb in parentheses.

1. The movie begins (later, latest) than the game.
2. Of all the choir members, Jan sings (highest, higher).
3. We go (most often, more often) to the beach than to the museum.
4. Sandra answers the telephone (most politely, more politely) than Sue.
5. The sun rises (earlier, earliest) in the summer than in the winter.
6. Our team paddled the canoe (most smoothly, more smoothly) of all the teams.
7. The small icicle melted (sooner, soonest) than the large icicle.
8. Of all the tumblers, Mary turns cartwheels the (more skillfully, most skillfully).
9. Of the two brothers, Sidney speaks the (more quietly, most quietly).
10. The kangaroo hopped (highest, higher) than the rabbit.

Practice Power

How many different African animals can you name? Imagine that you are a photographer on a safari. Write five sentences that describe the actions of different animals. Use adverbs that compare in your sentences. Here is an example sentence.

The elephants walk *slower* than the giraffes.

Lesson 3 Using Adverbs Correctly

Good and *Well*

> **The word *good* is an adjective.**

Adjectives modify nouns or pronouns. *Good* describes persons, places, or things, answering *what kind*.

> I read a *good* book. (Adjective: *what kind* of book?)

> **The word *well* is an adverb.**

Adverbs usually modify verbs. *Well* describes the actions of verbs. *Well* answers the question *how*.

> This author writes *well*. (Adverb: *how* does this author write?)

Exercise 1

Complete each sentence with *good* or *well*.
1. Cynthia rides horseback _____.
2. Is Margo a _____ magician?
3. This is _____ chili.
4. Irma cleaned the elephant's tusks _____.
5. Frost the cake _____.
6. The fable has a _____ ending.
7. Otters swim _____.
8. Can you spell new words _____?
9. Chuck explained the math problem _____.
10. Saturday is a _____ day for the bike rodeo.

No, Not, Never

> Only *one* negative word is needed to express a negative idea in a sentence.

Here are some words that express a negative idea.

can't	never	no one
don't	nobody	nothing
haven't	none	nowhere

Do not use two negative words in the same sentence.

INCORRECT: I *don't* have *nothing* to do.
CORRECT: I *don't* have anything to do.
            I have *nothing* to do.

INCORRECT: I *haven't* found *none*.
CORRECT: I *haven't* found any.
            I have found *none*.

Exercise 2

Choose the word in parentheses that will correctly complete each of these sentences. Each sentence should express a negative idea.

1. This sandwich hasn't (any, no) cheese.
2. We didn't see (anyone, no one) at the front door.
3. There are (any, no) tadpoles in this stream.
4. Nothing makes (any, no) difference to Ralph.
5. None of us saw (any, no) shooting stars.
6. Haven't you (nothing, anything) to read?
7. There weren't (any, no) animal tracks around the tree.
8. The keys were (anywhere, nowhere).
9. There should be (any, no) broken eggs.
10. I've never seen (anything, nothing) as funny as a baboon.

Exercise 3

These sentences are incorrect because they contain more than one negative word. Express each one correctly.

1. Tom doesn't have no sugar for the horse.
2. Nothing makes no sense to me in this book.
3. None of us can go nowhere without a bike.
4. Nobody knows nothing about the class party.
5. There isn't no show at the planetarium today.
6. I don't have no bananas on my cereal.
7. Joshua has never been nowhere in Canada.
8. No one should write nothing in the wet cement.
9. The Rockets haven't won no games this season.
10. The team never had no excellent players.

You Are the Author

Choose one.

1. Glinda told Dorothy about the power of the Silver Shoes. Imagine that you had these shoes—or magic boots with the same power—for one day. Write a story about your adventures. Give your story a beginning, a middle, and an end.
2. Pretend that you are Dorothy or one of her companions. Think about your journey along the yellow brick road. Write an entry in your journal about some of your experiences.

Chapter Challenge

Read this paragraph carefully, and then answer the questions.

¹Finally the wild animal acts were completed. ²Now it was time for the main event of the circus. ³The famous new acrobat would swing fearlessly above the heads of the excited crowd. ⁴He climbed up the ladder quickly and smiled down at the vast audience below. ⁵The drums rolled loudly and then became silent. ⁶Grasping the bar, the bird-like figure swung forth, tumbled skillfully, and swooped to the other side. ⁷The crowd breathed easily again and applauded enthusiastically. ⁸Wasn't that a courageous act!

1. In sentence 1, name an adverb of time.
2. In sentence 2, name an adverb of time.
3. In sentence 3, name an adverb of manner.
4. In sentence 4, name at least one adverb of place.
5. In sentence 4, name the adverb that modifies the verb *smiled*.
6. In sentence 4, the adverb *quickly* answers the question *how* about which verb?
7. In sentence 5, name an adverb. What kind of adverb is it?
8. In sentence 6, name at least one adverb. What kind of adverb is it?
9. In sentence 7, the adverb *enthusiastically* modifies what verb?
10. In sentence 7, name two adverbs of manner.

Creative Space 6

What Is Red?

Red is a sunset
Blazy and bright.
Red is feeling brave
With all your might.
Red is a sunburn
Spot on your nose,
Sometimes red
Is a red, red rose.
Red squiggles out
When you cut your hand.
Red is a brick and
A rubber band.
Red is a hotness
You get inside
When you're embarrassed
And want to hide.
Fire-cracker, fire-engine
Fire-flicker red—
And when you're angry
Red runs through your head.
Red is a headdress,
A Valentine heart,
The trimming on
A circus cart.
Red is a lipstick,
Red is a shout,
Red is a signal
That says: "Watch out!"
Red is a great big
Rubber ball.
Red is the giant-est
Color of all.
Red is a show-off
No doubt about it—
But can you imagine
Living without it?

Mary O'Neill

352

Exploring the Poem...

This poem begins by asking the question *What is red?*
Name some *feelings* the speaker describes as red. Name
some *things* the speaker lists as red.

What is the speaker describing in the lines: *Red squiggles
out/When you cut your hand?* Do you think *squiggle* is a
good word? Why?

Why do you think the speaker calls red a *show-off?*

★ What is your favorite color? What things have that
color? Write four lines about your favorite color. If
you'd like, you can experiment with rhyme. Before
you begin your poem, read these poems written
by students.

In America's flag
Red is a stripe.
When it comes to
tomatoes
Red is ripe.

When the sky is blue
My heart feels glad.
But when I feel blue
My heart is sad.

Chapter 7

Punctuation and Capitalization

Trouble

by Nicholasa Mohr

from *Felita*

"Now be friendly. Remember, you will make good friends here."

I stood on the **stoop**, watching the group of girls I had seen from my window. They had stopped playing rope and were now playing hopscotch. One of them saw me and then whispered to the others. They all stopped playing and looked at me. I made sure to turn in the other direction. Slowly I went down the steps to the sidewalk and leaned against the stoop railing. Then I walked toward them and stood only a few feet away. They were having a good time, using bottle caps and keys to toss on the chalked squares. Hopscotch was one game I was really good at!

"Hi! Hey you!" a girl with short brown hair and glasses wearing blue jeans called out. "You wanna play with us?"

"Sure." I walked over and waited my turn. There were six of them playing. They were all about my age. They played a fair game of hopscotch. One girl with bright carrot-colored hair and lots of freckles was the best. But she wasn't as good as me. At last my turn came. I did the whole ten boxes forward and backward without one mistake.

"You're real good," one of the girls said.

"Even better than Molly." The girl with the glasses pointed to the girl with the bright hair and freckles. "What's your name?" she asked.

"Felita."

Detail from *Orchard Street* by David Levine

"Wow," she said, "that's real pretty! My name is Katherine. This here is Molly . . . and Mary Beth, Wendy, Thelma, and Margaret Jean."

"You must've played hopscotch before," said Molly.

"I did. On my old block we played it a whole lot."

"Let's play some more," said Katherine.

We all played. When it was my turn, I got to play over and over because I was the best one. Molly was second best. Margaret Jean was the slowest, and she hardly got a full turn because she kept stepping on the lines.

"After this," Margaret Jean said, "let's play jump rope again."

We all agreed and played for a long time.

"Are you going to our school, Felita?" Katherine asked.

"I think so."

"What was the school you went to?" asked Wendy.

"Oh, **P.S.** 47. That was near our old neighborhood."

"Our school is P.S. 91. It's real near here," said Molly.

"I'm sure you will be going to our school," said Katherine. "Everybody in this neighborhood goes there. We walk together every morning. You wanna walk with us when school starts again?"

"That's neat. Thanks," I said. They were really nice. Maybe it wouldn't be so bad here after all.

"You know, sometimes we get together at each other's homes and have, like, a meeting," Wendy said. She was the tallest one and had two long straw-colored braids and bangs. "We might even form a club. It's not a sure thing yet. We have to plan it. Listen, would you like to come to our next meeting?"

"Sure. I would really like to come to your next meeting very much."

"You live in this building, right?" asked Katherine.

"On the third floor in front." I nodded.

"I live down the block in that house." She pointed to another gray brick building about midway down the street. "But Mary Beth and Thelma live in your building."

"I been living there all my life," said Mary Beth. "Thelma moved here when she was real little."

From Williamsburg Bridge
by Edward Hopper

"We seen you move in," said Thelma.

"I was real little when I moved into my old block . . ." I said.

"I was four," Thelma said. "That's what my mother told me anyway."

"Mary Beth, what are you doing?" a woman called out. She stood with several men and women near my stoop.

"Playing, Mama."

"Get over here!"

"Wendy, Thelma, Molly . . . all of you, come here. Right now!"

All the girls walked over to the grown-ups except Katherine.

"I gotta be getting on home," she **murmured** and walked off.

The other girls huddled together with the grown-ups. They all spoke in low voices. I waited. Were they coming back to play? They all stared silently at me. I smiled at them and waited, but there were no smiles for me. I glanced up at our window, hoping that Mami might be watching. No one was there. I looked around at the unfamiliar street. Katherine had already disappeared into her building.

Suddenly I felt frightened and all alone. I wanted to get home, upstairs, where I would be safe with Mami. I decided to head for my apartment. Now the adults and girls were standing in a group beside the stoop steps. As I **approached** my building, I lowered my eyes and quickened my **pace**. I figured I would walk around them and get up the steps as fast as I could.

Thelma quickly stepped in front of me, blocking my way. "Why did you move here?"

"Why don't you stay with your own kind?" Mary Beth stood next to Thelma.

"Yeah, there's none of your kind here, and we don't want you." As I tried to get by them, the other three girls ran up the stoop and formed a line across the building entrance.

The Writer's Craft

1. Felita missed her friends in her old neighborhood. How would you feel about leaving your neighborhood and moving into a new one? What would you do to make new friends?
2. At first the girls were happy to include Felita in their games. Later they did not want her. What do you think caused the change in attitude toward Felita?
3. The author, Nicholasa Mohr, lets the reader see events through Felita's eyes. How does this add to the story?
4. Mohr's use of dialogue helps set the mood of the story. Find some sentences within quotation marks that create a mood of acceptance at the beginning of the excerpt and then other examples that show the change in attitude at the end.
5. Punctuation in writing gives clues to what sentences mean just as the voice does in speech. Notice the punctuation used when the grown-ups called the children over to them. What does the punctuation help to tell the reader?

Recalling What You Know

1. What do the punctuation marks tell the reader in this sentence? *"You want to play with us?"*
2. We use capital letters for the names of particular persons, places, and things. Give the reasons for the capital letters in this sentence: *Felita visited Puerto Rico in the book* Going Home.

Lesson 1 The Period

Capital letters and punctuation marks help you to write clear sentences.

When you speak, your voice helps the listener to understand your thoughts. When you write, capital letters and punctuation marks help the reader understand your thoughts.

Notice how difficult it is to read and understand this paragraph from *Felita* without any punctuation or capitalization.

> you know sometimes we get together at each others homes and have like a meeting wendy said she was the tallest one and had two long straw-colored braids and bangs we might even form a club its not a sure thing yet we have to plan it listen would you like to come to our next meeting

Now read the paragraph as the author wrote it. Does the punctuation help you to understand the paragraph? Does it help you to read the paragraph with expression?

> "You know, sometimes we get together at each other's homes and have, like, a meeting," Wendy said. She was the tallest one and had two long straw-colored braids and bangs. "We might even form a club. It's not a sure thing yet. We have to plan it. Listen, would you like to come to our next meeting?"

> **1. A period is a stop sign. It marks the end of declarative and imperative sentences.**

A *declarative sentence* states a fact. It is followed by a period.

Felita missed her friends in the old neighborhood.

An *imperative sentence* gives a command or makes a request. It is followed by a period.

Come here.

Exercise 1

Tell whether each of the following sentences is *declarative* or *imperative*.

1. Felita missed her best friend, Gigi.
2. Felita's mother wanted her to meet new friends.
3. Go out and play, Felita.
4. Put on your blue-and-white sailor dress.
5. The people in the new neighborhood were not kind to Felita and her family.
6. Felita's grandmother, Abuelita, still lived in Felita's old neighborhood.
7. Come to my house tomorrow.
8. Felita liked talking with her grandmother.
9. She told Abuelita about the girls in her new neighborhood.
10. Read more about Felita and her family in the books *Felita* and *Going Home*.

2. A short form of a word is called an abbreviation. A period is used after many abbreviations.

Abbreviations are often used in lists and addresses. Abbreviations are usually not used in sentences. Look at these common abbreviations.

U.S.	United States	N.	North	min.	minute
St.	Street	S.	South	hr.	hour
Ave.	Avenue	E.	East	sec.	second
P.O.	Post Office	W.	West	mo.	month
				yr.	year

The *months of the year* are often abbreviated.

Jan.	January	Sept.	September
Feb.	February	Oct.	October
Mar.	March	Nov.	November
Apr.	April	Dec.	December
Aug.	August		

The months with short names—May, June, and July—are not abbreviated.

The *days of the week* are often abbreviated.

Sun.	Sunday	Thurs.	Thursday
Mon.	Monday	Fri.	Friday
Tues.	Tuesday	Sat.	Saturday
Wed.	Wednesday		

Metric symbols do not begin with capital letters and they are *not* followed by a period.

l	liter	m	meter
g	gram	cm	centimeter

A period is *not* used after postal abbreviations for states. In the United States, the Post Office asks that these special state abbreviations be used on all mail.

AL	Alabama	**KY**	Kentucky	**ND**	North Dakota
AK	Alaska	**LA**	Louisiana	**OH**	Ohio
AZ	Arizona	**ME**	Maine	**OK**	Oklahoma
AR	Arkansas	**MD**	Maryland	**OR**	Oregon
CA	California	**MA**	Massachusetts	**PA**	Pennsylvania
CO	Colorado	**MI**	Michigan	**RI**	Rhode Island
CT	Connecticut	**MN**	Minnesota	**SC**	South Carolina
DE	Delaware	**MS**	Mississippi	**SD**	South Dakota
DC	District of Columbia	**MO**	Missouri	**TN**	Tennessee
		MT	Montana	**TX**	Texas
FL	Florida	**NE**	Nebraska	**UT**	Utah
GA	Georgia	**NV**	Nevada	**VT**	Vermont
HI	Hawaii	**NH**	New Hampshire	**VA**	Virginia
ID	Idaho			**WA**	Washington
IL	Illinois	**NJ**	New Jersey	**WV**	West Virginia
IN	Indiana	**NM**	New Mexico	**WI**	Wisconsin
IA	Iowa	**NY**	New York	**WY**	Wyoming
KS	Kansas	**NC**	North Carolina		

Exercise 2

Name the state for each of these abbreviations.

AK	IN
CA	ME
DE	TN
GA	VT
HI	WY

Name the abbreviation for each of these states.

Alabama	Rhode Island
Oregon	Nevada
Ohio	Florida
Colorado	Louisiana
Iowa	Texas

Exercise 3

Name the word or words for each of these abbreviations.

g	cm
Sept.	S.
mo.	Tues.
Dec.	Ave.
Fri.	P.O.

Name the abbreviation for each of these words.

August	October
North	Monday
meter	minute
hour	East
Street	United States

3. A period is used after titles and initials.

The titles *Mr.*, *Mrs.*, *Ms.*, and *Dr.* are often abbreviated. When they are used with persons' names, they may be abbreviated within a sentence.

Sometimes a person will use an *initial* in place of his or her name. The *first letter* of a name is an initial. John Paul Jones, for example, may be known as J.P. Jones, or as John P. Jones, or as J. Paul Jones. Every initial should be followed by a period.

Exercise 4

Add periods where needed in these sentences.
1. Ms Jennie E Tamillo spoke to the computer club
2. Swimming lessons are given by Mr Al E Gator
3. *One of Our Dinosaurs Is Missing* was written by D Forrest
4. Mr and Mrs Anthony Kane own the skating rink
5. This is addressed to Steve D Miller
6. My dentist is Dr Molly B Gibson
7. The scientist's name is Dr F G Stein
8. Ms Carol D Sullivan's name was in the newspaper
9. Her signature is M E Rupert
10. P J Schwartz will give a book report today

Exercise 5

Find the abbreviations in these sentences. Write the word
for each abbreviation. Remember, except for titles and
initials, most abbreviations should not be used
in sentences.

1. On Tues., Dr. Walsh will look at the llama.
2. How many cm are there in a m?
3. Sunny St. and Ocean Ave. are lined with tulips.
4. Mar. came in like a lion!
5. The IN state fair begins Aug. 12 and ends Sept. 25.
6. Heat the caramel for one min. and stir.
7. They moved the tepee on Mon.
8. Every hr. a bus leaves the station.
9. Is the U.S. your native country?
10. Winston bought a bicycle on Jan. 12.

Practice Power

Here are some other words that can be abbreviated. Try
to find the correct abbreviation for each.

Expressway   Shore
Hospital   Lane
Parkway   River
Turnpike   Village
Lake

Lesson 2   The Comma

> **1. Commas set off words in direct address from the rest of the sentence.**

When you speak to a person, you will find that you usually address him or her by name. This is called *direct address*. There is usually a pause before or after the person's name. Read these sentences aloud, as if you were speaking to Elaine.

>Elaine, do you want to play volleyball?
>Can you swim underwater, Elaine?
>Do you think, Elaine, that you can come to my party?

In writing, use a comma to show the pause before and after the person's name. If the name is the *first* word in a sentence, it is *followed* by a comma.

>John, your shoelace is untied.

If the name is the *last* word in a sentence, the comma is placed *before* the name.

>Your shoelace is untied, John.

If the name comes anyplace in the sentence, other than first or last, two commas are needed. One comma is used *before* and another is used *after* the name.

>Your shoelace, John, is untied.

Exercise 1

Add a comma or commas to set off the word in direct address in each sentence.

1. Why did the turtle cross the road Bennie?
2. Art it crossed the road to get to the shell station!
3. Run girls or you'll miss your bus.
4. Katie your sister is in the library.
5. Frankie did you write this computer program?
6. Some deep-sea fish glow in the dark Sonya.
7. Do you know how marbles are made Peter?
8. Australia Ruth is the smallest continent.
9. How much pepperoni Bettina do we need?
10. Paul hold the canoe while I climb in.

Complete each sentence using a person's name in direct address. Use commas where necessary.

11. When the clay has dried _____ you can paint it.
12. Watch the eclipse with us _____.
13. _____ take the mail to the post office.
14. When _____ does the record store close?
15. _____ say "cheese."

> **2. A comma is used after the words *yes* and *no* when they introduce a sentence.**

A sentence that begins with *yes* or *no* usually answers a question. A comma is placed after the *yes* or *no* to set off the word from the rest of the sentence.

Yes, I like scrambled eggs.
No, I don't like raw eggs.

Exercise 2

Add a comma where needed in each sentence.
1. Yes there is a lion loose.
2. No the Braves didn't win the game.
3. No this year is not leap year.
4. Yes the pepper is hot.
5. Yes the bell rang.
6. No school wasn't canceled.
7. Yes this dollar is for you.
8. No it didn't snow last night.

Exercise 3

Answer each question with a *yes* or *no*.
1. Do you know anyone who likes spiders?
2. Did six dwarfs take care of Snow White?
3. Does a cat have nine lives?
4. Have you ever seen a peacock feather?
5. Are there seven days in a week?
6. Can a cow jump over the moon?
7. Are bats really blind?
8. Do bees buzz?
9. Are there sixty minutes in an hour?
10. Have you ever flown in a plane?

3. Commas are used to separate words in a series.

You may use several words to describe an object, to express actions, or to explain how something is done. If you write three or more *words in a series*, use a comma after each word in the series except the last one.

Each of these sentences shows a series of nouns.

> Jay collects *stamps*, *marbles*, and *old coins*.
> (things)
> *Janet*, *Peggy*, and *Cathy* worked together.
> (persons)
> Our family visited *Boston*, *New York*, and *Philadelphia*.
> (places)

Each of these sentences shows a series of verbs.

> The children *ran*, *jumped*, and *played* in the park.
> The gymnasts *tumbled*, *rolled*, and *flipped* across the mat.

Each of these sentences shows a series of adjectives.

> *Funny*, *exciting*, *interesting*, and *scary* stories were told around the camp fire.
> *Red*, *white*, and *blue* streamers floated in the breeze.

Exercise 4

Add commas where needed in these sentences.

1. Lizards spiders and snakes are unusual pets.
2. Paint stripes dots hearts and stars on the eggs.
3. Bats balls and gloves are in the locker room.
4. We gave the scarecrow eyes ears and a smile.
5. Ms. Aldo cut nailed and sanded the swing.
6. Washington Jefferson Adams Monroe and Madison were presidents.
7. The cool ripe and juicy watermelon was refreshing.
8. We need balloons glue and yarn for the project.
9. The haunted house is dark gloomy and scary.
10. He forgot to bring a flashlight sleeping bag and matches.

Complete each of the following sentences by using words in a series. Add commas where needed.

11. We'll eat _____ _____ and _____ at the picnic. (*add nouns*)
12. Kangaroos _____ _____ and _____ across the plains. (*add verbs*)
13. The unusual T-shirt is _____ _____ and _____. (*add adjectives*)
14. _____ _____ and _____ were played at the sports festival. (*add nouns*)
15. We _____ _____ and _____ during our vacation in Colorado. (*add verbs*)

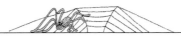

> ### 4. A comma is often used to set off short direct quotations.

When you write the exact words of a speaker, you write a *direct quotation*. A comma is often used to separate the quotation from the rest of the sentence.

> Russ said, "We repainted all the screens."
> "It was a hard job," said Gus.

Exercise 5

Add commas where needed in these sentences.
1. "There's a cobweb in that corner" said Paula.
2. "My dog is a collie" said Fran.
3. "The current is strong" warned the lifeguard.
4. "This horse is a good jumper" said Rachel.
5. "I'll grant you three wishes" explained the genie.
6. Mrs. Hernandez said "The lobsters are cooking now."
7. Maria remarked "That new skyscraper is unusual."
8. "Help me carry these logs inside" said Daniel.
9. Farley said "The stone cottage is cool in the summer."
10. "I can't see the screen" whispered Lucy.

When the speaker asks a question, a question mark is used. When the speaker expresses strong or sudden emotion, an exclamation point is used. If the words spoken are at the beginning of a sentence and followed by a question mark or exclamation point, the comma is *not* used.

> "Did you finish your work?" asked Paul.
> "Yes, let's go!" exclaimed Russ.

Exercise 6

Look at these sentences. Add a question mark if the speaker asks a question. Add an exclamation point if the words show strong or sudden feeling.

1. "What big teeth you have" exclaimed Red Riding Hood.
2. "What is the largest desert in the world" asked Nick.
3. "We won" shouted the players.
4. "Rain is pouring through the tent" yelled Sid.
5. "How many teeth does a chicken have" joked Margot.
6. "How loud the fireworks are" said Andrew.
7. "Are leprechauns real" asked the little boy.
8. "I just saw a shooting star" Anita shouted.
9. "Who made our first flag" asked the teacher.
10. "Do you have a CB radio" asked the truck driver.

Exercise 7

Add commas where needed in these sentences. Remember all the rules for commas that you have studied.

1. Yes I found my shoes.
2. "I want a double cheeseburger" said Gary.
3. No I've never been to Florida.
4. How many pets do you have Annie?
5. I mowed trimmed and weeded the grass.
6. We saw model airplanes ships and trains at the museum.
7. Andrea announced "I am the winner."
8. Jessica please tell us another story.
9. I saw a robin Teddy in your backyard.
10. "Guess a number from one to ten" said Julio.

Practice Power

Write three questions that use names in direct address. Then answer each question. Begin each sentence with *yes* or *no*. Before you begin, look at these sentences.

> Randy, did you make the baseball team?
> Yes, the coach told me on Saturday.

Here are four sets of words in a series. Write each set in a direct quotation. Try to write quotations that ask questions or show exclamations. Before you begin, look at this example.

> raisins, juice, pretzels
> Mom asked, "Do we need raisins, juice, and pretzels?"

cows, horses, pigs
purple, red, green, orange
encyclopedia, almanac, dictionary
aunts, uncles, cousins

Lesson 3 The Apostrophe, Exclamation Point, and Question Mark

The Apostrophe

> **1. An apostrophe is used to show ownership or possession.**

To show that *one* person owns something, place an apostrophe and the letter s ('s) after the noun.

> The cat's tail is long. (*One cat*)

To show that *more than one* person owns something, place an apostrophe *after* the *s*. If a plural noun does not end in *s*, place an apostrophe and *s* ('s) after the noun.

> The cats' tails are furry. (*More than one cat*)
> The children's kittens purr. (*More than one child*)

Exercise 1

Make these nouns singular possessive.

SINGULAR NOUNS	SINGULAR POSSESSIVE
cat	_____
Jean	_____
bird	_____
goose	_____

Make these nouns plural possessive.

PLURAL NOUNS	PLURAL POSSESSIVE
geese	_____
women	_____
boys	_____
ants	_____

Exercise 2

Add an apostrophe where needed in each sentence.

1. The natives houses had grass roofs.
2. Kim wants to play Michaels guitar.
3. Before winter, bears fur grows thicker.
4. Did you feed Ralphs pet pigs?
5. Moms umbrella broke today.
6. The sound of the wolfs howl made me shiver!
7. Tigers stripes help them hide in the grass.
8. The clowns hair was bright red.
9. Mens hats used to be very tall.
10. I found a secret room in my aunts house!

> **2. An apostrophe marks the place where one or more letters have been left out in a contraction.**

A *contraction* is a short way to write some words. When two words are joined to form a contraction, one or more letters are left out. Use an apostrophe to take the place of the missing letter or letters. Here are some contractions you have studied.

I'm	I am	don't	do not
I've	I have	can't	cannot
we'll	we will	aren't	are not
we've	we have	wasn't	was not
it's	it is	hasn't	has not
they've	they have	won't	will not

Exercise 3

Use a contraction in place of the words in italics in each sentence. Use an apostrophe to take the place of the missing letter or letters.

1. *I will* make chocolate chip cookies.
2. My team *did not* score any runs.
3. *She is* training for a black belt in karate.
4. A dog *cannot* run backwards.
5. *Is not* that your homework under the desk?
6. The lions *will not* eat marshmallows.
7. Tina *has not* walked on her hands yet.
8. Our class *could not* solve the puzzle.
9. *It is* summer now in Australia.
10. *They have* never been to the desert.

The Exclamation Point

> **An exclamation point marks the end of an exclamatory sentence.**

An *exclamatory sentence* expresses a strong feeling such as joy, surprise, fear, or pain. Exclamatory sentences often begin with the words *how* or *what*.

How I love summertime!

The Question Mark

> **A question mark is used at the end of an interrogative sentence.**

An *interrogative sentence* asks a question.

Does the moon shine during the day?

Exercise 4

Add an exclamation point or a question mark at the end of each sentence.

1. How many rides will you take on the roller coaster
2. What are the names of Santa's reindeer
3. What a strange plant this is
4. How quiet this house is
5. Watch out for that hole
6. How many sides are there in a rectangle
7. What a funny face that camel has
8. How did you solve this problem
9. Did you read the book *My Side of the Mountain*
10. What a sad movie that was

Practice Power

Imagine that you are at your favorite playground. Write two exclamatory and two interrogative sentences about some of the fun things you do. Use two apostrophes—one that shows possession and one in a contraction.

Lesson 4 Quotation Marks

Quotation marks are used before and after the exact words of a speaker.

When you write the exact words a person says, you write a *direct quotation*. Use quotation marks before the *first* and after the *last* words spoken. These marks show that you are writing the exact words spoken.

> Mr. Lopez said, "Be here at seven o'clock."
> "Where are we going?" asked Frank.
> "I can't wait!" shouted Jessie.

In a direct quotation
—a comma is placed before or after the speaker's exact words.
—if a question mark or an exclamation point appears at the end of the quotation and the name of the speaker follows, the comma is *not* used.
—the first word begins with a capital letter.
—the punctuation at the end is placed before the final quotation marks.

Exercise

Add quotation marks before and after each direct quotation.

1. I hear footsteps, whispered Marjorie.
2. It's too hot to go to the beach, said Tom.
3. She asked, Where are the runners for this race?
4. Ginny replied, My brother is afraid of the dark.
5. Who likes garlic bread? Jerome asked.
6. They answered, We found the hamster this morning.
7. Let's go! said Kelly.
8. She replied, Your skateboard needs paint.
9. What does an octopus eat? asked Billy.
10. Our dairy has two hundred cows, said Luke.

Add your own quotations. Use quotation marks and other punctuation where needed.

"The water is icy cold!" exclaimed Daniel.

11. _____ Jason explained.
12. Mr. Havlis announced _____.
13. Sheila asked _____
14. _____ Dawn whispered.
15. _____ Gerald shouted.

Practice Power

Write four lines of imaginary conversation between two of your friends. Talk about something they like to eat or a place they like to visit. Before you begin, look at this example.

"Do you like Chinese food?" asked Sue Ling.
Sarah replied, "I love it!"
"Then let's go to Wing Wong's," said Sue Ling.
"Can you teach me to use chopsticks?" questioned Sarah.

Lesson 5 Capital Letters

> **1. The first word of every sentence begins with a capital letter.**

A *sentence* is a group of words that expresses a complete thought. Punctuation marks—like the period, the question mark, and the exclamation point—signal the end of the sentence. The capital letter tells where the sentence begins.

> The brownies are delicious.
> Is jogging good exercise?
> How that wind is howling!
> Zipper your jacket.

Exercise 1

Use a capital letter to show where each of these sentences begins. Use the correct mark of punctuation to signal the end of the sentence.

1. i can swing from that vine
2. how did he learn to type
3. what amazing tricks the stunt plane did
4. have you ever seen a silent movie
5. how I enjoyed the sailing trip
6. what kind of insect is crawling up her back
7. do you keep a diary
8. an opossum protects itself by playing dead
9. look at those giant hailstones
10. did you remember that funny joke

2. A proper noun begins with a capital letter.

A proper noun names a particular person, place, or thing. Proper nouns begin with a capital letter.

Here are some examples of proper nouns.

Persons: Benjamin Franklin, Margaret Mead
Cities: Paris, Cleveland
Countries: China, Canada
Holidays: Columbus Day, Memorial Day
Days of the week: Sunday, Monday
Months of the year: July, January

Exercise 2

Begin each sentence and each proper noun with a capital letter.

1. that brass lamp was aladdin's.
2. carol, gail, and I are going to greenway park.
3. we read fairy tales by hans christian andersen.
4. isn't richmond the capital of virginia?
5. birds ate the crumbs that hansel and gretel dropped.
6. captain john smith was saved by pocahontas.
7. hummingbirds fly from south america.
8. the united nations building is in new york.
9. her doll was made in greece.
10. a mouse just ran under ms. smith's desk.
11. robert fulton named his ship the *clermont*.
12. france gave the statue of liberty to the united states.

Exercise 3

Use capital letters to begin the names of months, days of the week, and holidays in these sentences.

1. A good month for flying kites is march.
2. We learned that flag day is in june.
3. The hot-air balloon race starts sunday.
4. The first monday of september is labor day.
5. My birthday is in july.
6. When is independence day?
7. Why is halloween on october 31?
8. On october 12 we celebrate columbus day.
9. We made a cherry cheesecake on washington's birthday.
10. Canadians celebrate thanksgiving in october.
11. We watch fireflies on june nights.
12. On the last monday in may we celebrate memorial day.

> **3. The first word in a direct quotation always begins with a capital letter.**

You have learned that the exact words of a speaker are called a *direct quotation*. The first word of the quotation always begins with a capital letter. The words spoken may be the first words in the sentence, or they may follow the name of the speaker.

"It will be ready tomorrow," he replied.
Elizabeth said, "This is my favorite book."

Exercise 4

Add capital letters and quotation marks where needed in these sentences.

1. Tad said, try my cinnamon rolls.
2. what color is ocher? asked Marcia.
3. i know the secret to that magic trick, said Cyndie.
4. how tired my feet are! exclaimed the centipede.
5. Daisy said, i have directions to the pool.
6. come sit beside me, said the spider to the fly.
7. Ms. Wilson said, please use a dictionary.
8. this music is great! exclaimed Joanie.
9. Smokey warned, only you can prevent forest fires.
10. where did all the cookies go? asked Kim.

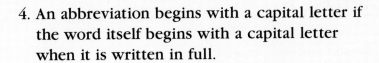

> **4. An abbreviation begins with a capital letter if the word itself begins with a capital letter when it is written in full.**

The name of a particular person, place, or thing always begins with a capital letter. The names of months, days, and holidays also always begin with capital letters. Use capital letters to begin the abbreviations.

Titles used with people's names and parts of proper nouns are capitalized even if they are abbreviated.

Dr. Ralph Conley	Jan.
U.S.	N. State St.
Mr. John Kane	KY
ND	MS
ID	WA

> 5. An initial is always written with a capital letter.

General U.S. Grant   John F. Kennedy

> 6. The pronoun *I* is always written with a capital letter.

I have one brother, but I have two sisters.

Exercise 5

Use capital letters for abbreviations, initials, and the pronoun *I* in these sentences.

1. i used the abbreviation nov. in my note.
2. mr. and mrs. Martin j. Boyd study rare birds.
3. Jay f. Greef, m.d., has an office on Indian rd.
4. Ulysses s. Grant was both a general and a president.
5. The speech was given by dr. j. g. Keenan.
6. ks is the abbreviation for the home of the Jayhawks.
7. i think Robert e. Lee's horse was named Traveler.
8. ave. is the abbreviation of what word?
9. The date on the letter was sept. 1.
10. me is the abbreviation for Maine.

> **7. The important words in titles of books and poems begin with capital letters.**

A *title* is the name a writer gives his or her work. Each important word in a title begins with a capital letter. The first word of a title *always* begins with a capital letter.

Little House in the Big Woods is my favorite book.

Exercise 6

Give the reason for each capital letter in these sentences.

1. "Ida skates on Lake Spruce," said Jeff.
2. Alaska and Hawaii became states in 1959.
3. Mr. Alfred B. Watkins likes the Green Bay Packers.
4. Did you read the poem "Ickle Me, Pickle Me, Tickle Me Too" by Shel Silverstein?
5. Do you know what I did last Saturday?
6. My cousin Michael had a Halloween party.
7. I'd like to read *Robin Hood and His Adventures*.
8. Next Sunday will be Father's Day.
9. Philip went to the Blackstone Theater on his birthday.
10. "You hide and I'll find you," said Tammy.

You Are the Author

Choose one.

1. Nicholasa Mohr tells the story at the beginning of the chapter from Felita's point of view. Think about an experience you have had of making a friend or being a friend. Write about that experience from your point of view. Be sure to include dialogue in your story.

2. Think about the story from *Felita* that you read. If you could change the ending in some way, how would you change it? Rewrite the ending as you would like it. Share your ending with a friend.

Orchard Street by David Levine

Chapter Challenge

Read each of these sentences carefully, and then answer the questions.

¹It was Monday afternoon at Jefferson Elementary School. ²Jerry listened carefully as their guest speaker, Mr. Gray, told the class about birds of prey.

³"Birds of prey come in all shapes and sizes," he said.

⁴Jerry discovered that they include falcons, hawks, eagles, and vultures.

⁵"Mr. Gray, are owls also birds of prey?" Jerry asked.

⁶"Yes, they are," Mr. Gray answered.

⁷Jerry learned that only owls hunt at night, and the others hunt during the day. ⁸He was amazed that some birds' wingspans are almost ten feet. ⁹Did you know that birds of prey have three eyelids? ¹⁰Yes, Jerry and his class were going to learn much about these magnificent birds.

1. In sentence 1, why do *Monday* and *Jefferson Elementary School* begin with capital letters?
2. What kind of sentence is sentence 2?
3. In sentence 3, why are quotation marks used?
4. In sentence 4, why are commas used?
5. In sentence 5, name a noun in direct address.
6. In sentence 6, what are the exact words of Mr. Gray?
7. In sentence 6, why is *Mr.* abbreviated?
8. In sentence 8, why is an apostrophe used?
9. What kind of sentence is sentence 9?
10. In sentence 10, why is a comma used after *Yes*?

Index

Acknowledgments

Text

121 "Why Nobody Pets the Lion at the Zoo" from *The Reason for the Pelican* by John Ciardi. Copyright © 1959 by the author. Reprinted by permission of J. B. Lippincott Company, a division of Harper & Row, Publishers, Inc. **122** "Oh, Who Will Wash the Tiger's Ears?" by Shel Silverstein. Reprinted by permission. **124** "The Umbrella Brigade" from *Tirra Lirra: Rhymes Old and New* by Laura E. Richards. Copyright © 1932 by Little, Brown and Company. **125** "Halloween" by Marie Lawson from *The Arbuthnot Anthology of Children's Literature* by May Hill Arbuthnot. Scott, Foresman & Company. **127** "The Wozzit" from *The Snopp on the Sidewalk* by Jack Prelutsky. Copyright © 1976, 1977 by the author. Reprinted by permission of Greenwillow Books, a division of William Morrow & Co., Inc. **133** "A Matter of Taste" from *Jamboree: Rhymes for All Times* by Eve Merriam. Copyright © 1962, 1964, 1966, 1973 by the author. All rights reserved. Reprinted by permission of Marian Reiner for the author. **133** "Galoshes" from *Stories to Begin On* by Rhoda W. Bacmeister. Copyright © 1940 by E. P. Dutton; copyright renewed © 1968 by the author. Reprinted by permission of E. P. Dutton, a division of NAL Penguin, Inc. **133** "Choosing Shoes" from *The Very Thing* by Frieda Wolfe. Copyright © 1928 by the author. Reprinted by permission of Sidgwick & Jackson, Publishers. **133** "The World Is Full of Wonderful Smells" from *Jingle Jangle* by Zhenya Gay. Copyright © 1953 by the author. All rights reserved. Reprinted by permission of Viking Penguin, a division of Penguin Books USA, Inc. **134** "Mud" by Polly Chase Boyden from *Child Life Magazine*. Copyright © 1930, 1958 by Rand McNally & Company. **134** "That May Morning" from *Is Somewhere Always Far Away?* by Leland B. Jacobs. Copyright © 1967 by the author. Reprinted by permission of Henry Holt & Co., Inc. **134** "The Kite" from *Windy Morning* by Harry Behn. Copyright © 1953 by the author; copyright renewed © 1981 by Alice Behn Goebel, Pamela Behn Adam, Prescott Behn, and Peter Behn. All rights reserved. Reprinted by permission of Marian Reiner. **135** "Homework" from *Egg Thoughts and Other Frances Songs* by Russell Hoban (text only). Text copyright © 1964, 1972 by the author. Reprinted by permission of Harper & Row, Publishers, Inc. **135** "That Was Summer" from *That Was Summer* by Marci Ridlon. Copyright © 1969 by the author. Reprinted by permission. **143** Fourteen entries and pronunciation key from *Scott, Foresman Beginning Dictionary* by E. L. Thorndike and Clarence L. Barnhart. Copyright © 1979, 1983 by Scott, Foresman & Co. Reprinted by permission. **165** From *Jimmy Yellow Hawk* by Virginia Driving Hawk Sneve. Copyright © 1972 by the author. Reprinted by permission. **194** "The Box" from *A Crazy Flight and Other Poems* by Myra Cohn Livingston. Copyright © 1969 by the author. Reprinted by permission of Marian Reiner for the author. **197** From *Henry Reed's Think Tank* by Keith Robertson. Copyright © 1986 by the author. Reprinted by permission of Viking Penguin, a division of Penguin Books USA, Inc. **224** "The Park" from *Crickety Cricket! The Best Loved Poems of James S. Tippett*, originally published in *I Live in a City* by the author. Copyright © 1927 by Harper & Row, Publishers, Inc.; copyright renewed © 1955 by the author. Reprinted by permission of the publisher. **227** From *Ben and Me* by Robert Lawson. Copyright © 1939 by the author; copyright renewed © 1967 by John W. Boyd. Reprinted by permission of Little, Brown and Company. **258** "E Is the Escalator" from *All Around the Town* by Phyllis McGinley. Copyright © 1948, 1976 by the author. Reprinted by permission of Curtis Brown Ltd. **261** From *Fireworks, Picnics and Flags* by James Cross Giblin. Text copyright © 1983 by the author. Reprinted by permission of Clarion Books/Houghton Mifflin Co. All rights reserved. **286** "Butterflies" by Oemaru from *Faces and Places*. Copyright © 1971 by Scholastic Book Services. Reprinted by permission of Scholarship, Inc. **289** Text excerpt and two illustrations from *Mufaro's Beautiful Daughters* by John Steptoe. Copyright © 1987 by the author. Reprinted by permission of Lothrop, Lee & Shepard Books, a division of William Morrow & Co., Inc., with the approval of the Estate of the author. **293** "Things to Do If You Are a Subway" by Bobbi Katz. Copyright © 1970 by the author. Reprinted by permission. **328** "Leavetaking" from *It Doesn't Always Have to Rhyme* by Eve Merriam. Copyright © 1964 by the author. All rights reserved. Reprinted by permission of Marian Reiner for the author. **331** From *The Wonderful Wizard of Oz* by L. Frank Baum, in the public domain. **352** "What Is Red?" from *Hailstones and Halibut Bones* by Mary O'Neill. Illustrated by Leonard Weisgard. Copyright © 1961 by Mary LeDuc O'Neill. Reprinted by permission of Doubleday, a division of Bantam Doubleday Dell Publishing Group, Inc. **355** From *Felita* by Nicholasa Mohr. Copyright © 1979 by the author. Reprinted by permission of Dial Books for Young Readers, a division of Penguin Books USA, Inc.

Fine Art

34 *Album* Quilts, c. 1840-1850. Collection of Dr. and Mrs. Donald M. Herr. **66** *Fourth of July on the River* by Susan Slyman. Courtesy of Jay Johnson America's Folk Heritage Gallery, New York. **81** From *Life before Man,* 1972, Artia, Prague. Thames and Hudson, Ltd., London. **84(L)** *Head,* British Columbia, Nootka people. Courtesy of The Menil Collection, Houston. **84(R)** *Funerary Mask,* late 19th-early 20th century, Gabon and Congo, Shira-Punu people. Courtesy of The Menil Collection, Houston. **85(L)** *Funerary Mask,* Middle Kingdom, c. 1700 B.C. Egypt, Nubia. Courtesy of The Menil Collection, Houston. **85(R)** *Noh Mask,* Muromachi period, 15th century. Tokyo National Museum. **114** *Adam Winne,* 1730, by Pieter Vanderlyn. Courtesy of The Henry Francis du Pont Winterthur Museum. **115** *Adam Winne,* 1730, detail, by Pieter Vanderlyn. **154** *A College Football Game—1890.* The Bettmann Archive. **173** *Buster,* 1982, from *Creatures* by Beth Van Hoesen. Copyright © by the artist. Reprinted by permission. **184** *Polar Bear,* 1985, from *Creatures* by Beth Van Hoesen. Copyright © by the artist. Reprinted by permission. **196** *Country Girl Diner,* detail, by Ralph Goings. Oil on canvas (48 x 68 in.). Courtesy of O. K. Harris Works of Art, New York. **199** *Country Girl Diner,* detail, by Ralph Goings. **205** *Abraham Lincoln* by an unknown artist. Courtesy of Illinois State Museum, Springfield. **205** *Summer Day* by Setsko Karasuda. Courtesy of American Telephone and Telegraph Company. **226** *Benjamin Franklin* by Charles Wilson Peale. Oil on canvas. The Historical Society of Pennsylvania. **229** Engraving. The Bettmann Archive. **231** Engraving. Emmett Collection; Arts, Prints and Photographs Division of the New York Public Library; Astor, Lenox and Tilden Foundations. **232** Book title page. The Bettmann Archive. **260** *The Spirit of '76,* 1876, by Archibald Willard. The original painting hangs in The Selectmen's Meeting Room, Abbot Hall, Marblehead, Mass. **354** *Orchard Street,* detail, by David Levine. Watercolor on paper. Copyright © 1972 by the artist. Courtesy of the Forum Gallery, New York. Reproduced by permission. **357** *From Williamsburg Bridge,* 1928, by Edward Hopper. Oil on canvas (29 x 43 in.). The Metropolitan Museum of Art, New York; George A. Hearn Fund, 10.37. Reproduced by permission. **386** *Orchard Street* by David Levine.

Photographs

Cover: Alan Shortall

i Jeff Lane. **ii** Don Klumpp/The Image Bank. **iii** M. Timothy O' Keefe/Tom Stack & Associates. **xviii–xix** Gerrard Champlong/The Image Bank. **xx** PEI Canada/The Image Bank. **6** Arepi Sigurd/The Image Bank. **31(TL)** Marc St. Gil/The Image Bank. **31(TR)** Index Stock Photography. **31(BL)** Steve Vidler/Nawrocki Stock Photo. **31(BR)** Paul Koinik. **42, 43** James L. Ballard. **60** American Foundation for the Blind. **71** Olaf Sööt Photography Associates. **72** G. Ziesier/Peter Arnold, Inc. **76, 86** Index Stock Photography. **90** James L. Ballard. **116** Index Stock Photography. **117** G & J Images/The Image Bank. **120** John Shaw/Tom Stack & Associates. **135** H. Feurer/The Image Bank. **138** Arthur Meyerson Photography, Inc. **147** Tom Stack & Associates. **158, 159** James L. Ballard. **162–163** Comstock. **164, 167** Steven Trimble. **189** Anna Flynn/Stock Boston. **204** William Albert Allard/Magnum Photos. **221(T)** Kaz Mori/The Image Bank. **221(B)** Index Stock Photography. **224** Bullaty Lomeo/The Image Bank. **247** Gibson/Tom Stack & Associates. **252** Mount Wilson and Palomar observatories. **257** Dieter Blum/Peter Arnold, Inc. **263, 264** The Bettmann Archive. **276** Franco Villani/The Image Bank. **313** Art Wolfe/The Image Bank. **328** Steve Dunwell/The Image Bank. **341** Charles Gupton/Stock Boston. **362** David W. Hamilton/The Image Bank. **363** The Image Bank.

Illustrations

Callie Blasutta, 214(B), 376 (B), 377(B). **Mary Lynn Blasutta,** xvi, xvii, 1, 2, 3, 12(T), 23(B), 28, 29(T), 34, 40, 62, 67, 68(T), 69(T,M), 78, 91(M), 97(T), 105(M), 122, 123, 140, 141, 142, 144, 145(T), 146(T), 159, 160, 161(T), 172(M), 173(M), 178(B), 179, 189, 190, 191(T), 203(B), 205, 208(T), 212, 213, 218(M), 222(B), 223(M), 238, 239, 256, 257, 269(T), 272(B), 273(B), 274, 280, 282(B), 302(T), 307(M,B), 312, 326(T), 327(T), 330, 334-335, 336, 337, 350(T), 351, 368, 369(T), 373(B), 374, 375, 376(T), 377(T). **Susan Blubaugh,** 145(B), 148, 191(B), 321(B). **Frank Bozzo,** 178(M). **Nan Brooks,** 97(B), 98(B), 99(B). **Ted Carr,** xv, 22(B), 109, 228, 229, 230, 231, 232, 233, 296(B). **Ralph Creasman,** 26(B), 27, 137(M), 359(B). **David A. Cunningham,** 10(B), 11, 33(B), 38-39(B), 47, 51(B), 57, 58, 59, 152-153(B), 155(B), 220(B), 246(B), 290, 291(T), 292, 293, 337, 385(B), 386(B). **Pat Dypold,** 13(M), 120(T), 121(T), 234(B), 326(B), 327(B), 347. **Jean Cassels Helmer,** 8, 9(B), 16(B), 119, 139, 151, 171, 182(B), 208(B), 340(M). **Kerry Gavin,** xii(B), 15(M,B), 91(B), 93(B), 94(B), 96(B), 102(B), 103(B), 180(B), 181(M,B), 219(B), 283(B), 302(B), 338(B), 339(B), 366, 367(B). **Linda Gist,** 286. **Cynthia Hoffman,** 30(T), 39(T), 69(B), 158, 269(T), 359(T). **Paul Hoffman,** 30(B), 134(B). **Mary Jones,** x, xi(B), xiii(B), 24, 64(B), 70(T), 72(T), 100, 116(T), 117, 124, 125, 132, 133, 146(B), 193(B), 194, 195, 201, 206, 207, 216(T), 217, 235(M), 250, 251(B), 254, 255(T), 293, 294, 295, 300, 301(B), 304, 305, 313, 320, 321(T), 342(M,B), 343(B), 359(M), 365(B), 370, 371, 378(T), 382, 383. **G. Brian Karas,** xiv(M,B), 4, 5(B), 14(B), 21, 32, 33(T), 36(B), 37,43, 50, 54, 55, 60, 61, 81, 83(B), 113(M), 118(B), 126, 127, 156, 157, 185(M,B), 186, 187, 211(M,B), 222, 236, 237, 242(B), 243(B), 258, 259, 270(B), 271(B), 272(T), 273(T), 275(B), 318(B), 319(B), 346, 348, 349, 350(B), 381(B). **Arist Kirsch,** 44(B). **Carl Kock,** xi(T), xii(T), xiii(T,M), xiv(T), 5(T), 6, 7, 9(T), 10(T), 13(T), 14(T), 15(T), 16(T), 17(T), 18(T), 19(T), 22(T), 23(T), 25, 26(T), 31, 35(T), 36(T), 38(T), 41(T), 44(T), 45, 46, 48, 49, 51(T), 56, 63, 64(T), 65(T), 71, 73, 74, 75, 76, 77(T), 79(T), 80(T), 82, 83(T), 86, 87, 88, 89, 92, 93(T), 94(T), 95, 96(T), 98(T), 99(T), 100, 101, 102(T), 103(T), 104, 105(T), 106(T), 107(T), 110, 111(T), 112, 113(T), 118(T), 128, 129, 130, 131, 134(T), 135, 136(T), 137(T), 143, 147, 149(T), 150, 152(T), 153(T), 154, 155(T), 166, 167, 168, 169, 170, 171, 172(T), 173(T), 176, 177, 180(T), 181(T), 182(T), 183, 184, 185(T), 190(T), 192, 193(T), 198, 199, 200, 201, 202(T), 203(T), 209, 210, 211(T), 212(T), 214(T), 215(T), 218(T), 219(T), 220(T), 221(T), 222(T), 223(T), 233, 234(T), 235(T), 242(T), 243(T), 245(T), 246(T), 247, 248, 249, 251(T), 252, 253, 262, 263, 264, 265, 266, 267, 268(T), 270(T), 271(T), 275(T), 276, 277, 278, 279, 281, 282(T), 283(T), 284, 285, 296(T), 297(T), 298(T), 299(T), 301(T), 303, 306, 307(T), 308(T), 309(T), 310, 311, 314, 315, 316(T), 317(T), 318(T), 319(T), 324, 325, 338(T), 339(T), 340(T), 341, 342(T), 343(T), 356, 357, 358, 359, 360, 361, 362, 363, 364, 365(T), 367(T), 369(B), 372, 373(T), 378(B), 379, 381(T), 382(T), 383(T), 384, 385(T), 386(T), 387. **Joan Landis,** 20, 136(B), 202(B), 308(T,B), 309(T,B). **Eileen Mueller Neill,** 68, 77(M), 79(B), 90(cut paper set), 108(B), 111(B). **William Seabright,** 65(B), 106(B), 107(B), 255(B). **David Sheldon,** 120(M), 121(M), 161(B), 174, 175, 204, 268(B), 297(M), 352, 353. **Slug Signorino,** 17(B), 18(B), 19(M), 35(B), 41(B), 172(B), 215(B), 216(B), 218(B), 240, 241, 298(B), 299(B), 322, 323, 344, 345. **John Steptoe,** 288, 291(B). **Mark Ulrich,** 12(B), 29(B), 80(B), 244, 245(M,B), 316(B), 317(B). **Lynn Westphal** (handwriting), 46, 49, 56, 70, 71, 73, 74, 75, 76, 77, 78, 80, 82, 83, 84, 85, 87, 92, 93, 94, 98, 99, 101, 102, 105, 116.

Editors

First Edition: George A. Lane, S.J.; Joseph F. Downey, S.J.; Jeanette Ertel; Jane Guttman.
Revision: Pam Bernstein, Stephanie Iverson, Suzanne Mazurek, Jane Samuelson, Richard F. Weisenseel.

Production Staff

First Edition: April Uhlir Lemke, David Miller, Kristina Lykos.
Revision: Nancy Gruenke, Mary O'Connor, Gloria Dallmeier.

The type for this book was set by Jandon Graphics, Inc.; the revised type was set on Macintosh computers; the film was made by H & S Graphics, Inc.; and the book was printed by R. R. Donnelley & Sons Company.